This book examines the reli Simone Weil in the context out of which it grew. It also explores illuminating parallels between these ideas and ideas that were simultaneously being developed by Ludwig Wittgenstein.

Simone Weil developed a conception of the relation between human beings and nature which made it difficult for her to explain mutual understanding and justice. Her wrestling with this difficulty coincided with a considerable sharpening of her religious sensibility, and led to a new conception of the natural and social orders involving a supernatural dimension, within which the concepts of beauty and justice are paramount.

Professor Winch provides a fresh perspective on the complete span of Simone Weil's work, and discusses the fundamental difficulties of tracing the dividing line between philosophy and religion.

MODERN EUROPEAN PHILOSOPHY

General Editor

RAYMOND GEUSS, COLUMBIA UNIVERSITY

Editors

HIDE ISHIGURO, BARNARD COLLEGE

ALAN MONTEFIORE, BALLIOL COLLEGE

MARY TILES, ROYAL INSTITUTE OF PHILOSOPHY

SIMONE WEIL

SIMONE WEIL

"THE JUST BALANCE"

PETER WINCH

Professor of Philosophy
University of Illinois at Urbana/Champaign

CAMBRIDGE
UNIVERSITY PRESS

Published by the Press Syndicate of the University of Cambridge
The Pitt Building, Trumpington Street, Cambridge CB2
40 West 20th Street, New York, NY 10011-4211, USA
10 Stamford Road, Oakleigh, Melborne 3166, Australia

© Cambridge University Press 1989

First published 1989
Reprinted 1994

Printed in the United States of America

Library of Congress Cataloging-in-Publication Data is available.

A catalogue record for this book is available from the British Library

ISBN 0-521-30086-X hardback
ISBN 0-521-31743-6 paperback

CONTENTS

ACKNOWLEDGEMENTS

I am very grateful to the Leverhulme Foundation which awarded me a Senior Research Fellowship during the academic year 1976–7. This freed me from my teaching and administrative duties at King's College, London, and I was able to devote myself to intensive study of Simone Weil's work. The foundations were thus laid for my treatment of her in this book, although I did not feel nearly ready to undertake the writing at that time. In fact, the prospects of ever writing the book seemed to me to diminish steadily in the next few years for more than one reason. However, a small group of undergraduates asked me to give a course of lectures on Simone Weil in 1983 and 1984; I agreed to this at first rather reluctantly, as I felt that the issues to which I had once felt close had slipped away from me. But discussion with the students brought things alive again and I felt that absence had given me a clearer perspective; I resolved to bring the work to fruition if I could. I do not think the book would have been written but for this stimulus and I should like to thank those undergraduates for that most warmly.

In 1985 I moved to the University of Illinois at Urbana/Champaign; the Department of Philosophy and the university were generous in giving me leave of absence in the Fall Semester of 1986 so soon after my arrival. I spent that semester at the remarkable Institut für die Wissenschaften vom Menschen in Vienna as Senior Visiting Fellow and completed a substantial draft of the book there. I should like to say that I have never known such congenial conditions for working as I found at the Institut. I want to thank Monika Fense, Christine Huterer, Krzysztof Michalski, Klaus Nellen, and my other friends there for all they did to make this possible.

Many individuals have helped me at various times with encouragement, discussion, ideas, and criticism, and some of them have given generously of their time and energy in commenting on earlier drafts of the book, which would otherwise be much more defective than it is. I shall not attempt to specify each individual's contribution but want to express my particular gratitude to Marina Barabàs, Steven Burns, Hugh Chandler, David Cockburn, Cora Diamond, Rai Gaita, Lars Hertzberg, Alan Montefiore, Dewi Phillips, and Rush Rhees.

And I thank the editors of the Modern European Philosophy series for their patience.

1

INTRODUCTION

The purpose of this book is to explore some of the most important philosophical issues underlying Simone Weil's thinking. She did not herself discuss the distinction between questions that are philosophical and those that have some other character. I do not wish to suggest that she should have done this. In so far as it is necessary to draw such lines at all, the best attitude towards them seems to me to be a pragmatic one: to wait until some particular issue makes the drawing of a line desirable and then to draw it in a way which clarifies that issue. I mean to imply by this that it will be appropriate to draw the lines in rather different places in relation to different issues. It will also undoubtedly be the case that writers who work in different philosophical traditions will have a multiplicity of ideas about where, if at all, such lines should be drawn. This is to be expected and not, in my judgment, to be deplored.

But while there is no point in trying to legislate in a comprehensive way about what is philosophy and what is not, it does seem to me that sometimes one needs to raise a question of that form. One needs to be clear where a particular discussion belongs in order to determine how precisely it is to be understood, what kinds of criticism it is appropriate to develop in relation to it, what kinds of reasoning one should look for as a defence, what are its further implications. And according to the tradition within which I work, these are types of question it is peculiarly the responsibility of a philosopher to press.

Such questions are likely to arise in the course of studying the work of any thinker of a radically innovative kind. Innovation in the intellectual, and especially in the philosophical, realm more

1

often than not takes the form precisely of pressing questions in contexts in which they have hitherto not been asked. A question asked in a new context may thereby become a rather different sort of question; and the nature and significance of this shift may not be easy to determine.

Difficulties of this kind do arise, sometimes acutely, for someone trying to assess the significance of Simone Weil's work. At least they have done so for me. This is particularly true in relation to the writings springing from the later part of her life, when considerations of a religious nature came to be more and more important. Indeed, the penetration and audacity of her religious thinking are, understandably and rightly, high amongst the things which have attracted attention. Often her religious observations are continuous with, or developments of, ways of thinking which earlier had not had this religious dimension, at least not obviously or to the same degree. At these points questions of the kind I have mentioned concerning how, precisely, they are to be understood can hardly be avoided; neither do I think one should attempt to avoid them, for it is through pressing such questions that one is likely to help Simone Weil's work make its proper contribution to our intellectual, spiritual, and cultural life.

This book does not claim to be a comprehensive exposition of Simone Weil's philosophical thinking. What I have written is intended as a quite personal reaction to a particular theme which undoubtedly runs through Simone Weil's work, my interest in which is shaped by the philosophical background and concerns which I have brought to it. I have made no attempt to disguise this perspective, the nature of which will be very soon evident to any reader. This perspective explains the emphasis given, especially in the earlier chapters, to parallels with certain ideas of Wittgenstein's which I find particularly interesting. But I think that the theme that I have tried to develop, particularly in the forms it takes in Simone Weil's earlier writings, would be recognized by any philosopher. Her thinking takes off from positions which she sees in writers who are central figures in most branches of the western philosophical tradition: Plato, Descartes, Spinoza, Kant, Marx, for example. She is concerned, roughly, with the nature of human beings, material beings in a material world, who think; and with the relation between human thinking and the materiality of the human world. She explores what thinking is and tries to show how it can develop out of the peculiarly active relationship human beings have to their world and to each other. She also tries to show the consequences of such a development for the nature of human society and the lives which human beings live together.

Chapters 2 to 8 of this book try to set out the main lines of her thinking about this topic in her early writings and the difficulties into which they led her. Chapter 2 deals primarily with a work, "Science et perception dans Descartes," her student dissertation, which attempts to deal with the development of human thinking in terms of a modified Cartesianism from a first-person, "subjective," point of view. In *Lectures on Philosophy*, representing her lycée teaching immediately after her graduation from the École Normale Supérieure, she abandoned that point of view in favour of what she called (with tongue *slightly* in cheek perhaps) "the materialist point of view." Chapters 3 to 6 explore the nature of this change, the reasons for it, and its wider implications. Chapters 7 and 8 discuss the repercussions of this view, the fully worked-out view of her early maturity, on her thinking about social and political questions. This discussion is based primarily on *Oppression and Liberty*.

The remaining chapters, 9 to 15, try to bring out the sort of impasse to which this line of thinking had brought Simone Weil in the late 1930s and very early 1940s and the new direction which her thinking took in response to this situation. The most extensive single work of this period was *The Need for Roots*. My own discussion, however, is based more directly on certain important essays written during this time, along with certain entries in her notebooks. The essays I have mainly used here are "Essai sur la notion de lecture," "Classical Science and After," "The *Iliad* or the Poem of Force," "Human Personality," and "Are We Struggling for Justice?" I have also discussed certain sections of the collection *Waiting for God*.

These really very radical changes in her thinking during the last years of her short life are partly to be understood as responses to the internal philosophical difficulties generated by her earlier line of thought. But, at this stage of her work especially, one cannot leave out of account the increasing, or at least increasingly explicit, religious strain, without which her response to those philosophical difficulties would not have been, could not have been, what it was. My own procedure in dealing with this has been to try for as long as possible to display these late thoughts in "secular" philosophical terms. This is *not* because I regard such terms as in any way more acceptable than the religious language which she increasingly speaks. It is in part, I expect, because I feel much more at home operating with such terms. But, more important, it is also because I have wanted to see how far one could go in terms acceptable to philosophers who do not wish to, or find themselves unable to, use the language of religion. My hope is that, by doing this, I have been able to exhibit something of the conflict between secular philosophy and religion which anyone who wants to understand Simone Weil has to come to terms with.

Two philosophers with whom I sometimes compare and sometimes contrast her in the course of the book are Spinoza and, much more extensively, Wittgenstein. The role of Spinoza in my discussion needs little explanation; Simone Weil had thought deeply about his philosophy and she is at times clearly directly influenced by him; at other times she is equally clearly developing her own position in opposition to him. But my use of Wittgenstein is different. As far as I know, neither knew the other's work; there is certainly no direct influence in either direction. There are, however, great affinities between the way they conceived and approached philosophical questions, as well as equally striking divergences. I have not attempted any systematic comparison between them; but I have frequently exploited both the affinities and the divergences in the interest of trying to clarify the nature of, and the difficulties confronting, Simone Weil's philosophical positions. In doing this I have sometimes permitted myself to use terminology drawn from Wittgenstein. More particularly I have spoken of the "grammar" of certain expressions important to Simone Weil's discussions in a way which may give some people difficulty. As a matter of fact, Simone Weil herself sometimes expresses herself in a very similar way. When she does so, she has in mind the way in which our use of these expressions has to be understood not merely in terms of their relation to other linguistic expressions that we use, but in terms of the roles they play in human attitudes and aspirations, activities, lives, and relationships. That is included in what Wittgenstein understood by "grammar" too. And that is how I am using the word here.

2

THE CARTESIAN BACKGROUND

Simone Weil is best known for her remarkable life, her striking religious insights, and certain aspects of her social and political thought. Philosophers generally have taken comparatively little interest in her work; this is especially, though not exclusively, true of the Anglo-Saxon academic philosophical world. Of course her philosophical thinking cannot, without a quite unacceptable degree of distortion, be prized apart from the rest of her work. There are deep difficulties at many points even in knowing where to draw the line, or whether a line can be drawn at all, between what should be treated as belonging to philosophy and what to, say, religious meditation. There are difficulties even in being sure one understands what one is asking in trying to raise such a question. These difficulties themselves often raise issues of deep philosophical interest, issues which we should lose sight of were we simply to drop the distinction between discussions which are properly speaking philosophical in character and those which are not. I shall raise such issues from time to time in the course of the present work, and more especially in my concluding chapter.

Simone Weil was trained as a philosopher: at the Lycée Henri IV in Paris and at the École Normale Supérieure. The teacher who most influenced her was the philosopher Alain (nom de plume of Émile Chartier). She wrote an interesting student dissertation, "Science et perception dans Descartes." And the first years of her adult life were spent as a teacher of philosophy at French lycées, teaching to the austerely, not to say pedantically, academic curriculum of the French Ministry of Education – though no doubt not in a way envisaged or approved by the administrators of that curriculum. The ideas and habits of thinking which she developed during those years were vigorous and arresting; but they changed and evolved in quite radical ways as time went on, and were it not for these developments she would hardly be remembered as she now is. However, the structure even of her mature thought still owes a great deal to those early ideas; and where there are divergences, we shall often find it hard to grasp the significance of her later thinking if we do not relate them to the earlier positions she is abandoning.

That is one reason why in this book I shall devote a good deal of attention to the thinking which Simone Weil developed in her early adult years. But it is only one reason. As will, I hope, emerge, that thinking is in any case of considerable interest on its own account. I shall also, especially in my early chapters, at several points suggest parallels between her treatment of certain issues and discussions in various works by Ludwig Wittgenstein, who was her contemporary (though their thinking developed of course quite independently). In drawing these parallels, which I think are often striking, I do not intend to suggest that there is anything like a "common position" which they hold. Their emphasis and direction of interest are usually rather different; but these very differences may often illuminate what each of them is concerned about. One major difference is that Wittgenstein was much more self-conscious about the precise nature of the questions he was concerned with, much more quick to see that questions expressed in the same, or closely similar, words may nevertheless be quite different kinds of question. In this respect at least, his work is a valuable reminder of the need to be on one's guard at those (increasingly frequent) points where philosophical and religious thinking seem to merge in Simone Weil's work.

In 1934 she wrote "Reflections Concerning the Causes of Liberty and Social Oppression," which now constitutes the main body of the volume called *Oppression and Liberty*. In it the main issue she confronts is, very sketchily expressed, the following: Human beings are essentially active beings. Their greatest good lies in the exercise of their activity. Social life, in the complex forms we are familiar with today, has developed through the attempts of human beings to further and safeguard their active nature in the teeth of the obstacles thrown up by those natural forces to which they themselves as well as the environments in which they live are equally subject. But the outcome of this social evolution has not after all been the enhancement of people's active natures, but rather their enslavement. – The thought owes much to Rousseau, whom Simone Weil greatly admired and by whom her own thinking was often influenced: "Man is born free, but everywhere he is in chains."[1] Her task in *Oppression and Liberty* is to give a detailed account of the mechanism of this enslavement and to consider what, if anything, can be done about it.

Her former teacher, Alain, wrote to her about this essay, and in her reply[2] she sketches some of the ramifications of the questions she had raised. She starts with an important criticism of Descartes's "method." Between the *Regulae* and the *Discourse on Method*, she suggests, Descartes went off the rails and lost the conception of "order" as simply a mode in which the terms composing it are interrelated; he allowed it to assume independent status as "a thing," by trying to express it with a sign. (What she means by this may become clearer soon: it is closely related to Descartes's substantializing of "I" in the *Cogito*.) Mathematics, therefore, which is *par excellence* the study and development of forms of order, must be conceived "from as materialist and, as it were, cynical a point of view as possible; it must be conceived as consisting purely and simply in combinations of signs." But at the same time we must recognize that the theoretical as well as the practical value of mathematics is to be found in the *analogies* that are to be seen between these symbolic combinations and the practical problems which arise in the lives of human beings. This will involve a study of perception: *active* perception, that is, such as is characteristic of a person *at work;* a study, therefore, that must extend to the tools and instruments used in work, not merely from a technical point of view, but in respect of their relation to persons themselves – and in particular to human *thought*. Such a study will have to extend to an investigation of the social conditions of work and of the relation between "the struggle against nature" and "social oppression."

The issues outlined in this letter continued to preoccupy Simone Weil throughout her life. But of course, as is to be expected, her conception of the true nature of the problems to be tackled changed quite drastically as her thought matured. The change appears quite dramatic if one compares the early essays collected in *Oppression and Liberty* with the posthumous *The Need for Roots*. I shall be concerned, roughly from Chapter 8 onwards, with the nature of this change and with the intellectual and spiritual pressures that were responsible for it.

However, we cannot properly understand even her statement of these questions in *Oppression and Liberty* without grasping central notions such as *activity, natural force, obstacle* which are deployed in her exposition. As the letter to Alain already suggests, this will embroil us in some very wide-ranging philosophical issues. I shall devote my first five chapters to discussing them and return to the questions raised in *Oppression and Liberty* only in Chapter 6.

The concepts in which we are interested are treated in some detail in *Lectures on Philosophy*. But this treatment already represents an important development in Simone Weil's thinking from a position expounded earlier in her student dissertation, "Science et perception dans Descartes." It will be useful for us to investigate what she wrote in that juvenile essay, because the difficulties that it reveals will help to highlight the significance of some of the central ideas in *Lectures* and in *Oppression and Liberty*.[3]

"Science et perception" has the form of a Cartesian "meditation," expressed in the first person singular. – I start with an entirely self-contained consciousness involving no knowledge or awareness of an external world. How, given this starting point, can I be intelligibly thought to develop awareness of such a world?

The first stage in answering this question is to establish how I might form any articulate thought at all in such a state, which Simone Weil conceives in entirely *passive* terms, comparing it with the state of consciousness of someone wallowing with eyes closed in a warm bath. Her procedure at this point is modelled quite consciously on that of Descartes in the *Meditations*, in which he starts with a doubt so radical as to sever all the links between thought and the object of thought that it seems to him possible to sever. He then asks whether, from the point of view of such a doubt, there is anything that can be said certainly to exist, given that there is thought (and thought is of course given in the very asking of this question). I myself (he answers), a thinking being, must exist. The essential feature of Descartes's soliloquy, which is retained in Simone Weil's argument, is the attempt to assume nothing over and above the thinking which is constitutive of the argument itself. The only thought that she will acknowledge as possible in the primitive state of consciousness from which she imagines herself starting is one that makes no use of materials beyond just what is involved in the very conception of that state.

Now a criticism that has been levelled against Descartes from the beginning has been, precisely, that he *does* make use of material to which, on his own terms, he is not entitled. In modern times for instance, Bertrand Russell, echoing an earlier remark of Lichtenberg's, has complained that Descartes had no business to say "I think": that he was entitled to say no more than "There is a thought," given which alone there will of course be no route to concluding the existence of a thinking substance. In her student dissertation Simone Weil does not explicitly criticize Descartes on that score. But her own modification of the Cartesian argument does show her to be sensitive to the kind of objection made by Russell and many others. She replaces "Je pense, donc je suis" ("I think, therefore I am") by "Je puis, donc je suis," which might perhaps be rendered in English as: "I (can) act, therefore I am." At the same time she noticeably does not emphasize the existential conclusion in the way Descartes does. She quite deliberately does not regard her inference as a prolegomenon to asking Descartes's question: "What then am I?" What is important for her is the way the formula characterizes thought itself – as *activity*.

There is here an inchoate anticipation of a very important criticism which, at a somewhat later stage, she does direct explicitly at Descartes: a criticism I have already alluded to in discussing her reply to Alain's letter. In an early notebook she complains that Descartes, in the *Meditations,* was "much too ambitious." I shall come back to the nature of this alleged over-ambition shortly; it is closely related to the point I am dealing with at present.

"Science et Perception dans Descartes" explores how the "activity" of thought is to be understood, though with rather inconclusive results. Her central contention is that it cannot be conceived as a power *over* anything: and this for two related reasons. On the one hand, the argument does not establish that there is anything other than thought over which thought could be the exercise of power. On the other, more fundamentally, whenever I do, as common parlance has it, exercise power over, or act on, anything, I can see on reflection that it is a purely contingent matter that things behave as I try to make them behave. Simone Weil uses the French word *hasard* to express this. Her point is close to that elegantly expressed by Wittgenstein in *Tractatus Logico-Philosophicus,* Proposition 6.374:

> Even if all we wished for were to happen, still this would only be a favour granted by fate, so to speak: for there is no *logical* connec-

tion between the will and the world, which would guarantee it, and the supposed physical connection itself is surely not something we could will.

It is clear from the way Simone Weil develops her thought that she is not merely saying that thought is a *species* of activity, but that it is, rather, activity itself, or at least involved wherever there is activity – as it were, the active ingredient in any true activity. She thinks of it as pure spontaneity. Other forms of so-called activity are all, so to speak, polluted by contingency *(hasard):* they are not characterized by pure spontaneity.

Her thoughts on this subject were to change very radically in ways we have to understand if we are to see the significance of other developments in her thinking. Changes in her conception of thought and activity are already marked in the notes taken of her philosophy teaching at the Roanne lycée *(Lectures on Philosophy).* But an indication of how much further still these changes were to go is the following, from an important essay of 1942:

> Thought never knows affliction except by constraint. Unless constrained by experience, it is impossible to believe that everything in the soul – all its thoughts and feelings, its every attitude towards ideas, people, and the universe and, above all, the most intimate attitude of the being towards itself – that all this is entirely at the mercy of circumstances.[4]

But these further developments will be hard to appreciate unless we first explore a bit further the ramifications of her early position in "Science et perception dans Descartes."

I remarked on the substitution of "je puis" for "je pense" in Simone Weil's version of Descartes's *cogito* formula. She spells out the significance of this in a number of remarks. For instance:

> Existing, thinking, knowing, are merely aspects of a single reality: ability to act *(pouvoir).*

And again:

> What I am is defined by what I can do.

So what *can* I do?

As I have already noted, my ability to act excludes everything that is a matter of *hasard* (chance, contingency): any brute fact, that is, which is as it is whether I will or no, everything of which, as she puts it, I can ask Figaro's question from Pierre de Beaumarchais's *Le mariage de Figaro,* Act 5: "Pourquoi ces choses et non pas d'autres?" ("Why this rather than something else?")

But there is a problem about how we should understand this. In the common course of life, for instance, if I press the bell-push and the bell rings, there is (in normal circumstances) no room for the question why the bell has rung. I made it ring. But for Simone Weil at the time of the Descartes essay, on the contrary the ringing of the bell would undoubtedly have been a matter of *hasard* relative to my *pouvoir.* The ringing of the bell clearly depends on a great many conditions over and above my pushing of the button: the state of the wiring, the mechanical condition of the bell, the supply of electricity from the mains, and so on. To a very large extent the satisfaction of these conditions is outside my control at the time of my pushing the bell-push. Moreover, there is no such thing as a specification of "all" the conditions necessary for the ringing of the bell and hence no possibility of my controlling "all" the conditions. And again, following the suggestion in my quotation from Wittgenstein's *Tractatus,* we can say that the fact that these conditions are indeed necessary for the ringing of the bell is itself something that obtains independent of my will. It would be an exaggeration to say that no explanations of why such conditions are necessary could be given, but, as Wittgenstein remarked in another place, explanations come to an end. And in the end I have to accept that certain things and relationships are as they are and not raise any further questions about them, at least for the time being. To the extent that this is true I am dealing with matters that Simone Weil would have said, at this time, are not in my power but belong to *hasard.* A little reflection is enough to establish that this argument, if valid at all, can be applied to any supposed power over physical events.

It is tempting to say at this point that at least I have power (in the requisite sense) over my own thoughts. But this does not seem to be true. Thoughts often come unbidden; they do not always come when I want them; they may be forced on me by circumstances (in fact to an overwhelming extent they are); they may follow obsessive patterns; and so on. In other words, my thinking is subject to causal conditions as much as anything else.

These are difficulties which are going to plague any conception of thought as pure activity. And in fact Simone Weil was to leave such a conception far behind in later writings in which the concept of *attention* became central to her account. This concept was for her closely related to that of *obedience:* we must submit to the demands of the subject matter which is the object of attention rather than attempt to dominate it. With this shift in emphasis was to come a much clearer recognition that the individual thinker is not sovereign but dependent on surrounding conditions and that the achievement of intellectual clarity is not so much an achievement as a gift or grace.

Even in the early "Science et perception dans Descartes" her emphasis on the pervasiveness of *hasard* brings her to a point where the Cartesian framework of her argument is beginning to crack. In fact her criticisms of Descartes's position are really much more thoroughgoing than I have so far brought out. Her substitution of "je puis" for "je pense" does not merely refrain from drawing Descartes's existential conclusion on the grounds that the premises of the argument do not entitle her to it. She also wants to make the more positive point that the word "I," at least as used in this context, does not stand for any sort of thing, or existent. *A fortiori,* we may conclude, it does not stand for something which is outside the realm of extended nature and which is not subject to the causal forces operating in that realm.

"Existing, thinking, knowing, are merely aspects of a single reality: willing" (or "being able to act": *pouvoir*). What Simone Weil wants to say is that my knowledge of myself as expressed in the *cogito* in *no* way goes beyond my thinking activity itself. The word "I" does no more than express the grammatical subject of the activity-verb; it does not refer to an entity which happens to perform this activity and which might do other things as well.

> And as far as my knowledge of myself is concerned, what I am is defined by what I can do *(puis)*.

A corollary is that the formula "je puis" does not express a *relation* between myself and anything else, since the word "I" in the formula does not stand for anything that could be a term in such a relation. So here is an additional reason why the *pouvoir* in question is not to be regarded as a power that I exert *over* anything: that would be a relation between myself and something else and the only "myself" involved is not something that could enter into such a relation: it is not *something* at all, just a grammatical requirement.

Simone Weil follows Descartes in conceiving thinking as essentially involving *order*. So the introduction of the thought "je puis, donc je suis" into her meditation is essentially a recognition of the possibility of order. As I remarked earlier, in her "Reply to a Letter from Alain," written in 1935, she wrote that Descartes, between writing his early work the *Regulae ad directionem ingenii* and the *Discourse on Method,* somehow went off the rails. He failed to prevent the order which he had discovered from becoming "a thing instead of an idea"; which is what happens, she continued, when one tries to express a series by means of a sign and thus represents it as a reality distinct from the terms that compose it. So, we may perhaps conclude that if the introduction of the word "I" into the meditation of "Science et perception" signals the introduction of order into consciousness, the temptation to substantialize the "I" (to which Descartes notoriously succumbed) precisely *is* the temptation to substantialize, or hypostatize, order.

But how does this hypostatization of order manifest itself in Descartes? The order Descartes is interested in establishing is a relation between existents. This can be achieved, he thinks, only through methodical thinking. In the *Meditations* and the *Discourse* methodical thinking starts with hyperbolical doubt, the professed aim of which is *not* to establish an intelligible order between terms the existence of which is taken for granted. This existence, indeed, is what is above all subjected to doubt. The first positive aim of the "method" is rather to establish the existence of something (the "thing that thinks"); everything else can subsequently be related to this and thereby be authenticated. Descartes's *cogito* and the arguments for the existence of God which immediately follow are the first steps in this process.

So the line of argument developed in "Science et perception" leads to a criticism of Descartes a good deal more radical than Simone Weil explicitly acknowledges there. It leads to a rejection of the view that hyperbolical doubt, and the *cogito* which flows from it, should be expected to lead to a genuinely existential conclusion. As Descartes had recognized earlier in the *Regulae,* method is concerned with establishing a proper order between elements which are in some sense already given. (Naturally, in the course of establishing order we may recognize that we are forced to abandon some of the ideas we had previously accepted, as well as that we need to fill in gaps that exist in what we so far know.) This is to see method as a kind of critique of existing intellectual disciplines, not as something that replaces them. In the period immediately following the end of Simone Weil's formal student days this thought is developed rapidly and ruthlessly.

An entry in one of her early notebooks reads:

> There is no way of opening broad vistas which the mind can observe without entering them. One must enter the subject before one can see anything.
> This is true of speculation, even in its purest form: "im Anfang war die Tat." Whence the necessity and the role of *critique*. From this point of view Descartes was much too ambitious.[5]

Descartes's over-ambition lay in supposing he had a method for discovering the truth of a kind which could *replace,* wholesale, existing methods of discovery already in use, and which would legitimate wholesale scepticism concerning the results of those existing methods. By contrast, "criticism" has to be applied to existing methods and results. It is essentially discriminatory; and it exploits (while, if necessary, improving) the techniques of discrimination involved in existing methods. Only in terms of such techniques (which have to be *learned,* not invented *de novo*) do we have any understanding of what "discrimination" would amount to. We cannot reflect discriminatingly on the existing given results while at the same time rejecting wholesale the existing methods of inquiry which have produced those results, if only because, amongst other reasons, the significance of the results can normally only be understood by someone with a grasp of the kind of inquiry from which they spring. Philosophy is no "pure intellectual inquiry" of the sort Descartes envisaged; and there is no such thing. There are only particular inquiries the forms of which are historically shaped. Philosophers can and should reflect on the adequacy of such particular historical forms; but if they try to dispense with them all, they will necessarily lose their grip on the concept of "adequacy" in this context.

There is another important point concealed in the brief notebook entry just quoted. The line from Goethe's *Faust* ("Im Anfang war die Tat" – "In the beginning was the deed") and the talk of "opening broad vistas" ("One must enter the subject") emphasize activity in a particular way. You will not understand a subject simply by contemplating it as a spectator; you have to practise it. And Descartes's hyperbolical doubt seems to take hold only when one does merely contemplate its object as a spectator. The point is similar to the one Wittgenstein was making when he spoke of "language going on holiday" – a way of putting it which directs our attention much more sharply to the source of our philosophical difficulties than does Hume's observation concerning their disappearance when one sits down to play backgammon. The way to rid ourselves of our difficulties is not to stop thinking but to see the confusions inherent in the mode of thinking which led to them.

What Simone Weil says here is, I believe, connected with her earlier emphasis on the word "I" when she discussed activity. Why "I," one may feel inclined to ask, rather than "he or she," "you," or "we"? The answer is that if we try to express activity in anything but the first person we do not get what we wanted – an *expression* of activity – but merely a *description* of activity. J. L. Austin's discussion of promising is relevant here: the words "I promise," in a suitable context, actually express the *making* of a promise, whereas the words "he promises" express only the *report* of the making of a promise.[6]

To consider this further, take as an example the activity of arithmetical calculation. It might be objected to what I have just been saying that I can clearly recognize the exercise of this activity in another whom I observe writing calculations on a piece of paper. I am not aware of (active) calculating only in myself; it is not the case that all I can observe in a third party is a going through the motions of calculating. And if I describe what I see, of course I describe what the third party is *doing*, namely calculating. So does not "Elizabeth is calculating" report the execution of an activity just as much as does "I am calculating"?

Yes, it does. But this is superficial. We need to compare the way language is used in the actual performance of the calculation with its use in the description of that performance. Take the description first. I say: "Elizabeth is adding 355 to 489. First she adds 9 to 5 and gets 14. She writes down '4' in the units column and carries 1. Then she adds 8 and 5 and 1 and gets 14. She writes down '4' in the tens column and carries 1 again. Then she adds 3 and 4 and 1 and gets 8, which she writes down in the hundreds column. This gives the answer: 844."

Notice particularly the constant recurrence of the third-person pronoun "she" in this report.

What does Elizabeth herself say in the performance of the calculation? "9 plus 5 make 14. That's 4 and carry 1. 8 plus 5 plus 1 make 14. That's 4 and carry 1 again. 3 plus 4 plus 1 make 8. The answer is 844." The first-person pronoun does not occur at all here. Elizabeth *could* of course have used it. "I add 9 and 5 and get 14. Then I write '4' and carry 1 . . . " This would be artificial, but that does not much matter. What *is* important however is that the use of the word "I" here is inessential, whereas the use of the word "she" in the third-person report is not. That is, the "I" is expressed in the performance of the activity itself. In the fussy second version of Elizabeth's performance, she was not using the word "I" to designate anything: it was merely an (inessential) adjunct to the execution of the activity itself.[7] It would be wrong to say (as Simone Weil comes close to doing in the Descartes essay) that the "I" here *designates* the activity; it is rather that the execution of the activity is itself an expression of the "I."

Awareness of the grammatical differences between first- and third-person utterances in such cases (of which the example above is a mere fragment) does seem to be essential to the grasp of a certain notion of activity. The important point is *not* that this is a form of activity the nature of which I can come to understand only through *awareness* of it in myself. On the contrary, I do not come to understand it through being aware of it at all, but through grasping the first-person use of certain expressions.[8] One very important way in which I manifest this grasp is in using the expressions in the first person singular myself. I think that in "Science et perception" Simone Weil emphasizes this too exclusively however; and this creates problems which she was only able to see round later, when she saw the importance of language as something which for the individual is *given* and has to be learned from third parties.[9] But my previous example will help to bring out how central nonetheless is my ability to use such first-person expressions myself and my ability to describe others as using them. When I say of Elizabeth: "She *adds* 9 to 5 and *gets* 14," I do not simply mean that she contemplates the figures "9" and "5" and then writes down "14." I mean what I do by it by virtue of my own ability to add and arrive at a result. "Getting" 14 by "adding" 9 and 5 involves the concept of getting it *right,* in the sense that the description of what Elizabeth is doing in these terms opens the door to the question whether she has calculated correctly. This much I have to understand in using such terms in the description. I have to know what it is like to distinguish a correct from an incorrect answer. Even if the calculations I am describing are of a kind the techniques of which I do not master, they must bear a recognizable relation to calculating techniques that I *do* master if I am to identify them as "calculations" at all. Mastery of such techniques is manifested on the one hand in the ability to calculate and on the other hand in the ability to recognize and understand similar expressions in the mouths of others. One way in which I exhibit this understanding is in basing my own third-person descriptions of what others are doing on what I hear them say. But these third-person descriptions are not, as it were, *translations* of the first-person utterances on which they are based; the latter are not "descriptions" at all but fill a quite different grammatical role. It is that role that Simone Weil is indicating when she emphasizes the special connection between the notion of activity and the use of verbs in the first person singular.

3

THE SENSATIONS OF THE PRESENT MOMENT

I tried to show in the preceding chapter how the modifications Simone Weil introduced into Descartes's original method of inquiry were leading her right away from the Cartesian conception of method as, so to say, radically creative, towards the idea of *criticism*. Now the whole point of this movement is to insist that thinking must start with some material: it cannot, as Descartes's *cogito* argument claimed to do, create, or even constitute, its own material. Furthermore, the difficulties with which "Science et perception dans Descartes" tries to deal, but in the end gets bogged down in, show that the "material" on which thinking must work cannot be an inarticulate splurge of passive sensation. If methodical thinking is critical in character, its object must be of such a form that it will make sense to speak of "criticizing" it. It must express a positive claim and have an articulate order. That means that it must at least purport to be a coherent, ordered thought; criticism will take the form of investigating this thought. All this, at least, is involved in Spinoza's observation, with which I associated Simone Weil, that thinking must start with "a given true idea."

And so the first chapter of *Lectures on Philosophy* contains the important remark

> When we are on the point of giving birth to thought, it comes to birth in a world that is already ordered.[1]

The "materialist point of view" which that first chapter elaborates is designed to show how such a thing is possible.

18

Now, given the context in which I have tried to show that the issue arises, this may seem no light undertaking. For the argument of "Science et perception" (which is, after all, what leads to the point we are at) had represented thought as the same thing as activity and hence the same thing as the creation of order. For order involves a series of elements arranged in such a way that we can pass from one to the other in a methodical way; and this is conceivable only to the extent that they have already been arranged in a quasi-methodical way. This doctrine, articulated in "Science et perception," also dominates the first two chapters of *Lectures on Philosophy*. (And indeed, I do not believe that Simone Weil ever gives it up.) Combined with the conception of thought as criticism (and with its corollary: that thought essentially needs ordered material to work on), the doctrine seems to require something like a creation of order, or, what comes to much the same thing, a formation of concepts, prior to any exercise of thought.

A warning is needed here. I am expressing the matter – and I have followed Simone Weil in this – as though what were in question is the description of some "cognitive process" ("creation of order," "formation of concepts"); and this sounds like a task for a psychologist: someone like Piaget, perhaps. But that is not what is really in question. We might try saying that what is required is the description of a logical structure: the structure, namely, of the ability to exercise concepts. But this way of putting it can easily be just as misleading as the other. (There are plenty of examples in intellectual history to bear this out: consider, as a recent example, the mythology of "innate ideas" associated with Chomsky's rather similar way of conceiving the ability to speak grammatically.)

What we need, I shall say, is a description of the difference between someone who does exercise concepts and one who does not. (This way of putting it is itself by no means immune from difficulties: where, for instance, are we supposed to find a being who does not exercise concepts? But let that pass.) Now, the quasi-Cartesian conception of "Science et perception" is that such a description will have to be given from the point of view of the subject who exercises the ability. I tried to show in the last chapter what lies behind that presupposition: that activity is only properly expressed in verbs conjugated in the first person singular; that if we describe the application of concepts otherwise than from the point of view of the subject, we are left with nothing but a description of events, of "things happening." ("Pourquoi ces choses et non pas d'autres?'') But if, as the argument claims to have shown, the ability to exercise concepts presupposes something *already* conceptually structured ("a universe that is already ordered"), we may seem to have returned all the way to our starting point without having made any progress.

In a way this is true, but in another not. For we have at least seen that progress cannot be made in the Cartesian way; another approach is needed. We cannot expect, however, to be comfortable with an alternative approach until we have freed ourselves from what seemed to make the Cartesian approach necessary: that is, the presupposition that the exercise of concepts must be described exclusively from the point of view of the agent.

One way in which Simone Weil tries to achieve this is through showing that there is an incoherence in the way that point of view is conceived in the Cartesian enterprise. This is an important part of the argument of Chapter 1 of *Lectures on Philosophy*, occurring, roughly, between pages 41 and 47 and yielding the conclusion, on page 43:

> What we can say about the operation of the senses apart from movement is that we have an infinite variety of sensations and that they teach us nothing at all.

The aspect of her argument that I shall concentrate on is this. According to an ancient and widespread empiricist tradition, the formation of concepts involves a certain passively given material (sensations) the inherent characteristics of and relations between which are then discerned through an activity of the mind, which then, on the basis of what it has thus discerned, regroups this material under concepts. This is the view that is being rejected in that last quotation.

I shall discuss Simone Weil's case by comparing it with, and amplifying it from, section v of Wittgenstein's *Philosophical Remarks*, which I think deals with the same subject from a very similar point of view, but which is often more explicit. In order to understand what both of them are saying, it is important to remember that the conception of sensation that is under attack is that found in empiricist epistemology. Outside the context of that epistemology, in our ordinary lives, we do of course speak of learning things from our sensations. (A sensation of heat may show me the presence of a hidden radiator, for instance.) We also speak of our sensations as having certain relations to each other. The sensation of taste I get from this wine is mellower than that I had a moment ago from another wine; or than the sensation of taste I had a moment ago when I drank the wine immediately after eating something sweet. In such talk, however, we are employing a developed, structured concept of sensation which has its life and its sense in its relation to talk about many other things *besides* sensations (radiators, wines, and so on). Empiricist epistemology, on the other hand, needs a concept of sensation that can be understood independent of any such talk. It is supposed to *underlie* these other kinds of talk and to make them possible. It is this latter conception of sensation that is under attack in what follows.

The following remarks come from pages 46 to 47 of *Lectures on Philosophy*.

> Do they [sc. sensations] give us [the idea] of time? A sensation is after all something that lasts, but for sensations to be able to give us the idea of time it would be necessary for us to be able to attach some significance to past sensations.[. . .]
> . . . As far as the sensation itself is concerned, one cannot think of it, except by actually feeling it. A past sensation, or one to come, is then absolutely nothing, and, as a result, since sensations have significance only in relation to the present moment, there is in them no passing of time and they do not give us the idea of time. It is difficult for us to believe that they do not give us the idea of time because they possess some kind of duration. But, in this case, one should call to mind Bergson's analysis and his distinction between time and duration. Time is something homogeneous and indefinite; duration is a single characteristic of the quality of a sensation. If we have the impression of duration in the case of a sensation, that only means that sensations are not brought about in an isolated way: there is a continuity, an overlapping of sensations. The duration of sensations does not mean that they involve time. On the contrary, it is impossible[2] to limit sensations to the present moment; to say that sensations are limited to the present moment would be to locate them once again in time.

I said just now that it is important for us to remember that Simone Weil's arguments are directed at a particular philosophical conception of "sensations." We must bear a similar point in mind concerning the use of the word "present" in this context. Of course, sensations, *as ordinarily understood,* are located in time, *as ordinarily understood.* Empiricist epistemology, on the other hand, requires something given out of which the familiar temporal distinctions of past, present, and future can be *constructed.* In that epistemology, the words "sensation" and "present" are supposed to belong to the description of that given. The empiricist's "sensations," then, cannot be thought of as already presupposing such distinctions. So they have to be thought of as occurring in a "present" which is understood independent of any "past" or "future."

What is the source of the idea "that sensations are limited to the present moment" which is criticized in the passage above? It will be helpful to compare this passage with one from Wittgenstein's *Philosophical Remarks* which deals with the same issue.

> The stream of life, or the stream of the world, flows on and our propositions are, so to speak, verified only at instants.
> Our propositions are only verified by the present.
> So they must be so constructed that they can be verified by it.[3]

I shall digress for a while here to consider Wittgenstein's use of the words "verified" and "proposition" *(Satz)* in this context. This will help us not merely to understand the position that he describes here (and goes on to criticize), but also what issue Simone Weil is raising in her discussion of "sensations."

The German word *Satz* is sometimes appropriately translated "sentence," sometimes "proposition." The use of the term "proposition" in philosophy is itself the result of philosophical and logical preconceptions and can raise philosophical difficulties. The association of talk about propositions with talk about verification, as in the passage above, inevitably brings to mind the so-called Verification Principle of the Vienna Circle and its logical-positivist followers. This has indeed led some commentators (Norman Malcolm for instance) to speak of *Philosophical Remarks* as representing a "verificationist" phase in Wittgenstein's thinking. If this word is intended to imply any close kinship between Wittgenstein's position at this point and that of the Vienna Circle, I think it is wide of the mark, although of course it goes almost without saying that the philosophical *problems* that concern him here are closely connected with those that preoccupied the philosophers of the Vienna Circle.

For some philosophers at least, the "Verification Principle" (roughly that the meaning of a *Satz* is the method of its verification) involved treating a sentence or proposition as something that can be detached from the particular circumstances of its being thought or uttered by someone at a given time and place. Interpreted in this way a *Satz* is analogous to what Frege understood by "a thought" – something that could be entertained on different occasions in different circumstances by the same or different people.[4] The meaning of the sentence "Caesar crossed the Rubicon" is taken to be rendered by describing what anyone would have to do in order to determine whether it is true or false. This method of verification would of course take time to apply – it might for instance involve cross-checking of records, determining the relative weight of different, and perhaps conflicting, sources of evidence, and so on. It is certainly not something which could be thought of as taking place "at an instant"; even less as something which always takes place "in the present" (the meaning of which striking but obscure phrase I shall consider shortly).

This is not the way in which Wittgenstein, in *Philosophical Remarks,* understands either *Satz* or "verification." The context makes it plain that by *Satz* we are to understand something which someone utters, or thinks privately, on some occasion. It is something like the expression of a judgment. Or perhaps we should say "the *attempted* expression of a judgment," since an aspect of the issue Wittgenstein is discussing is: What makes an utterance (public or private) into a genuine expression of a judgment? If for instance, as I write these words sitting in Vienna under a cloudless sky, I utter (or think) to myself the words "These wretched monsoon rains will continue for a long time yet," it is clear that those words do not express a genuine judgment. The context is not such as to allow us to attach that sort of significance to them.

I believe that Wittgenstein is here discussing what it is that makes an utterance into the genuine expression of a judgment. If, when I uttered the words above, I were sitting in Kuala Lumpur in the middle of the monsoon season, it would be a different matter. And if I, who utter these words, am familiar with the climate in Malaysia, have some idea how long the rains have already lasted and what is their normal duration, that, in the absence of countervailing considerations, would be enough to qualify my utterance as a genuine expression of a judgment. I think it is clear that considerations such as these belong to what Wittgenstein is discussing as the "verification" of a *Satz* in this context. Of course there is another, perhaps more usual, use of the verb "to verify" according to which my judgment has not been verified until a long time has passed without the rains ceasing. Thus, according to Wittgenstein's usage here, to say that the circumstances in which, at a given time, I utter a certain *Satz* constitute a "verification" of it is compatible with allowing that the judgment thus made will later turn out to have been *false*. To say that my utterance is verified at the time at which I make it is to say that my circumstances are such as to give me good reason for thinking it to express a true judgment; the idea is that this much is required if the utterance is to be counted as the expression of a judgment at all – true or false.[5]

The account I have given so far explains, perhaps, why Wittgenstein says that "our propositions are, so to speak, verified only *at instants.*" But why does he immediately go on to say that they "are only verified *by the present*"? At first blush that seems to be quite a different matter. For example, I wonder whether a book which I see to be missing from my shelves has been borrowed by a friend. I verify this by being told by him that he has taken it: I can now be said to judge that he has taken it. That verification, we may say, takes place at a certain "instant." At the time when I am making it, that is at the time when I am being told that my friend has taken it, it can be said (even if the locution is somewhat artificial) that the proposition is being verified "by the present," that is by those present circumstances in which I find myself. However, the following day I shall be able to say: "It was *X* who took my book; I verified this *yesterday.*" So while it may be true that my verification took place at a certain *instant,* it does not look as though I can say (at all times) that my proposition is verified by the *present.*

But these considerations do not go far enough to reach the problem Wittgenstein is discussing. Even if now, the day after I have spoken with my friend, it is natural to say that I verified *yesterday* the proposition that it was he who took the book, it may be that the circumstances I am in *at present* do not allow me to make the same judgment. For instance, I may have suffered some injury which afflicts me with amnesia concerning all that happened yesterday; or overwhelming evidence may have come to light indicating that my friend had been lying in order to protect someone else who had stolen the book; and so on.

We may then feel inclined to say that what gives me warrant for making the judgment is not so much the fact of what happened yesterday as the fact of my present knowledge, which is a survival from what happened yesterday. It seems as though yesterday's confrontation with my friend, if it is now to provide me with any warrant for my claim that *X* took the book, can do so only *through* some mark it has left on my present "cognitive state." And so it now seems that what "verifies" today's judgment is different from what verified yesterday's judgment to the same effect. Yesterday it was my actual confrontation with X. – Or rather, having embarked on this line of thought, we may want to modify that too and say: it was my perception of, or experience of, that confrontation (since if I did not experience it, it would have given me no warrant for making the judgment in question . . . !). – Today it is the knowledge that I retain as a result of that confrontation. We are now on the brink of saying what is said in the quotation from Wittgenstein:[6] that my proposition is verified "by the present." A crucial part of the road that leads over the brink is the idea that my present knowledge is part of my present state of consciousness on the basis of which I judge as I do. That is to treat the situation as on a par, say, with some sensation, like an itch, which I am experiencing at the present moment and which warrants me in judging that there is a source of irritation at a particular point on my body. The distortion involved in thinking of the matter in this way is of course an aspect of what Wittgenstein so relentlessly criticized in the later *Philosophical Investigations:* the idea that such epistemologically central words as "know," "understand," "remember," "intend" designate so-called mental states.

The general line of argument I have tried to express above does not turn on any features peculiar to the particular example. If sound, it could be adapted so as to justify saying quite generally that what "verifies" any judgment made at a particular time is some state of consciousness of the one who makes the judgment. And this, I think, is the position Wittgenstein is trying to express in the words "Our propositions are only verified by the present," the position which he is combating in that section of *Philosophical Remarks.*

It is essentially the same position that Simone Weil is criticizing on page 47 of *Lectures on Philosophy:*

> Sensations tell us nothing about the world: they contain neither matter, space, time and they give us nothing outside of themselves, and in a way they are nothing.
>
> Nevertheless we perceive the world; so what is given us is not simply sensations. Far from sensation being the only thing that is immediately given to us, it is, as such, only given us by an effort of abstraction, and by a great effort at that.

A central part of her argument for this conclusion is that, as stated in my earlier lengthier quotation, it is *impossible* to "limit sensations to the present moment." The conception of sensations as "limited to the present moment" is precisely the conception of "the present which verifies our propositions" involved in the discussion of Wittgenstein above. Simone Weil's assertion that sensations "tell us nothing about the world" is a rejection of what Wittgenstein is also trying to show is a confusion: the idea that our propositions are verified "only by the present." She, like Wittgenstein, is concerned with the question of what is involved in our having a conception of, being able to make judgments about, a determinate world. What they both argue is that we cannot find the answer in the conception of "sensations of the present moment." Their arguments also are remarkably similar: they attack the conception of *the present moment* involved here.

Having said, in the remarks already quoted, that sensations "do not give us the idea of time," Simone Weil goes on to amplify and strengthen this observation by saying that it is a mistake even to suppose that they are "limited to the present moment," since that would be "to locate them once again in time." I insisted earlier that the word "sensations" in this context must be understood as being used in a special way: that characteristic of a certain epistemology. It is not, for instance, being denied that I can say, with sense and with truth: "Half an hour ago I had a twinge of toothache but it did not persist," and the like. The concept of toothache is itself a temporal notion: it *presupposes* the concept of time, in the sense that mastery of it involves the ability to deal with such questions as "When did you last have it?" "Did it last long?" "Have you had it more than once?" and so on. But Simone Weil's discussion belongs precisely to an investigation of what makes such abilities possible, of the features of human life and experience out of which they are fashioned. She is criticizing the idea that these abilities are somehow constructed out of experiences that we can grasp and speak about independently of such abilities.

Her claim that we cannot speak of "sensations" in *this* sense as "limited to the present moment" is identical with the claim made by Wittgenstein in the following passage from section v of *Philosophical Remarks* (p. 85):

> If someone says, only the *present experience* has reality, then the word "present" must be redundant here, as the word "I" is in other contexts. For it cannot mean *present* as opposed to past and future. – Something else must be meant by the word, something that isn't *in* a space, but is itself a space. That is to say, not something bordering on something else (from which it could therefore be limited

off). And so, something language cannot legitimately set in relief.[. . .]
. . . And so it is a meaningless epithet.

Let us apply this to my earlier example. I considered a situation in which I think *today,* on the basis of something said to me by my friend *yesterday,* that it was he who had taken my book. The argument was: it must be inaccurate, or at least elliptical, to say that what I think today is based on something that happened yesterday; since nothing that happened *yesterday* can have any bearing on what I think today except in so far as it appropriately modifies my *present* situation. I say "appropriately" because not any sort of modification will do. What is required is that I should in my present circumstances have *grounds* which will make it intelligible that I should have such a thought as "It was X who took my book." The idea is that for it to be intelligible that I should have a thought *about* something, there must be a link between me *now* at the time I have the thought and, as it were, a position in space and time at which my thought is directed. – It is necessary to express things in this cumbersome way in order to make room for the intelligibility of my having a thought that is *false:* even in that case there must be a route between me in my present situation and some state, or states, of affairs by way of which I could be shown that my thought is false. And that means that my understanding or awareness of my present situation must provide me with access to that route.

Of course the philosopher Wittgenstein is considering, who says that only the present moment is *real,* denies the possibility of any such route leading away from the present moment. That philosopher is a solipsist who thinks that thoughts *can* only refer to the experience of the present moment. That is a further step beyond the original empiricist emphasis on the epistemologically fundamental significance of the experience of the present moment. We do not need to consider that further step here, although, as we shall see later in the book, the temptations of the solipsist's position are relevant to the later development of Simone Weil's thinking.

If my present thought can be attached to the world only through something that is the case concerning me *now,* then what *was* or *will be* the case cannot have any relevant bearing on things as they are with me now. That is to say, everything relevant to the sense of my present thought must be now available to me: otherwise the sense of the thought would not at present be a determi-

nate one; it would have to wait on my making some epistemological contact with the past or the future – and then the same sorts
of question could be asked concerning the nature and basis of *that*
epistemological contact. But that must mean that what I mean by
"now" in this context cannot involve any *contrast* with past or
future. For if such a contrast *were* in question, then I should
indeed be involved, now at the present moment, in an immediate
relation with some other time of the sort which the argument
claims to show to be impossible.

Of course normally, when we speak of what is the case "now"
or "at the present moment," a contrast with what was or will be
the case *is* implied. "What's the weather like?" "It's raining at
present." That is, the dry spell is over; or: we shall have to wait till
the rain stops if we don't want to get wet. The word "now" and
its analogues would have no point if such contrasts were not in the
offing. But now, I, a philosopher, in the grip of the argument
under criticism, may say: In order to have the thought "It's raining
at present" I have to have – *now* – perceptual experiences, visual,
auditory, tactual sensations perhaps, which give me reason to
think that it's wet outside. And if, as was claimed at the beginning
of this paragraph, my thought does have implications about the
past or the future (as ordinarily understood), there equally has to
be something in my *present* circumstances which puts me in a position to have a thought with such implications. My present state of
mind must contain an epistemological residue of past experiences
of weather patterns: of rain showers coming to an end and the sun
coming out, and so on. The word "present" in the preceding sentence does not refer to any *content* of the original thought under
discussion ("It's raining at present"); it tries to refer to something
that makes it possible for me to have that thought. Wittgenstein's
characterization hits the nail on the head: "Something else must
be meant by the word, something that isn't *in* a space, but is itself
a space."

He draws the consequence that this is "something language cannot legitimately set in relief." A moment ago I attributed to empiricist philosophers the claim that "my present state of mind must
include an epistemological residue left by past experiences." But
it is clear that, in that context, the philosophers have no right to
use words involving a relation of the present to the past. And it is
also clear that they would be quite unable to say what they need to
say without using some such words. What they would like to be

able to say cannot be said. As Wittgenstein remarks, here the word "present" is a "meaningless epithet." Or, as Simone Weil puts the same point: "It's impossible to limit sensations to the present moment; to say they are limited to the present moment would still be to locate them in time."

I have tried to develop at some length the line of thought that seems to me to underlie what Simone Weil says about sensations in relation to time because this seems to me to hit the general position she is attacking in the opening pages of *Lectures on Philosophy* at its most central point. I shall now discuss more schematically some of the other points she makes against the attempt to base thought on sensations. I think it will be evident that these further points are intimately related to the difficulties about the relation of sensations to time.

From one point of view the claim that we can only think about sensations in a temporal context may be seen as a special case, or application, of the general thesis that sensations can be understood as making a contribution to thought only in so far as they are seen as (essentially) standing in certain *relations* to each other and to other things. So, where what is in question is a sensation's presentness, this can only be expressed by thinking of it as located in a network of temporal relations with other things; and more generally, thinking of a sensation as qualitatively determinate in some respect, is seeing it as belonging to a *system* of internally related qualities.

In putting the matter like this we are seeing temporality as just one instance of a general truth about *any* qualitative determinateness attributed to sensations. There is nothing wrong with this. And in fact Simone Weil's discussion of notions like colour, taste, smell, and so on does repeatedly make this general point. But there is a further, and perhaps stronger and more interesting, claim made in the course of her treatment of sensations. It is the claim that *only in the context of human action, which is an essentially temporal phenomenon,* is it possible to see anything (and *a fortiori* sensations) as systematically interrelated. Consider for instance the following passage, on page 42 of *Lectures,* which treats of the concept of colour and its relation to our visual sensations.

> It is impossible to give a name to the colours one sees. Every coloured point has its own peculiar colour which is not like any other colour. Are there greater or lesser differences, for sight, between colours? The degrees of difference imply series which we have to

construct and which we construct in our imaginations by making use of series which we can make from some material or other. Whenever there is a series there is an activity of the mind. One could make series of colours (blue to red through violet) in such a way that it would be difficult to distinguish each term from those immediately next to it. So one cannot speak of series, nor of greater or lesser differences, by reference to sight alone. So long as two colours appear different, they are so absolutely. One does not lay down a series between the two, because one cannot order colours in a series except by relating them to quantities (an increasing proportion of blue). But as far as sight alone goes, there is no quantity. There is, properly speaking, no quantitative difference between qualities. The differences between qualities are differences of kind, not of degree.[. . .]

So, each coloured point has its own colour which is not like any other, and each coloured point is completely changed from one moment to the next.

In order to understand this we have to try not to think of colours in terms of the colour *system* exemplified by the spectrum on which colours appear as internally related to each other. We have to think of them rather as simply given in visual experience. (This is by no means such a simple exercise as may be thought by the unwary!) It is of colours conceived of in this way that Simone Weil says that "it is impossible to give them a name," the reason being simply that the names of colours *do* imply such a system.

Now, it may be protested that the names of colours as such do not imply membership of anything as precise or articulated as the system of the spectrum. And it is no doubt true that, for instance, a child learns to talk of colours before it ever becomes acquainted (if it ever does) with the colour spectrum. However that may be, unless some fairly systematic interconnections are presupposed, it is difficult to see how there is going to be any sense to questions concerning whether colour A is more or less like colour B than colour C; or whether A is darker or lighter than C. Of course the question whether one *colour* is darker or lighter than another is quite different from the question whether one *coloured object* is darker or lighter than another. The first question concerns an internal relation, the second an external relation. An object that was once darker than another may become lighter than it while still remaining the same object. If we substitute "colour" for "object" in that last sentence, we produce nonsense. Furthermore, the external relations of *lighter and darker* between coloured objects in a sense presuppose the internal relations between col-

ours. To call these relations "internal" is, one might say, to recognize that *these relations are rooted in the colours themselves*. And this
suggests that our very identification of colours for what they are
is a locating of them within a system.[7] And that of course is just
Simone Weil's point.

She states the point, as we have seen, in terms of a distinction
between quantity and quality: "one cannot order colours in a
series except by relating them to quantities (an increasing proportion of blue)." That is one way of putting it. But the main point is
that the conception of a "proportion of blue" is not something
one could derive simply from "the sensation of blue"; one has to
learn certain ways of speaking and thinking, certain principles of
arrangement. In default of this, that is outside the context of the
ability to arrange things in a certain sort of order, "so long as two
colours appear different, they are so absolutely."

In any case the names of individual colours certainly presuppose
the general concept *colour*. That much at least is clear from Wittgenstein's discussion of ostensive definition in *Philosophical Investigations*. And that is already to concede that the relation in which,
say, blue stands to red is of an entirely different sort from that in
which it stands to, say, loud, or rough, or oblong. The important
thing is to recognize that we do not know how to operate with
terms like "different," "similar," "more or less different," and
so on except in so far as we presuppose some system of
interconnections.

Since such a system is not derivable from bare sensations and
since such comparative judgments as those above are the very least
that would be required if our sensations were to form the basis for
our empirical concepts, it seems that we still lack an adequate
account of what makes such concepts possible, or of what is
involved in the mastery of them. This is where what I called
Simone Weil's stronger point comes into play: that it is only in *the
temporal context of human action* that anything (and *a fortiori* sensations) can be seen as systematically interrelated. "The degrees of
difference imply series which we have to construct and which we
construct in our imaginations by making use of series which we
can make from some material or other."

The development of this point is the subject of the next chapter.

4

"LA SIMPLE PERCEPTION DE LA NATURE EST UNE SORTE DE DANSE"

The position we have reached might be summarized as follows. In her very earliest writings Simone Weil's concern is already to elicit those features of human beings' lives which make it possible to ascribe to them mastery of concepts and the ability to know and understand. She is investigating what sort of creature a human being has to be in order to develop such abilities. In "Science et perception dans Descartes" she takes the notion of thinking, conceived in a quasi-Cartesian way, as her primitive starting point and argues that it is identical with pure *activity*. "Je puis donc je suis." But since the very purity of the activity, as she conceives it at that time, precludes its being a power "over" anything (since this would at once introduce an alien element of contingency into the exercise of activity), thought would have to furnish its own material for the development of its concepts: material completely within the power of thought itself. Descartes had attempted to show how this could be so, but his attempt failed: and necessarily so. Thought is essentially critical in nature and criticism requires something to be criticized. Sensationalist empiricism attempts to supply this material in the form of passively experienced sensations. But just because sensations, *as they have to be conceived for the purposes of this argument,* represent pure passivity, they do not possess any form or structure on which critical thinking could be exercised. In fact, so radical is the formlessness of such "sensations" that nothing at all can be said about them. They can have no place in an account of human understanding.

This outcome points to a fundamental flaw in the whole conception of the enterprise. It creates the dilemma: order is the product of thought, but thought can only be exercised on what already exhibits order. Simone Weil's response to this dilemma is to abandon the thesis that all order is the product of thought. "When we give birth to thought, it will be born into a world that is already ordered." That remark can easily be misunderstood in such a way as to suggest that she is simply throwing in the sponge. Given that the whole project was to investigate what is involved in seeing the world as ordered, it would be a pretty lame outcome for her to say that the world is simply given to us as ordered! But, of course, that is not what she is saying: her point is that, though order is indeed a product of the activity of human beings, that activity itself does not, in the first instance, involve thought.

So it is the identification of thought and activity, the central thesis of "Science et perception," that she abandons at this stage. And this move opens the door to the remarkable reversal of the Cartesian, first-person-singular, point of view, characteristic of that early essay, in favour of what in *Lectures on Philosophy* she calls "the materialist point of view," the point of view of a third-person observer of human activity.

However, the argument as I have so far reconstructed it does not show how it is possible for Simone Weil to make such a move, given that one of its pivotal contentions is that activity can only be expressed in the first person. What are the consequences of abandoning that contention? The urgency of this question is recognized in a remarkable entry in the notebook she was keeping at that time:

> The behaviourist psychology is the only good one, on the express understanding that one does not believe it. Everything that can be thought about the human condition is expressible in terms of behaviour – even including freedom [*in the margin:* even free thought (problems), or the most generous feelings (Platonic love . . .). Try to describe all these things without ever mentioning soul, spirit, etc.] The only thing that escapes is that which, since it is thinking, cannot be thought.[1]

Of course, that entry hardly expresses a *solution* of the problem, or even an indication of where the solution is to be sought. And what she calls "the only thing that escapes" looks like quite a big fish.

I have not found in Simone Weil's writings any full and explicit treatment of the problem sketched here. However, I believe that she did reach a point of view from which the problem no longer appeared threatening. I also believe that there are materials in her thinking at that time which make a resolution of the difficulty possible. In what follows I shall use those materials in an attempted reconstruction of an argument which would achieve this.

The basic presupposition of the argument in "Science et perception" is, then – to repeat what I said at the end of Chapter 2 – that activity can only be grasped in the actual use of first-person conjugations of certain verbs. Any *description* will be only of "things happening," events. Simone Weil's often reiterated point was that we can always ask of mere happenings why they occur like that and not in some other way. If I intentionally do something, however – so it is implied – my grasp of *what* I am doing already comprises my *reasons* for doing it; and this is true *par excellence* of active thinking. For instance, my present thought that there is a difficulty in Simone Weil's position is what it is by virtue of my understanding of that position. To explain why I think what I do I need only give the reasons I have for thinking it – and these reasons are largely constitutive of the thought it is. That is, someone who did not have these reasons would not be in a position to "think the same thought"; we should not identify whatever thought that person might have as "the same" as mine.

There is a discussion of *language* in the first chapter of *Lectures on Philosophy* (pp. 64–75) containing some remarks which, though not fully worked out, are suggestive in relation to the problem we are considering. Having observed that language is "something that belongs to human beings alone," Simone Weil makes the rather cryptic remark that "it is something artificial in relation to the individual (but natural for society)." I take her to mean something like this: the very existence of society involves the use of language – we should not call, or think of, anything as "a society" which did *not* involve the use of language – whereas the human individual is born without language and has to learn it. We may now ask what is involved in this learning and what makes it possible. Simone Weil observes in this connection that individuals have something she calls "spontaneous language," by which she means certain natural, unlearned gestures, bodily postures, facial expressions which are, equally spontaneously, reacted to by others. "Language proper" (that is, the language that the child learns as it grows up in a society) still contains "traces of natural language"; and it is clear that she regards the "language proper," thus acquired, as developing out of, and made possible by, those unlearned spontaneous gestures and reactions.

Now the learning of language is, at the very least, closely connected with the formation of concepts. The remarks on language which I have just noted suggest that, in order to understand what is involved in this, we should not start with a conception of myself as isolated Cartesian intelligence faced with the task of constructing concepts out of the material provided by my own thinking or experience. We should begin instead by considering the human child, equipped with certain natural propensities and born into an existing human society, the language of which it learns from others. And we should recognize that this learning is itself in large part a development of the child's own natural propensities.

The distinction between the propensities which the learner brings to his learning and the material which is learned is of course not the same as the distinction between activity and passivity; but the two distinctions are closely connected. It would be natural to speak of the learner's "active" contribution to the process of learning. Moreover an analogous active contribution has to be made by the speakers of a language, once learned. I mean that the distinction between, for instance, the ("active") role of the one who speaks and the ("passive") role of those addressed is essential to our understanding of what language is.[2]

This last point is suggested by Simone Weil's remark that the language that is *learned* still contains "traces" of the "spontaneous language" of which it is a refinement; it is intimately connected with the problems surrounding the notion of activity which are central to her thinking at this stage. Another comparison with something discussed by Wittgenstein may help to bring out what is at stake.

In *The Blue Book* he discusses the type of solipsist who wants to say: "Only my own experiences are real" or "Only I have experiences." This discussion is closely related to that which I dealt with in the last chapter from *Philosophical Remarks*, and the concept of "experience" involved in the discussion of the solipsist is virtually the same as the concept of "sensation" involved in that previous discussion of "the present."

Wittgenstein suggests in *The Blue Book* that the solipsist is dissatisfied with the notation of our present ordinary language in which the linguistic formulae used to express experiences are invariant as between speakers. For example, in that notation it is correct for each of us, given suitable circumstances, to say "I have a headache." If I take the position of Wittgenstein's solipsist I shall feel that my relation to my own experience is special. – Indeed it is, I shall think, the *only* experience to which I have any relation. Because of this, in the language that I speak and understand, the word "experience" as applied to myself means something quite different from the same word as applied to other people. Hence, according to what *I* mean by the word "experience," it is a necessary truth that only I have experiences. This important truth, I feel, ought to be built into the language I speak by reserving the use of the word "experience" for application to myself.

Wittgenstein imagines a situation in which I succeed in persuading or compelling everyone else to adopt this modified usage. In this language the correct way to express what *I* now express with the words "I have a headache" is "There is a headache." That is, when, as we *now* say, P.W. has a headache, this will be correctly expressed, both by P.W. and by everyone else, as "There is a headache." But if anyone else, N.N., has, as we *now* say, a headache, this will be expressed as "N.N. is behaving as P.W. behaves when there is a headache." That is, this is what will be said by both N.N. and everyone else in order to express what in our present language N.N. expresses with the words "I have a headache" and everyone else with the words "N.N. has a headache." From my assumed solipsistic point of view this revised language appears to have the important feature that in it I express only facts of which I am myself aware. I say "There is a headache" only when I experience a headache. I say "*X* is behaving as P.W., behaves when there is a headache" only when I am aware of *X*'s behaviour and of its similarity to my own behaviour on other occasions, which I now remember. Similarly, no one else is permitted to say anything that I cannot understand in terms of facts of which I myself am aware. So it looks as though nothing that I say or hear requires justification by way of an interpretation of others' behaviour in terms which go beyond what I am, or could be, aware of.

This, at any rate, seems to be what Wittgenstein's solipsist supposes will be achieved by the new notation. But is this so? Imagine my friend N.N. with a hangover, clutching his forehead and saying "N.N. is behaving as P.W. behaves when there is a headache." Imagine that I, P.W., utter the same sentence. Do N.N. and I express the same fact? And *what* fact? If both N.N. and I say what we do on the same basis – by observing the similarity between

N.N.'s and P.W.'s behaviour in given circumstances – then it might seem that we do indeed express the same fact; but it is *not* the fact at present expressed in ordinary English when N.N. says "I have a headache" and I say "N.N. has a headache." Because (in ordinary English) N.N. does *not* say what he says on the basis of observation of behaviour, though I do say what I say on that basis. That is, as far as ordinary English is concerned, it is essential to my (P.W.'s) and N.N.'s expressing the same fact (that N.N. has a headache) that our respective utterances do not have the same relation to what we are both expressing. That is to say, I confirm N.N.'s remark "I have a headache" when I say "N.N. has a head-ache" only to the extent that I base my remark on observation of N.N.'s behaviour and N.N. does not. And the same must hold for the solipsistic language if, as Wittgenstein seems to intend, it is to be taken as having the same expressive resources as ordinary English and simply a more (solipsistically) satisfying *notation*.

But even this does not go far enough. It is incoherent to think that N.N.'s utterance and mine might have the same relation to the fact reported. Each of us says "N.N. is behaving as P.W. behaves when there is a headache." But what are N.N.'s grounds supposed to be for saying that the behaviour of P.W. that is in question occurs *when there is a headache?* According to my, the solipsist's, story, only I have any relation to *headache* and only I, therefore, am able to refer to it.

To put the matter another way: there is no way for N.N. to draw any distinction between "There is a headache" and "P.W. is behaving as he does when there is a headache." Indeed there is presumably no use for the latter expression by anyone other than the solipsist himself in the solipsist's language. *For us,* however, these two sentences do mark a distinction: between the case where P.W. genuinely has a headache and the case where he is shamming. This is a distinction moreover which, for us, may be drawn in the third person; and that possibility is essential to our understanding the sense of "behaves as P.W. does when there is a headache," that is, in our language, "behaves as P.W. does when he, P.W., has a headache." But this means that the apparent reference to the occurrence of a headache in what N.N. says is spurious and might as well be left out. But if it *is* left out, the solipsist's language seems to collapse, since there is no way of expressing N.N.'s entitlement to say anything corresponding to what we now say using the term "headache." And that has the consequence that he cannot even express *what* behaviour of P.W. he is supposed to want to refer to, namely the behaviour that occurs "when there is a headache." When is that? N.N. cannot even ask the question. That is, he cannot learn the language which I, P.W. (the solipsist), want him to speak.

We might express what is shown by the discussion of this case as follows: when I (P.W.) have a headache and tell you so in the (ordinary English) words "I have a headache," the manner in which I utter these words is essential to their conveying what they do convey. If the utterance were a consequence of my examining the colour of my skin and the lines on my face in the mirror, my noting that I had just taken a heavy dose of aspirin, that I was unable to concentrate, and so on, then the utterance would *not* express what we usually understand by the words "I have a headache." On the other hand, when you hear my words you show that you understand them by, for instance, examining me and noting my behaviour in the way just described. That "the same thing" is meant by the speaker and understood by the listener is shown precisely by the *difference* between the moves made by speaker and listener in the conversation. This sort of complexity, or relativity, was of course one of the important things that Wittgenstein was trying to highlight with his notion of a "language game," a notion which in its suggestion of the diverse roles played by speakers of a language emphasizes their active character as essential to it.

The point is so important that it is worth mentioning another discussion of Wittgenstein's that relates, though not obviously, to the same issue. *Philosophical Investigations,* §300, speaks of the relation between the representation of *behaviour* and the representation of *pain*. (I have discussed this passage at length in *Trying To Make Sense,* pp. 76–8, though from a different point of view.) He says that the representation of pain enters into our language game with the word "pain," "only not as a picture," whereas the language game *does* involve a picture of behaviour. One way of putting his point would be to say that the representation of *pain* in language is achieved through a distinctive grammar in the way we talk. One of the most important features of that grammar is undoubtedly the quite different conversational role of the one who says, for example, "I have a headache" as compared with the one who hears and understands this, or as compared with the one who reports in the third person that X has a headache.

What I have been discussing is not an *isolated* area of language. Linguistic communication is shot through and through with analogous distinctions between roles which give different speakers different kinds of relation to what is said. And the existence of these differences helps to determine what it is that is being said. It belongs, in Wittgenstein's phrase, to its grammar. Hearers can understand speakers – that is, can understand the *same* thing as is meant by the speakers, only in so far as speakers and hearers express their understanding of what is being said quite *differently.*

Let me return now to Simone Weil's discussion of language. The digression above was intended to provide an amplification of what she says about the traces of what she calls "spontaneous language" in the language we *learn.* The point I wanted to bring out was that it belongs to the sense of (very, very many at least of) the things we say that the speakers of the language stand to each other in many and varied roles. In the context of my overall argument, it will be remembered, this notion of "spontaneity" in language is important for our understanding of how Simone Weil freed herself from the impasse into which her earlier, quasi-Cartesian, conception of *activity* had led her. It is important to emphasize in this connection too her insistence, in *Lectures on Philosophy,* on what I might call the "describability" of language. "Language has a reality of its own because it is fixed, permanent, artificial" (p. 67). – I do not think she would have contested that the "fixity" and "permanence" are only relative. What is important in the present connection in the idea of "a reality of its own" is that language, and the sense that is expressible in it, are not *reducible* to anything else – to the personal experiences and sensations of its speakers, for example. On the contrary, these experiences can achieve characteristically linguistic expression only because of the, in a sense, "impersonal" reality of language.

> It enables us to express ourselves: our tears, cries, groans are states of our own, often brought about unconsciously, but they are always felt as our own; on the other hand the word "pain" has nothing painful about it. As soon as one has given a name to one's feelings one can look on them as objects which have a reality of their own.

And again:

> So language is for this very reason a means of purification; it is a source of health in the sense that it expresses all the things that

torment us. As soon as it is expressed it becomes something general, human, so something we can overcome. . . .

Once Goethe had expressed his despair in *Werther* it became a phase through which all people pass.[3]

We have reached a point where we can say that the active–passive distinction is a feature, a fundamental feature, of the "impersonal," and hence *describable,* reality of language. We are no longer compelled to say, we no longer can say, that the notion of activity appears only to the agent who is speaking in the first person. It no longer appears true that observers' descriptions capture only events, things happening. For the notion of activity involved in first-person uses of activity-verbs is only possible *in* that – describable – language. And *descriptions* of the practice of speaking in the first person *are* accounts, descriptions, of the relevant notion of activity.

It remains of course the case that these descriptions of first-person uses have a very different sense, and function, from the first-person uses themselves. The description of what making a promise consists in is very different from the making of a promise. And that, perhaps, is what made Simone Weil say, in the entry from her early notebook that I quoted previously in this chapter, "The behaviourist psychology is the only good one, on the express understanding that one does not believe it." I do not find that a very good way of putting the point, though. Better is the subsequent remark: "The only thing that escapes is that which, since it is thinking, cannot be thought."

Acting is not the same as describing someone acting. But that does not mean that we *cannot* describe someone acting. No doubt too there is an understanding involved in acting, a practical understanding, which is not the same as the understanding involved in being able to give a description of acting.[4] But that does not mean that this latter understanding is *not* an understanding of acting.

It is time to return to the difficulty with which I opened this chapter. I said that, in order to make room for an account of thinking as *criticism,* Simone Weil needed to show how there could be any sufficiently articulate material for criticism to be exercised on, *given* her previous insistence that the requisite articulated order is itself the result of thought. How is it possible for thought to be "born into a world that is already ordered"? I noted that she continued to regard order as a product of human activity. And the clear consequence was that she needed an account of activity which gives it a certain independence of thought.

Now the original identification of activity and thought rested on the presumption that activity as such cannot contain any element of contingency: just so far as what takes place depends on factors which do not spring from my will, it is not purely something that *I do*. But any description from a third-person viewpoint of what takes place implicitly sets the occurrence in a network of contingent conditions. That can only be avoided, so she seems to have held, through an expression in the first person which is not a description at all but a direct manifestation of activity; and such an expression can only be articulated as a thought. The intention of my long digression has been to show how some of the considerations developed in *Lectures on Philosophy* in fact enabled Simone Weil to escape from the straitjacket of this position. The crucial consideration is that articulated thought is only conceivable in a context of action which is understood as *temporal* and which, as such, is subject to all the contingencies that go with temporality.

Her escape was expressed in the following beautiful metaphor:

> C'est le rapport essentiel entre nous et l'extérieure, rapport qui consiste en une *réaction,* un réflexe, qui constitue pour nous la *perception* du monde extérieure. *La simple perception de la nature est une sorte de danse;* c'est cette danse qui nous fait percevoir.

> Our *perception* of the external world constitutes the essential relation between us and what is outside us, a relation which consists in a *reaction*, a reflex. The elementary perception of nature is a sort of dance; this dance is the source of our perceiving.[5]

We are far away from the "warm bath" of sensations from which we are supposed to start in "Science et perception dans Descartes." It is not just that the emphasis is now on bodily movements. We are positively invited to look at ourselves as from the standpoint of a third-party observer: the concept of a *dance* is not of course an exclusively spectatorial one, but it certainly does require that the spectator's point of view be taken into account in its implication of a *pattern* of movements. Of course, dancers do not necessarily have to think of that pattern in executing their movements. But if there *is* no spatio-temporal pattern of movements, they have not executed a dance. Furthermore, a dance is an *activity* – an activity, then, which can be described from a spec-

tator's standpoint. The whole argument of the earlier essay had
rested on a denial of this last possibility.

Here is an example in which the central features of this new
conception are embodied. Let us imagine a woman walking across
fields on a fine spring day. She keeps her eyes constantly fixed on
the peak of a distant mountain and the route she takes consistently
takes her towards that landmark. Sometimes she comes to obstacles like woods, streams, fences and then she deviates from the
straight line she follows when she is in open country. If she comes
to a stream she stops momentarily and her eyes span the distance
between the two banks; if the distance is small she jumps; but if it
is great she turns away and rummages amongst the dead branches
lying around. Those which she cannot move she leaves alone; she
discards those which are seriously crooked and eventually finds a
straight broad one which she is able to lay across the stream: she
then clambers over. Birds sing in nearby trees; she stops and
searches the branches with her eyes; when her eyes focus on a
bird, she smiles and after a while goes on. Sometimes her eye is
caught by a flower beside the path; she stoops and sniffs it and
smiles again. In the woods she follows the path through the trees;
sometimes she stops and looks at a particular tree with a puzzled
expression, fingers its bark, picks a leaf and holds it in front of her
eyes; then she shrugs her shoulders and goes on. There is a distant
roll of thunder; she stops and looks up at the sky where clouds are
thickening. She turns round and retraces her steps, always keeping
in front of her the spire of the church in the village from which
she started out. When it begins to rain she quickens her pace. And
so on.

Everyone would recognize this as a description of a woman pursuing certain goals, expressing certain interests, and taking notice,
with varying degrees of attention, of different features of her surroundings. What she does, that is what she can be observed to be
doing, shows what she is aiming at, what she is interested in, what
she is taking notice of, what is forcing itself on her attention, and
so on. There is little need to spell this out any further.

The suggestion in Simone Weil's metaphor is that our understanding of what it is for a human being to perceive things of different sorts requires familiarity with, and ability to interpret, this
sort of "dance": a familiarity and an ability which all normal
human beings possess. Her discussion distinguishes two aspects of
the dance: on the one hand, reactions which depend on the com-

plex *physiology* of the human body; on the other hand, movements the description of which introduces *geometrical* concepts.

We are interested in how this account is going to make room for the perception of an *ordered* world without presupposing an original activity of *thought*. Let us start with the physiological reactions. Simone Weil uses the Greek distinction between the "limited" and the "unlimited" to make the point.

> If we examine the relation between reactions and stimuli, we see that the latter are limitless in number, while the former are limited. The salivary gland, for example, always secretes saliva, whatever the food is. It is as if it were able to discern the general character of food throughout the infinite variety of foods. Other reflexes are more remarkable: the salivary glands secrete at the very sight of food, and yet the food never has the same look about it (change of colour, of shape).
>
> So, by means of our reactions we generalize stimuli. If there were a different reaction corresponding to each stimulus, each reaction would only be produced once in a life time, and then life would be impossible.
>
> It is in this way that the body classifies things in the world before there is any thought. (Example: the chick leaving the egg distinguishes between what is to be pecked and what not.)
>
> So, from the very fact that we have a body, the world is ordered for it; it is arranged in order in relation to the body's reactions.[6]

The "limited" character of the body's reactions, then, in relation to the "unlimited" character of the stimuli to which it is subject, already creates a sort of primitive classification: the stimuli are, as she puts it, "generalized" in so far as certain stimuli are always reacted to *in the same way,* for example by salivation, and are *thereby* classified together, for example as food. That is, the "classification" in this instance *consists* in the fact that the stimuli all evoke the same reactions: it is completely unreflective, not mediated by thought. We do not salivate *because we recognize* what is before us as food; our recognition of it as food manifests itself in our salivating in its presence.

I said: *"in this instance."* Of course, Simone Weil is not suggesting that there is no such thing as a response to an environment which is mediated by thought or reflection. The point is, first, that not all our responses are like that; second and more important, that not all our responses *could* be like that, since the concepts necessary for thought and reflection require unmediated, unreflective responses for their formation.

Simone Weil uses the terminology of "conditioned reflexes" in her account of how these original, instinctive responses are modified by experience and learning. But in substance her thinking about how such learning is to be understood owes very little in the end to the mechanistic straitjacket of that Pavlovian concept. Her understanding of "behaviourist psychology" as, it will be remembered, she speaks of it in her early notebook is not at all a mechanistic one. And her account of how genuine thought and reflection develop through the *methodical* organization of primitive reactions in the light of the agent's projects and interests is not compatible with a mechanistic outlook. I shall say more about this account in the next chapter.

At present I want to emphasize that though, as I have said, Simone Weil is by no means denying the importance of the fact that very many of our actions and reactions *are* based on thought and reflection, many of the concepts in terms of which we think about our surroundings, *even such as obviously enough have to be learned,* are manifested in responses which are not at all reflective. Connected with this is her insistence that our reactions are characteristically to "wholes" and systems of relations rather than to atomic properties. We recognize (react to) a chair as such without needing to recognize the details of its appearance. A chair is something one sits in; a staircase is something one climbs.

> Everything that we see suggests some kind of movement, however imperceptible. (A chair suggests sitting down, stairs, climbing up, etc.)[7]

Similarly, our concept of three-dimensional space is formed out of our natural propensity to *grasp* certain objects. It is important to distinguish her view about this from an empiricist doctrine like that of, say, Berkeley in *A New Theory of Vision.* Though she shares with Berkeley the idea that the concept of a three-dimensional object cannot be formed with visual material alone, for him the important thing is that we should have both visual and tactual (including kinaesthetic) *sensations,* whereas for Simone Weil what is needed is not more "given" material at all. It is through our own active *movement* itself (and not just the kinaesthetic sensations associated with movement) that we reach the concept of objects in three-dimensional space. "The sensible changes which are perceived in movement still do not give us space."[8]

This last point has important connections with the difficulties about time discussed in the last chapter arising out of the attempt to account for our concept formation purely in terms of sensations. If it is only through our bodily movements that we form the concept of three-dimensional space, then since movement is essentially a temporal notion, time is necessary to the framework within which this concept formation is described. The framework is *not* that of a "timeless present" of sensation. Time enters Simone Weil's account, of course, in more than one way. For instance, any movement involves a before and an after. But her account also emphasizes our repetition of the same movements on different occasions (for instance in its explanation of how "by means of our reactions we generalize stimuli").

I have reached a point at which I need to introduce Simone Weil's discussion of the way in which *geometry* enters into the body's perceptual "dance."

> *Il y a donc toute une géométrie élémentaire déjà dans la perception.* Tout se passe comme si notre corps connaissait des théorèmes géométriques que notre esprit ne connaît pas encore.
>
> Dans la perception normale il y a déjà géométrie. *Donc, il n'y aura pas à s'étonner s'il y a imagination dans la géométrie puisqu'il y a déjà imagination dans la perception.*[. . .]
>
> C'est la même cause essentielle (imagination) qui fait que nous percevons les choses les plus vulgaires et que nous faisons de la géométrie, qui est à la base de toutes les sciences, et aussi que nous sommes émus par la flèche d'une cathédrale ou par une symphonie (*cf.* Paul Valéry dans *Eupalinos*).
>
> C'est le rapport essentiel entre nous et l'extérieure, rapport qui consiste en une *réaction,* un réflexe, qui constitue pour nous la *perception* du monde extérieure. *La simple perception de la nature est une sorte de danse;* c'est cette danse qui nous fait percevoir.

> There is already, then, an elementary geometry in perception. Everything happens as if our bodies already knew the geometrical theorems which our mind does not yet know.
>
> There is already geometry in normal perception. So we should not be surprised if there is imagination at work in geometry, since it is already at work in perception.[. . .]
>
> It is the same cause really (imagination) which enables us to perceive the most ordinary things, and do geometry, which is at the foundation of all the sciences; it is this too which moves us in a cathedral spire or in a symphony (cf. Paul Valéry in *Euphalinos*).[9]

Consider again the country walk which I described by way of example. There are various ways in which geometry enters into it.

There is, for example, the way in which the walker navigates by reference to the distant mountain or church spire. She focuses her eyes on the landmark and walks in a straight line towards it. The disposition to return to the line indicated by the landmark after detours, while it could be, as it were, "justified" in terms of certain geometrical theorems, is clearly not, in most cases, actually *based* on any reflective knowledge of such theorems. Similar points could be made about the walker's other movements, her examination and manipulation of the various objects she encounters, for instance her judgments about the suitability for bridge-building purposes of branches lying in her vicinity, and so on.

There are other facts, relating to geometrical structure, of a sort which Simone Weil in several places alludes to in her discussion of tools, which have to do with the "elementary geometry involved in perception." There are, for example, the mechanisms of our various joints (compare: elbow, shoulder, and hip), which condition the ways in which we move about and our abilities to manipulate things. Since our concepts of objects, and hence the ways in which we perceive them, are built up on the basis of these various sorts of bodily activity, Simone Weil is suggesting that the geometry involved in these facts of anatomical mechanics contributes to the structure of our perceptual fields.

An important essay from 1941 makes the point very clearly:

> All tools are instruments for ordering sensible phenomena, for combining them in definite systems; and in handling them men always think of the straight line, the angle, the circle, and the plane.

The instruments a worker uses, and the movements involved in using them, create "a closed and limited and definite world." For instance,

> In using a spade I hold the handle, place my foot on the blade, and assume definite positions of the body in relation to the spade; I handle it with the thought of a straight line in relation to an angle; and all the various material turned by the spade falls into a series of continuous magnitudes according to the greater or less resistance each movement encounters.[10]

Before I leave this subject I want just to draw attention to the connection between it and notions belonging to aesthetics – to our abilities to find beauty in what we perceive. "It is this too [sc. the elementary geometry in perception] which moves us in a cathedral spire or in a symphony." The line of thought suggested here is hinted at again and again in the *Lectures* and in Simone Weil's other writings belonging to this time. It was to be much more fully developed later in a way which brought with it fundamental changes in her account of concept formation. I shall have more to say about this later.[11]

5

LANGUAGE

Prométhée

Un animal hagard de solitude,
Sans cesse au ventre un rongeur qui le mord,
Le fait courir, tremblant de lassitude,
Pour fuir le faim qu'il ne fuit qu'à la mort;
Cherchant sa vie au travers des bois sombres;
Aveugle quand la nuit répand ses ombres;
Au creux des rocs frappé de froids mortels;
Ne s'accouplant qu'au hasard des étreintes;
En proie aux dieux, criant sous leurs atteintes –
Sans Prométhée, hommes, vous seriez tels.

Feu créateur, destructeur, flamme artiste!
Feu, héritier des lueurs du couchant!
L'aurore monte au coeur du soir trop triste;
Le doux foyer a joint les mains; le champ
A pris le lieu des broussailles brûlées.
Le métal dur jaillit dans les coulées,
Le fer ardent plie et cède au marteau.
Une clarté sous un toit comble l'âme.
Le pain mûrit comme un fruit dans la flamme.
Qu'il vous aima, pour faire un don si beau!

Il donna roue et levier. O merveille!
Le destin plie au poids faible des mains.
Le besoin craint de loin la main qui veille
Sur les leviers, maîtresse des chemins.
O vents des mers vaincus par une toile!
O terre ouverte au soc, saignant sans voile!
Abîme où frêle une lampe descend!
Le fer court, mord, arrache, étire et broie,
Docile et dur. Les bras portent leur proie,
L'univers lourd qui donne et boit le sang.

Il fut auteur des rites et du temple,
Cercle magique à retenir les dieux
Loin de ce monde; ainsi l'homme contemple,
Seul et muet, le sort, la mort, les cieux.
Il fut l'auteur des signes, des langages.
Les mots ailés vont à travers les âges
Par monts, par vaux mouvoir les coeurs, les bras.
L'âme se parle et tâche à se comprendre.
Ciel, terre et mer se taisent pour entendre
Deux amis, deux amants parler tout bas.

Plus lumineux fut le présent des nombres.
Les spectres, les démons s'en vont mourant.
La voix qui compte a su chasser les ombres.
L'ouragon même est calme et transparent.
Au ciel sans fond prend place chaque étoile;
Sans un mensonge elle parle à la voile.
L'acte s'ajoute à l'acte; rien n'est seul;
Tout se répond sur la juste balance.
Il naît des chants purs comme le silence.
Parfois du temps s'entrouvre le linceul.

L'aube est par lui une joie immortelle.
Mais un sort sans douceur le tient plié.
Le fer le cloue au roc; son front chancelle;
En lui, pendant qu'il pend crucifié,
La douleur froide entre comme une lame.
Heures, saisons, siècles lui rongent l'âme,
Jour après jour fait défaillir son coeur,
Son corps se tord en vain sous la contrainte;
L'instant qui fuit disperse aux vents sa plainte;
Seul et sans nom, chair livrée au malheur.[1]

The point from which I started in Chapter 2 was the concept of the human being as essentially an active being which forms the basis of Simone Weil's analysis of oppression in *Oppression and Liberty*. I have been tracing the development of her understanding of the meaning of "activity" in some of her earliest writings: more particularly, the development from the quasi-Cartesianism of "Science et perception dans Descartes" to the "materialist point of view" of the *Lectures on Philosophy* and early notebook. In my treatment of this latter position I have so far emphasized the primitive bodily reactions which she represents as the foundation of concept formation. I want now to explore her account of how these bodily reactions are transformed into truly methodical procedures in connection with which it is more natural to speak of an "exercise of concepts."

I have emphasized the radical break with Cartesianism which her abandonment of the first-person perspective signals. But there remains a strain in her thinking which suggests a continuing Cartesian influence: namely a certain kind of individualism. This individualism is not logically required by "the behaviourist point of view" as it is by Descartes's first-person perspective, but is still nevertheless present in her thinking at this stage. In some of the most important sections of *Oppression and Liberty* it makes itself felt very strongly and interacts decisively with her social and political ideas. In *Lectures* this tendency competes with countervailing influences, especially in the sections on language. I have the impression that she had not satisfactorily synthesized the various elements in her thinking at this stage.

The picture suggested in *Lectures on Philosophy* by its quasi-physiological starting point is of an individual human being, bringing into the world certain innate propensities to active movement, propensities expressing his or her inner wants and needs. The growing child adapts its movements to the environment it encounters, thereby learning how to satisfy its wants and fulfil its needs; in the course of this process it forms concepts of the objects of which the environment is composed and of their properties and modes of interaction with each other. The suggestion here that what is important to the development of thought is the individual's interaction with the natural environment rather than with other people certainly had very strong appeal for Simone Weil at this time. The following passage from her early notebook is characteristic:

> To be in direct confrontation with nature, not with men, is the only discipline. To be dependent upon someone else's will is to be a slave. And that is the fate of all men. The slave depends on the master and the master upon the slave. This situation makes men either suppliants or tyrants, or both at once (omnia serviliter pro dominatione). On the other hand, when confronted with inert matter one is obliged to resort to thinking.[2]

I shall come back to this in Chapter 7 when I consider the notion of "free action," which is the basis of her discussion in *Oppression and Liberty*. But the role which she ascribes to *language* in the development of thought introduces considerations of a quite different, indeed opposing, sort. I have already had occasion to argue that the existence of language is important to the third-person conception of activity on which the epistemology of *Lectures* is based. There is more to be said about this however.

> We can, thanks to language, call to mind anything we please; it is language which changes us into people who act.[3]

What she is getting at here is less easy to fathom than may appear on the surface. The immediate point is that the production of words is something over which we have far greater control than we have over most of the things words stand for. I can make the word "sun" present to myself any time I wish; I cannot do that with the sun itself. All right; it is of course a very important feature of language that we can (normally) produce words more or less at will. But this hardly seems to support the further claim later in the same section that "we have power over almost everything *through* words *(par les mots)*" (my emphasis). That we normally have more or less complete power over the production of words themselves seems on the face of it not to show at all that this power extends over anything *beyond* language itself.

Simone Weil's reason for making this much stronger and more interesting claim is made more explicit in her next section, from which I shall quote *in extenso*.

> *Language as a means of coming to grips with the world.*
>
> 1. Through it we possess everything that is absent (it is a support for memory). We can, of course, have for a moment a general feeling of something being absent without language; but, apart from language, we cannot call to mind its characteristics exactly.
>
> Without language, one would never be able to relate what one sees to what one does not see or to what one has seen. Language is a bridge crossing over the moments of time. The past, without language, would only exist as a vague feeling which could not help us to know anything. Likewise, the future only exists thanks to language.
>
> 2. It gives us order. Thanks to language the world is like the playthings which children take to pieces and put together again. Order is something which unfolds in time, and depends on a relationship between successive operations. Without language there is no recollection: so, an operation which has taken place would no longer exist.
>
> It is language that enables us to represent the world to ourselves as a small machine (eclipses of the moon using oranges). Language, by allowing us to recreate the world, makes us like the gods, but we only achieve this through symbols.[4]

The central thought in this passage is caught in the sentence "Order is something which unfolds in time, and depends on a relationship between successive operations." Or rather there are here two interlinked thoughts: first, about what makes grasp of a temporal order possible at all; and second, about the fundamental role played by time, temporal order, in the grasp of *any* kind of order. In both these respects Simone Weil must surely have been strongly influenced by Kant. I shall say more about the second point in the next chapter.

My discussion (in Chapter 3) of Simone Weil's treatment of "sensations" shows why some account of the roots of our idea of temporal order is needed. If the discrete, atomic sensation is taken to be the sole ultimate source of our concepts, it is hard to see how an individual consciousness can be anything but totally absorbed – engulfed, as it were – by the sensation of the present moment. Someone may object: but why should I not compare my present sensation with an image of a past sensation? But what *is* this "image of a past sensation"? How has that concept been formed? What is it about any present experience I might have that would justify me in so designating it? How indeed am I supposed to understand such a designation? Even if we can make sense of the idea that my present sensation might have a certain internal complexity such that I could compare one aspect of it with another (and there are difficulties enough about providing for the conceptual complexity that would be needed for that), this would take us no nearer to giving the sense required for talk about comparing a *present* with a *past* sensation.

We need, then, something more than sensations if we are to account for the conception of temporal order. We need, Simone Weil says, "a relationship between successive operations." In order to understand this we have to see why it is that she can allow herself to talk in this way after having ruled out, for the reasons stated, talk about a "relationship between sensations." An operation already incapsulates a relationship in that it involves a base on which it is performed as well as a result thus obtained. So, for example, to explain the operation of negation I need to say that it has to be performed on a given proposition, p, as a result of which we obtain another proposition, not-p. Moreover, because not-p is derived from p in that way, these two propositions are essentially, internally, interrelated. – I am, of course, drawing on Wittgenstein's *Tractatus Logico-Philosophicus* for this example. I do so because I believe that the way in which he talks about "operations" there has close affinities with Simone Weil's thinking in *Lectures*. I shall come back to this in Chapter 6.

It may be said, then, that an operation has an essential internal complexity: and a *temporal* complexity, at that – I *start* with the base and *finish* with a certain result. This is important in the present context if only because Simone Weil herself (drawing on contemporary ideas about the "specious present") allows for the possibility that *sensations* have an internal temporal structure, a before and after, but argues that this nevertheless does not give us the idea of a temporal relation between one sensation and another.

> Analysis of the memory of a sensation regarded as a pure quality (for example the blueness of the sky one sees while daydreaming,[5] a note of a double-bass). We always try: 1. to reproduce or rediscover something which resembles the past sensation; 2. to reproduce as faithfully as possible the reaction the sensation produced in us. As far as the sensation itself is concerned, one cannot think of it, except by actually feeling it. A past sensation, or one to come, is then absolutely nothing, and, as a result, since sensations have significance only in relation to the present moment, there is in them no passing of time and they do not give us the idea of time. It is difficult for us to believe that they do not give us the idea of time because they possess some kind of duration. But in this case one should call to mind Bergson's analysis and his distinction between time and duration. Time is something homogeneous and indefinite; duration is a single characteristic of the quality of a sensation. If we have the impression of duration in the case of a sensation, that only means that sensations are not brought about in an isolated way: there is a continuity, an overlapping of sensations. The duration of sensations does not mean that they involve time. On the contrary it is impossible to limit sensations to the present moment; to say that sensations are limited to the present moment would be to locate them once again in time.

It may seem as though parallel reasoning could be applied to the notion of an operation: the fact that there is an *internal* temporal structure provides no basis for the notion of a temporal relation *between* operations.

But to reason in this way would involve a misunderstanding. The notion of an operation has a role in what she says that is entirely different from the role of the notion of sensation in empiricist epistemology. We are not supposed to derive the idea of time from it by way of an act of mental abstraction. We simply do act, we operate; what is more, our actions, our operations, exhibit a pattern: that is, they do as matter of fact exhibit a pattern. The pattern emerges in the ways in which we (again, as a matter of fact) repeat our operations. This feature of Simone Weil's thinking is present, for example, in the second sentence of the quotation above: we react and, in certain circumstances, we *reproduce* our reaction; we also try to reproduce the original circumstances of our reaction. The idea of the *recurrence of a sensation,* she is arguing, depends on these regular repetitions in our behaviour.

I was following Simone Weil when I said just now that *we* act, that *our* operations exhibit a pattern. This can be taken in two ways: it may mean that the operations of *each one of us* exhibit a pattern; and it may also mean that, if we are considered collectively, there is a pattern in the ensemble of our operations. Simone Weil does not dwell on this distinction and probably at this stage hardly sees the full importance of it. (That is an aspect of the imperfect harmonization of disparate elements in her thinking that I suggested earlier.) But it will be remembered that she does emphasize the importance of "order" depending on "a relationship between successive operations" in her discussion of *language,* which, in the same connection, she calls "a bridge crossing over the moments of time," making *recollection* possible. And it will also be remembered that she insists on the social character of language: "it is something artificial in relation to the individual (but natural for society)."

The upshot is that the individual child, whose reactions to situations, involving both nature and other human beings, exhibit a pattern common to it and to other human beings, comes into relation with the order provided by language. This latter order is itself a structure involving ordered responses to the natural world. It is in this way that language is "a means of coming to grips with the world" and it is in this way that "we have power over almost everything through words." It is a power deriving from the possibility language provides of a *reflective* response to the environment. And the conception of nature as involving systematic interconnections between objects of determinate kinds is a product of the systematic interconnection, preserved in language, between the discriminatory responses to different situations which have evolved from the original primitive reactions described at the beginning of Simone Weil's *Lectures.*

This is part of the picture painted in the remarkable poem "Prométhée," which I put at the head of this chapter and which was written about 1937. The most striking and important connection made in this picture is probably that between the kind of "order" to be found in human behaviour and the notion of an "order of nature" within which the objects with which we have dealings are systematically interconnected *with each other.* I want to try to see how Simone Weil makes this connection. That will occupy the rest of this chapter and virtually the whole of Chapter 6.

How, first of all, are we to think of the development of a system of methodical responses to the environment out of our most primitive reactions? The notion of an *obstacle* is fundamental in this connection.

> Necessity only comes into view when thought comes up against an obstacle. . . .
>
> The mind makes a tool of the matter which would crush it. It is in so far as man controls nature, whether he does this really, or whether he does it by the use of signs, that he has the notion of necessity.
>
> For there to be necessity there must be encounter, there must be two elements: the world and man (mind). So materialism destroys itself when it comes up against the notion of necessity.
>
> All human progress consists in changing constraint into an obstacle.
>
> Why must man then run away from the world in order to rediscover himself, face to face, in mathematics? Because the world does not allow him any respite; it is impossible to create a series as long as one is grappling with the real world.
>
> Man is king as long as he is handling his symbols, whereas he is completely powerless before nature. Man cannot construct by placing his hand directly on the world: he can return to the world once he has an abstract construction.[6]

What she is here calling "the materialist point of view" is a point of view which treats human beings as a part of nature. That is what she was doing at the beginning of *Lectures* when she described certain elementary facts about the structure and workings of human physiology. The situations thus reacted to are not objects for thought; they are simply situations reacted to. It is when one encounters an obstacle that one has, as we say, to take stock of the situation, to explore ways of circumventing the obstacle: that is how Simone Weil understands the birth of thought (and, *pari passu,* of the concept of necessity).

Perhaps there is a difficulty in seeing how the notion of an obstacle is to be fitted in here. If all we have is the notion of a reaction to a stimulus, it may look as though all reactions and all stimuli should be treated as on the same level. To treat some "stimuli" as *obstacles* seems to presuppose a background that has not yet been painted in.

In a sense this is true. The notion of an obstacle clearly involves a *teleological* conception of the organism, and so far nothing has been said about this. Let us take one of Simone Weil's first examples: salivation. I do not salivate in the presence of food on purpose; but, on the other hand, we should hardly understand salivation if we did not see it as connected with the seeking of food in order to eat. It should be noted that this does not so far infringe her conception of "materialism," since a teleology of this sort does not have to involve thought on the part of the creature concerned. One might say: the primitive reactions are not performed "for" a purpose or "for the sake" of an interest. They do however, at least in very many cases, "express" or "manifest" interests, purposes, and concerns. And this is not a contingent matter. As I pointed out in the case of salivation, we should hardly understand what the reactions actually were if we did not see them in such a light. Perhaps something like Spinoza's concept of *conatus* is needed here. Our grasp of what an organism is is a grasp, amongst other things, of a teleological pattern in its reactions to its environment.

Such a pattern makes room for, and perhaps even requires, the possibility that an organism will be *thwarted* or *hindered* in its pursuit of a goal. There are also characteristic reactions to being thwarted. For example, rage. Or again: renewed attempts. In certain circumstances we should see such repeated attempts as a sign of perseverance and determination. That was how Robert the Bruce saw the spider. But in only slightly different circumstances determination would become stupid obstinacy and lack of *imagination*. Imagination would be displayed, for example, in the creature's desisting from doing the things that most *obviously* lead to the goal and doing things that rather seem to lead it, to begin with, *away* from the goal. For instance, if I repeatedly fail to scale a difficult rock face I descend to get new equipment or I explore in various directions till I find a manageable route. An image of which Simone Weil is very fond, and which she uses to striking effect even in the early "Science et perception," is that of a sailing boat tacking against the wind. The headwind is initially an obstacle; it is overcome and even used to advantage by the navigator's

turning the boat, in the first instance, *away* from his actual destination. This is *part* of what she means, in the passage quoted
above, by "running away from the world."[7]

But it is only part of what she means. Tacking, it may be said,
hardly involves running away *from the world;* only taking a longer
route within the world. She speaks of a flight into mathematics,
symbols, abstract constructions. Three questions arise here. First,
how are we to understand the creature described in Chapter 1 of
Lectures as undertaking such a flight? Second, how are we to
understand this symbolic world of "abstract constructions"?
Third, what is the relation between such abstract constructions
and the world of action to which one must return?

I shall end this chapter with some reflections on the first of
these questions. The other two I shall take up in Chapter 6.

I want to consider here the two stanzas dealing with language
and with numbers in the poem "Prométhée." It is true that the
poem was written a few years later than *Lectures* and that Simone
Weil's thinking had in the meantime matured; I think all the same
that it illuminates ideas already quite far advanced in the *Lectures.*

> Il fut auteur des rites et du temple,
> Cercle magique à retenir les dieux
> Loin de ce monde; ainsi l'homme contemple,
> Seul et muet, le sort, la mort, les cieux.
> Il fut l'auteur des signes, des langages.

These lines link the development of language with the performance of ritual. Rituals are not to be thought of, I think, as
engaged in for a purpose: they are not *zweckmässig.* Once established, they constitute "a magic circle to keep the gods away from
this world." That may have been Prometheus's purpose for
humankind, but he is a god; it was not a purpose humankind had
in establishing rituals. I take it that that is one reason why their
development is described as the gift of a god. Rituals do of course
share with other human activities the property of involving constantly repeated patterns of behaviour. Indeed they do so to a pre-
eminent degree: one could almost say that their chief characteristic is to highlight that very notion by separating it from the
pursuit of natural purposes. They constitute, then, a *shared* activity
exhibiting a high degree of *order.*

How is ritual to be thought of as "keeping the gods away from this world"? I understand this as meaning that they provide a space within which human beings are freed, temporarily, from their constant obsession with natural necessities. The gods who are in charge of these necessities are, as it were, given their own realm; and through ritual persons may communicate with them otherwise than through experiencing the heavy hand of those natural necessities.

It is interesting that the poem links rituals and language in the same stanza. It is also interesting that the stanza does not even mention the role of language in "coming to grips with the world": that is reserved for "numbers" in the stanza that follows. Here the emphasis is on the role of language in the kinds of life people lead: the handing down of traditions, the uniting in action and feeling of those distant from each other, the intimacies of friends and lovers; the discourse of the soul with itself. Language is part of the essential constitution, so the suggestion seems to be, of certain distinctive patterns of human life: patterns formed in the intercourse of people with each other and in their attempts to see, or give, form to their own lives as individuals.

One can see here too, though in a different sense from that in which this was said of ritual, a sort of "turning away from the world." And though this is not said in the poem, I think one can see, behind what *is* said, the idea that the notion of *the world in which we live our lives* takes determinate shape only in the context of these semi-autonomous patterns of human culture. I am sure, at any rate, that this thought was at work in Simone Weil and was playing its part even in the reflections on language in *Lectures*.

All this may seem, and is, quite a long way from the idea I started from: that thought is born in the encounter with obstacles. I do see an analogy, however, between the (temporary) turning away from one's immediate objective, characteristic of the human encounter with obstacles, and the turning away from the world, characteristic of so much of human life and culture. I think Simone Weil is suggesting that this too is a condition of the development and maintenance of language and, through it, of a kind of thought in which human beings may *encounter* nature and not simply be a part of it. That is, this is made possible through the *separateness* from nature emphasized in the stanza from "Prométhée" under review. Expressed in this way the tension with the remark referred to in note 2 above is all the more striking. As I

said, "Prométhée" may be later – the notebook in question runs
from 1933 to about 1939. To what extent it represents a new
development in her thinking and to what extent a strain which was
already present in her thinking alongside those with which it conflicts, I shall not try to determine.

6

NECESSITY

In this chapter I shall discuss Simone Weil's account of the natural world as an order of necessary relations. The main problem here is to see how the conception of an "order" in that sense is related to the "order" involved in human behaviour, and in particular to the ordered sequence of operations which constitutes a "method." This will involve some consideration of what she says about the formation of mathematical concepts and their application.

In Chapter 5 I compared her conception of an *operation*, and of a *sequence of operations*, to Wittgenstein's in the *Tractatus*. Wittgenstein's concern there is with the nature of logic. He conceives logical relations between propositions as depending on, even consisting in, the relations between the various conditions that make propositions true (their "truth-conditions"). By virtue of these relations certain propositions can be seen as interlinked in systems of "truth-functions": systems in which the truth of some propositions is displayed as depending on (as a function of) the truth or falsity of others. Such systems are generated through the application of certain operations on given propositions (which serve as the "bases" of the operations); in this way other propositions are formulated which are logically, truth-functionally, related to each other and to the original bases *by virtue of* the way they have been generated. In the *Tractatus* Wittgenstein held: (1) that there is only an apparent diversity between the operations that generate truth-functional systems – that they can all be reduced to the single operation of iterated negation; (2) that *all* logical relations between propositions, and hence all logical necessity, can be understood in this way; (3) that all necessity is logical necessity.

Simone Weil does not arrive at her account of necessity by the same route as Wittgenstein; and I do not want to suggest that their accounts are identical. There are however some very striking analogies between the ways in which they conceive necessity, consideration of which may, I believe, shed light on both. In particular, Simone Weil, along with Wittgenstein, believes that our perception of necessity is a product of our acting in ordered sequences of operations; and she also believes, with him, that all necessity is, in the end, of the same sort.

> L'acte s'ajoute à l'acte; rien n'est seul;
> Tout se répond sur la juste balance.

("One act follows another; nothing stands alone; everything answers to everything else on accurate scales.") Those two lines occur in the stanza of "Prométhée" that speaks of *numbers*. The following passage from *Lectures on Philosophy* makes a similar point more discursively:

> The elementary operation of arithmetic gives us order. . . . Order consists in always doing the same thing again and again. Numbers could not be applied to things or animals if one did not consider the operation which makes one move from one thing to another (pupils in a class, soldiers, etc.).
> There are no numbers in nature.[1]

It is worth comparing the operations involved in counting with ritual (discussed briefly in the last chapter). In both there is a rigorous insistence on always doing the same thing, a constantly repeated pattern. Counting in its actual application is not a ritual, of course. But if one considers how numbers are initially *learned* by children, it is obvious that there is something ritualistic about this. It is plausible to say, even, that it is partly the ritualistic nature of the exercise that gives it the appeal, even fascination, it has for children, for something very similar is certainly to be found in many children's games. But there is also obviously fascination in the sense of the unlimited systematic possibilities opened up by counting. (Remember the pleasure a child who is just mastering counting takes in counting up to very high numbers.)

I think both these kinds of fascination enter into Simone Weil's wonderment at arithmetic: on the one hand the ritualistic "l'acte s'ajoute à l'acte," and on the other the sense of mastering a great all-embracing system ("tout se répond"). This fascinated wonderment leads her both to profound insights and to dangerously distorting pictorial ways of speaking.

The idea that numbers relate everything to everything else in one great system of interlocking necessities is the result of something like the following line of reasoning, which recurs again and again.[2] Order is created by the repetition of operations, one act after another. Questions about the nature of the "acts" involved or what "repetition" amounts to can be asked later. The methodical procedures from which ordered series result are always, at bottom, the same in kind: first one operation, then another. So, at bottom, order and necessity (which presupposes order) are also of the same kind. All particular necessities are an expression of a fundamental single necessity to which all things are subject in so far as they belong to an ordered world (and only in the context of an ordered world can anything be thought of at all). The following passage from "Reflections Concerning the Causes of Liberty and Social Oppression"[3] is characteristic:

> But whatever may be the patterns taken by social transformations, all one finds, if one tries to lay bare the mechanism, is a dreary play of blind forces that unite together or clash, that progress or decline, that replace each other, without ever ceasing to grind beneath them the unfortunate race of human beings. At first sight there seems to be no weak spot in this sinister mesh of circumstances through which an attempt at deliverance might find its way.

I have noted the analogy between Simone Weil's way of thinking about necessity in relation to "operations" and the treatment of necessity in Wittgenstein's early work, the *Tractatus Logico-Philosophicus*. Now, Wittgenstein himself came to think there were serious confusions in that treatment and one, at least, of his self-criticisms can be applied to Simone Weil. As I said, the *Tractatus* treats iterated negation as the fundamental operation which generates the system of truth-functions from given propositional bases. According to that account the repetition of the operation of negation always results in reversing the truth value of the proposition to which it is applied. So: when we negate p we get not-p; when we negate not-p we get not-(not-p) (= p); when we negate that we get not-[not-(not-p)] (= not-p); and so on. (And so on?) At the time of the *Tractatus* Wittgenstein thought that this sequence is *determined* by the nature of the operation of negation in its first application. But, as he was later to point out, this is not at all clear. We can equally (and sometimes do) use the repetition of a negation to emphasize, rather than reverse, the first negation. If we do so, does it imply that we *meant something different* by the first application of the operation from what we meant by its first operation in the case where we went on to use its repetition differently? That would be pure mythology. This criticism, followed through, led Wittgenstein to a completely new conception of what is involved in a logical system.[4]

Consider now the sentence from page 79 of *Lectures on Philosophy* that I have already quoted: "Order consists in always doing the same thing again and again." There is a difficulty about this. Are we to understand that everything belongs to the *same* order in so far as it is always the same operation which is repeated, whatever the context? (That would be somewhat akin to the *Tractatus* contention that all operations are reducible to one: iterated negation.) This seems to be required by the thought that everything is in harmony with everything else: things can only belong to the *same* order in so far as it is the repetition of the *same* operation which has brought them into that order.

But how are we to determine what is to count as "always doing the same thing"? There is a game with which small children torment each other (or used to at any rate). One child, a boy let us say, performs certain acts and the other, a girl, is each time to "do the same thing." The first child points at his own face; what is the other to do: point at *her* or *his* face? Either response could count as "doing the same" in suitable circumstances. The point about the game is that there are no circumstances which determine the right answer; so the boy can torment the girl by condemning *any* answer she gives as wrong. I noticed in what I said about Simone Weil's use of the notion of an "operation" in the last chapter that an operation does not for her play the role of a datum from which one deduces the possibility of repeating it; but that the appeal is to the *fact* that we actually do repeat our operations. However, that thought needs to be pushed further: what we do actually count as "repeating our operations" differs from one case to another. This difficulty already affects the point Simone Weil is making in the quoted passage from page 79 of *Lectures*. She speaks of "the operation which makes one move from one thing to another." *Is* this really always the same operation? For instance, does counting the number of children in the class involve the same operation as, say, counting the number of red-headed children in the class, or counting the number of classes in the school? Though my question is in a sense rhetorical, this is not because I think the answer is obvious. It is rather because I think that there *is* no determinate answer; and in this case, that is as much as to say that the sense of the question itself is unclear.

This already undermines the idea that everything is harmoniously interrelated in a single systematic order, since our understanding of what is meant by such an order has been made to depend on the conception of "always repeating the same operation." An indeterminacy in *this* conception would bring with it an indeterminacy in the other; and the use to which Simone Weil wants to put it cannot tolerate such an indeterminacy. The difficulty shows that the belief that we have a clear idea of what it means to speak in this way is illusory.

I certainly do not want to suggest that Simone Weil was always completely blind to this sort of consideration. For instance, she points out that following a particular methodical procedure provides us with no guarantee that it will allow us to relate systematically everything to which we apply it. Consider for instance the extremely interesting point she makes about mathematical procedures on page 116 of *Lectures:*

> How can the working of the mind lead the mind itself to problems? (up to now the problems have arisen by chance). How can the mind, by methodical research, furnish itself with difficult problems to solve?
>   This happens whenever a definite method meets its own limit (and this, of course, happens, to a certain extent, by chance).

The example she considers is the difficulty faced by the Pythagoreans when they "ran up against the diagonal of the square which exhibited incommensurables." The difficulty could only be solved, she goes on, by making a clear distinction between magnitudes and relations. For present purposes the important point about this is that the need for such a distinction was not somehow already immanent in mathematics from the beginning. It was *created* by the difficulty which was thrown up by a particular, contingent, way in which mathematics developed. (Such a thing "happens, to a certain extent, by chance.") And one can only speak of a method running up against its own limits in so far as one recognizes the possibility of a fundamental diversity of methods.

But in spite of such insights the fascination of the thought that everything in the world belongs to a single all-embracing system of necessities was something Simone Weil never freed herself from. It is still very active even in her very last writings; it is involved, for instance, in the way she speaks of the "gravity" to which everything "here below" *(ici-bas)* is subject. But this takes me too far away from my immediate concerns. I shall be coming back to it more than once.

For the present I want to resume my discussion of the way in which Simone Weil thinks of the concept of necessity as being generated by the regular repetition of an operation. It is easy enough to see, first of all, how a concept of *practical* necessity would be involved here. For instance in counting it is *necessary* that the numerals should be recited in a definite order: 1, 2, 3, 4, 5, 6, etc. and *not*, say, 2, 6, 3, 1, 5, 4. It is an illustration of the point at issue that I cannot add "etc." to that second sequence as I did to the first, because that sequence exhibits no necessity in its continuation. (Or at least: some such necessity has got to be explained – by representing the sequence as the application of some particular mathematical formula – before "etc." would have any meaning.) The point of using the words "necessary" and "necessity" in this connection is that we are not going to recognize as a case of "counting" any sequence of actions which does not follow that order.

But now, in the light of these preliminaries, let us address ourselves to the most difficult question: what has this discussion of the practical necessities involved in human methodical procedures to do with the conception of an order of nature within which things and events are necessarily interrelated?

We must go back to the discussion of "overcoming obstacles" in Chapter 5. Simone Weil's treatment of this notion, in *Lectures on Philosophy* (but also as early as "Science et perception dans Descartes"), stipulates an important distinction between "obstacle" and "constraint." If, while engaged on some project, I am hit on the head by a falling rock and knocked unconscious, thereby being rendered incapable of completing the project, that is constraint. If, by contrast, there is a rock in my path and I think how I can circumvent it or get it out of my way, I am confronted by an obstacle. I *might* of course simply repeatedly hurl myself in despairing fury against the rock until I collapse from exhaustion: in that case the rock would again be for me a constraint.

So the distinction between constraint and obstacle involves a relation between thought and the world, a relation incapsulated in the notion of *method*.

> All human progress consists in changing constraint into an obstacle.[5]

This is not a pragmatic conception of progress. The point is not merely that we are more successful with our projects in so far as we transform constraint into obstacles, true though that may be. The deeper point is that progress in *understanding*, both of ourselves and of nature, consists in such a transformation. The important difference between obstacle and constraint is suggested by a grammatical distinction: when I try to find a way round the rock in my path I *see it as* an obstacle; but I do not see the rock which knocks me unconscious as a constraint: I do not see it as anything, I am simply overcome by it. When I see things as obstacles I am already on the way to investigating and developing systematic ideas about their properties and interrelations: about the necessities to which they are subject. That is how we are to conceive progress in understanding nature, which, so Simone Weil argues, involves at the same time progress in understanding ourselves, because "it is only those actions and thoughts which have a necessity about them that are truly human."[6] On the one hand, the development of a methodical approach to the environment, signalled by treating things as obstacles, of its nature represents an increase in our understanding of our own relation to that environment, since our own methodical procedures are transparent to our understanding. And on the other hand, it is of its nature also a development in self-discipline, an ordering of our own psychic forces, and this is a necessary condition of any self-understanding. – This last point plays a large role in Simone Weil's treatment of oppression.

An understanding of what has to be done in the face of various obstacles is an important element in our concepts of different kinds of object. A river is, from one point of view, something that will impede us if we want to get from one place to another; from another point of view it is something that may help us to overcome other obstacles (such as lack of land transport). Understanding what something is and what it is like is inseparable from understanding how it may impede or help us and how we need to treat it in order to carry through our projects. If a river lies between us and our destination we may need to build a boat or a bridge; neither of these would be much good if we were faced, say, with a tiger or a mountain.

To deal with an obstacle is to carry out a definite sequence of operations, and this of course is a *temporal* notion. But the way in which time enters into our understanding of method has an important complexity, about which Simone Weil has some interesting things to say, integral to the questions about necessity we are considering. On the one hand, my grapplings with the obstacle take place at a certain time and have a certain duration. On the other hand they involve a temporal ordering of before and after of the various operations involved. If I am building a boat, I first collect the materials and then process them in various ways before assembling the parts thus constructed. So far I have just been describing what I perhaps in fact did on a particular occasion: I *first* did this, *then* that, and *next* the other thing. But of course, if what I did is to be intelligibly described as "building a boat" at all, that is, if it represents the application of a certain *method* of doing something, it is no contingent fact that there is a definite order in certain sequences of my operations. If a sequence of operations is to constitute the application of a method, the temporal order of the sequence is often essential: that is, within the context of the method, it is *necessary* that A before B before C, and so on.

This conception of a necessary temporal order is incapsulated in *mathematical* methods: for example that of solving a quadratic equation. But let us consider geometry, of which there is an interesting discussion on pages 79 to 81 of the *Lectures* (and which plays an increasingly important role in Simone Weil's thinking in ways about which I shall have more to say in Chapter 11). She remarks: "We cannot construct a polygon before a triangle." What is the sense of the word "cannot" here? The procedure of geometrical construction involves a time order in the sense that certain operations can only be carried out after certain other operations have been carried out. "Can" in this context means something like: "nothing is going to count as 'constructing a square' which does not involve constructing a triangle as an intermediate step." Temporal notions like "before" and "after" have a place here, but not notions like "how long?" and "at what time?" This is connected with the fact that, considered purely formally, the procedure of construction is not at the mercy of contingencies. It would, for instance, be nonsense to interpolate in the specification of the procedure an instruction like "Take care the straight lines don't bend or snap." Of course, someone's execution of such a procedure does take place at a determinate time and lasts so long, and is subject to contingencies such as pencils snapping, rulers bending, and so on. But none of these features has a place in the description of the geometrical construction.

That last example concerns of course what Simone Weil calls an "abstract construction." Consider now a methodical procedure for achieving some practical end. Think of one of those pieces of household equipment supplied in a do-it-yourself kit, with a set of instructions on its assembly. Here too of course the instructions do not specify just a collection of operations but a series of operations in a definite temporal order. There may be reasons of different sorts for the ordering. In some cases it may be merely more convenient to do A before B rather than vice versa. But in other, more interesting, cases there are considerations somewhat analogous to those applying in the geometrical example. For instance, the description of one operation may include, or at least presuppose, the description of a state of affairs resulting from an operation carried out previously.

Suppose, for instance, that we are instructed to screw together two tubes which have been, by an earlier operation, fitted together so that their screw holes are lined up. There is a sense in which we "cannot" insert the screw before fitting the tubes together and aligning the holes. Someone who did not understand this would hardly be said to understand the instructions at all; we might even say that he or she would not understand what "insert" means in this context. In this respect the case is analogous to the geometrical: "Nous ne pouvons pas faire le polygone avant le triangle." But the analogy, though real, is limited. Contingencies are relevant in a way they are not in geometry. The "impossibility" of not inserting the screw unless the holes are aligned depends in part on the physical properties of the materials. Moreover, tubes may stick together, break into pieces. Of course, as I remarked in connection with geometry, pencils and rulers too may get damaged while someone is using them in the course of making a geometrical construction. But though a person uses them in making a construction, they are not elements in what is being constructed: their relation to what is being constructed is quite different from that of the tubes to the apparatus being assembled form the DIY kit. The

marks made by the pencil on the paper are also not elements in
what is being constructed in geometry. The triangle that I am constructing does not consist of pencil marks, though it may be said
to consist of straight lines and though too my use of the expression
"straight line" in this context depends on a certain relation, attitude, that I have to the marks that I have made with the pencil.
But pencil marks are subject to contingencies; straight lines are
not – not at least in anything like the same sense. There are other,
related, differences.

However, something like a geometrical order with its correlative
conception of necessity does permeate the conception of such an
ordered sequence of physical operations to a greater extent than
is brought out by what I have so far said. The description of the
fitting together and screwing operations in my example takes for
granted that the tubes and other materials will behave "as they are
supposed to behave." Sometimes they will not: and the way in
which we apply the instructions expresses our understanding of
that. If a tube snaps, even though it has been subjected to no
"undue" pressure, we do not blame the instructions for being
incomprehensible; we blame the tube manufacturer for shoddy
workmanship. But there are limits to what we should accept as an
intelligible deviation from the norm. If the reason why we cannot
carry out the specified operation is that the things we are handling
start squirming about and inflicting venomous bites, we won't
speak of faulty manufacture of the tubes. And if we were told to
go ahead and apply the instructions all the same as best we could,
I think we should find that injunction unintelligible. Lewis Car-
roll's description of the "croquet match" played with flamingos
instead of clubs and hedgehogs instead of balls is, as so often, a
joke which makes a philosophical point. The point is the close,
internal, connection between the possibility of carrying out, or
even understanding, a specified sequence of operations and our
understanding of what the things *are* on which those operations
are being carried out.

Simone Weil is suggesting, I believe, that the necessity involved
in an ordered sequence of operations such as is found in geometry
spills over, so to say, into the natural world through the *application*
of such ordered sequences in actual physical procedures. Or to
speak less metaphorically, our conceptions of the necessities which
characterize the behaviour and relations between things in the

natural world are a product of the application to them of procedures defined by certain necessary sequences of operations.

$$\left.\begin{array}{l} A = B \\ \\ B = C \end{array}\right\} \quad A = C$$

is an operation which defines a standard.

That is to say, we use that arithmetical operation in formulating
our descriptions of the relations between physical quantities. We
shall not describe three quantities as "equal" if they do not stand
in the relation defined by that operation.

> Why must man then run away from the world in order to redis-
> cover himself, face to face, in mathematics? Because the world does
> not allow him any respite; it is impossible to create a series as long
> as one is grappling with the real world.
> Man is king as long as he is handling his symbols, whereas he is
> completely powerless before nature. Man cannot construct by plac-
> ing his hand directly on the world: he can return to the world once
> he has an abstract construction.[7]

In the last few pages I have been discussing what Simone Weil
calls the "return to the world," or, in other words, the *application*
of "abstract constructions." I want now to make some remarks
about the claim that "man cannot construct by placing his hand
directly on the world."

> What language alone can give us is method, and it can do this for
> one reason: because it is so different from what is real. In the world,
> of course, we have to obey what is necessary. For example, we can
> carry no more than a certain number of kilos; beyond that all
> weights are the same for us since we are debarred from them all on
> the same score (they are too heavy). On the other hand we can speak
> of whatever number of kilos we wish, for the word kilo does not
> weigh a thing. Language allows us to lay down relationships which
> are completely foreign to our needs.[8]

Techniques of weighing enable us to have a conception of
aspects of physical things which would be quite inaccessible to us
if we were confined to lifting those things we were able to lift and
simply giving up on the others. But those techniques in their turn
depend on other techniques of a different sort: for instance, the
practice of counting, the rigorous, quasi-ritualistic aspect of which
I have already noted. The number 10 *has* to come between 9 and
11; because anything that does not come between 9 and 11 is sim-

ply not 10. Without the observance[9] of formal rules like this, it is not easy to see how there could be anything like the practice of weighing. And without *that* practice there could be nothing much like the concept of *weight*. This is an example of the general suggestion contained in the following note:

> All concrete knowledge of facts, including human facts, is the recognition of a necessity in them, either a mathematical necessity or something analogous.[10]

The general line of argument, then, is that the necessary order of operations which belongs to method introduces necessity into our conception of those things to which we apply our methodical procedures. The obverse of this conception of necessity is that of contingency: it is equally important to our understanding of the things around us that they may behave in ways which we do not and cannot foresee.

In the present context the word "contingency" or "the unforeseen" *(l'imprévu)* has to be distinguished from the *hasard* spoken of in "Science et perception dans Descartes." *Hasard* stands outside the distinction between necessity and (the present notion of) contingency; the latter *presupposes* the notion of necessity.

> The unforeseen is what stands in contrast to what is contained in the language expressing a method.[11]

It is because in "placing his hand directly on the world" one is subject to *hasard* that one has to "turn away" from the world and make abstract constructions; it is then in the application of those constructions (in which the "return to the world" consists) that the notion of "contingency" *(l'imprévu)* acquires sense.

Consider an example. If I work out a way of raising a weight by using a system of pulleys in an ordered sequence of steps, something may always happen which makes it impossible to achieve the desired result by following that predetermined sequence. A rope may break or a wheel jam; and then I have to undertake repairs or think of some other way, or give up. The description of the method adopted for raising the weight did not of course include these, or any other, unforeseen contingencies. But it *was* a description in which the possibility of such contingencies is provided for.[12] This is shown by the fact that I was able so easily to give examples of possible unforeseen contingencies. There are plenty of unforeseen things that could happen while I was carrying out the procedure with the pulleys which would not serve as examples: for instance the sun might go behind a cloud, someone might walk along the pavement opposite the house, and so on. Not even every unforeseen event that would put a stop to my operations would serve as an example: a nuclear explosion, a heart attack. My point (and it is also one of Simone Weil's points) is that the language in which I formulate my methodical procedure already imposes a potential order on what I *cannot* foresee. Although an accident disrupts the intended order of my operations, the very fact that I count it as an accident means that it in a way fits into the order created by my understanding of the project and the possible ways of executing it. "Accident" is to be understood relative to "order": to count something as an accident is already to relate it to a determinate order.

Before I conclude this chapter I should like to comment on a way in which Simone Weil's treatment of this matter seems to me to go dangerously adrift. The point is closely related to the way in which she thinks of everything as subject to one all-embracing necessity, on which I commented earlier in the chapter.

> Reality comes into view when we see that nature is not only an obstacle which allows us to act in an ordered way, but it is also an obstacle which infinitely transcends us.[13]

The valid point in this is that all our methods of dealing with things in nature provide for the possibility of disruption by unforeseen obstacles; that is, in Wittgenstein's language, part of the grammar of our talk about nature and of our methodical transactions with it. But in the remark quoted Simone Weil talks about nature itself as an obstacle, one that infinitely transcends us. It sounds as though she were thinking of nature as itself a natural object, only on an infinitely grander scale. (Perhaps the influence of Spinoza is making itself felt again, less happily this time.)

It would not matter very much if this were just a matter of overblown rhetoric, but I think there is more to it than that. I want to consider some remarks from an essay which Simone Weil wrote in 1941,[14] very late, that is, which seem to me to show that there were indeed confusions in that early way in which she expressed herself and confusions from which she was never to become altogether free. (They surface, in a different form, in the account of "free action" in *Oppression and Liberty* that I shall be discussing in the next chapter.)

"Classical Science and After" (p. 32), in the course of an examination of the relation between a geometrical figure and the figure actually drawn on a particular sheet of paper, speaks of the latter as being an "image" of the former and says that there is an "infinite error" involved in this relationship in so far as the geometrical straight lines, triangles, planes, and so on which the drawn figures allow us to "imagine" differ "abysmally, infinitely" from the latter.

For instance, a straight line (in Euclidean geometry) has no breadth, unlike what I draw, however thin. If I measure with sufficient accuracy the interior angles of the triangle I draw I shall find that their sum deviates from two right angles, more or less. What I draw may fade, get blotted out; and so on. Some of these facts are troublesome for the way Simone Weil speaks of our "imagining" these geometrical figures, if we are to understand by that anything like "having a mental picture." Mental pictures too are subject to contingencies – even if not the same ones as physical pictures – from which geometrical figures are immune.

I am not sure how harmless this is. It may be that she needs something like this way of speaking to give an appearance of sense to her talk about the "infinite error" involved. What, after all, *is* the error in question? It is certainly not the kind of error in calculation or construction that can occur in an attempted geometrical demonstration, since, according to her conception, the error she is speaking of is involved in *any* geometrical demonstration, whether "valid" in the normal sense or not. Nor is it the sort of error that would be committed by a child who, introduced to geometrical proof for the first time, took it to apply only to the particular drawn figure with which the child had been presented and thought that it needed to be done all over again with the next drawn figure. – It is, by the way, interesting and important that this is *not* a commonly made mistake. A child who did make it, at any rate persistently, would be regarded as mentally retarded or disturbed in some no doubt determinate way. – An "error" of this last sort would amount of course to not having grasped the concept of a geometrical demonstration, which precisely requires that one does *not* ask for a proof to be repeated with each new figure. But again, when Simone Weil speaks of "error" here, what is in question is precisely an error which is supposed to be committed by everyone who *does* correctly operate with the concept of a geometrical proof.

At the particular point in "Classical Science and After" at which she makes these remarks it is the relation between geometry and physics that is mainly under discussion. And the "error" allegedly involved in our relation to geometry is sometimes spoken of as though it were analogous to that of an experimental scientist who accepts a result lying outside the "margin of error" appropriate to the experimental technology he or she is using. Now, the phrase "margin of error" has no use in non-applied geometry, because geometry is not concerned with particular methods of measurement. It is, as one might say, agnostic with regard to these. It will tell you what the relation is between the hypotenuse of a rightangle triangle and its other two sides, but say nothing about how the lengths of the sides or the right angle are to be measured. In other words, geometry says nothing about how its theorems are to be applied to figures drawn on paper, though these theorems will be understood only by someone who has at least some familiarity with methods of application. To use a phrase from *Lectures on Philosophy* already quoted, an operation in geometry is "an operation which defines a standard." That standard *then* has to be applied; it is only at this point that the notion of a "margin of error" comes into play. It makes no sense, then, to speak of an error of this sort as being involved when we are doing pure geometry.

Still, to leave things there would be to miss an important point underlying Simone Weil's discussion. She wants, quite rightly, to draw our attention to important contingencies underlying our practice of geometry. She refers, for instance, to the fact that, when I press the chalk against the blackboard, something results which I can recognize as having a certain determinate shape and which remains stable. (The important thing is that it remains stable long enough for me to complete the proof.) She also refers to the fact that

> when we see a place and want to go there, we set off with the thought of a direction, that is to say, of a straight line; and although we make a number of movements infinitely different from a straight trajectory, *we arrive more often than not at the place we want*.[15]

It is the fact that we do have such "successes" more often than we have "failures" (and we are speaking here of *empirical* successes and failures) that "gives a value to geometry"; that is, there would otherwise be little point in doing geometry.

But what *is* this value? The answer given in "Classical Science and After" might seem a surprising one. It is *not* that it serves our practical ends (though of course she does not deny that it has such a value too). It is rather because these facts about geometry "reflect the contradictions of the human condition" that it has a value. Simone Weil is here speaking from the point of view of the religious interests which increasingly preoccupied her in her later years. At this point we run into an important example of the difficulties which arise from the intermingling of religious and philosophical concerns in her thinking. And it is very difficult to talk sense about these difficulties; but let me try.

Like many other of Simone Weil's later writings, "Classical Science and After" seeks to see science in general, and geometry in particular, as an image in terms of which a certain religious view of human life can be articulated. It is a view which attempts to understand the imperfections, afflictions, injustices of human life – but also its joys, beauties, and instances of nobility and sanctity – from a point of view "outside the world." My own opinion is that in developing this view she very frequently expresses insights of great beauty and extraordinary profundity. On the other hand, I do not see how anyone who reads her with attention could possibly agree with everything she writes in this dimension. To read her with attention is necessarily to reflect on the truth or falsity, adequacy or inadequacy, and so on, of what she writes. It would be absurd, therefore, to dismiss questions of truth as unimportant. On the other hand, it would also be absurd – perhaps "stupid" is a better word – to imagine that one should evaluate her stature as a writer and thinker against the extent to which one agrees with her opinions. It is, or should be, a commonplace that one can learn more from one person's mistakes than from another's multitude of correct opinions.

I do not offer these observations in a defensive spirit. It is rather that the criticisms which I believe have to be made of really quite central strands in her thinking will not be rightly understood by someone who is not clear about the general assessment of her stature and importance from which those criticisms spring. To put it more concretely, I do not think it is worth (unless for reasons springing from a particular unavoidable polemical context) criticizing a writer whose work one regards as worthless.

I return to Simone Weil's treatment of geometry. I am very far, then, from having anything against her attempt to display it as a paradigm of the dependence of human life on something which lies "outside this world" (and I shall try to say more about this later). Her view, moreover, that Greek mathematics and science represented a higher cultural achievement than their contemporary counterparts *because* they lent themselves to being thus displayed seems to me a serious, arguable position and one for which, indeed, she makes a strong case. However, the case she is making for such a view at this point in "Classical Science and After" seems to me to rest on a confusion. She is interpreting the fact that "we make a number of movements infinitely different from a straight trajectory" when we head for an intended destination as though we were somehow not merely in error in applying the geometrical notion of a straight line in this way, but necessarily and infinitely so. But the truth of the matter is, surely, that the phenomenon which she here describes is a characteristic feature of what we *mean* by "the application of a geometrical notion."

What we do mean by this is indeed a tangled matter of which it is very difficult indeed to give a clear and unexceptionable philosophical account: it is a philosophical puzzle. But a philosophical puzzle is not the same as a religious mystery. The enormous importance of geometry in human life, the complex interrelation of factors in our lives and in our relations to the world we live in which make geometry a possible study for us – these are a fitter object for religious wonder and gratitude than many things. But this wonder and gratitude are devalued to the extent that they are based on a charm which results from philosophical confusion.[16] And, on the other side, philosophical confusions will become even more difficult to remove if wrongly given the status of religious mystery.

7

EQUILIBRIUM

> The secret of the human condition is that equilibrium between man
> and the surrounding forces of nature "which infinitely surpass him"
> cannot be achieved by inaction; it is only achieved in the action by
> which man recreates his own life: that is to say by work.[1]

This overall conception of human life is filled out in the section
called "Analysis of Oppression" in the main essay of *Oppression
and Liberty*, "Reflections Concerning the Causes of Liberty and
Social Oppression." The phrase "which infinitely surpass him" is
a quotation from Spinoza, and "by which man recreates his own
life" echoes Marx. Both writers heavily influenced this essay.
There is much fundamental criticism of Marx in it, but also
acknowledgement of the debt owed him.

The notebook entry speaks of "an equilibrium between man and
the surrounding forces of nature." The concept of *equilibrium* was
very important to Simone Weil at all stages of her thinking. Her
view of how the equilibrium between people and their environment is to be understood changed a good deal as time went on,
but I think it is possible, and desirable at this stage, to say something in general about what she meant by this term.

Roughly speaking, x and y are in equilibrium when they are in
stable relations with each other of a sort which permits each to
retain its own essential nature. It follows that what is to count as
equilibrium in any given case will be internally related to how we
understand the essential natures of the entities involved. I express
myself with some caution here. I do *not* say: what is to count as
equilibrium will *depend* on the essential natures of the entities
involved. That would strongly suggest that it will always be possible

to give an account of the essential nature of something as independent of what will count as its being in equilibrium with its environment.

This is an important point. In "Reflections Concerning the Causes of Liberty and Social Oppression" Simone Weil *starts* with the conception of a person as an "active being" and then considers what it would be for such a being to be in equilibrium with its environment: an environment consisting of both other human (and hence active) beings as well as natural objects. It will throw the point into relief to contrast this procedure with a late, magnificent work in which the notion of equilibrium also plays a central part: "The *Iliad* or the Poem of Force."[2] The leading idea in this essay is *justice,* which is conceived as an equilibrium between human beings: indeed, as *the* form that equilibrium takes in the relations between human beings. Now, justice, as conceived here, is connected with the idea of *consent:* a just community is one in which nobody forces anything on anybody else without the other's consent. And this idea of consent is itself made essential to the characterization of human beings: to treat someone as a human being *is* to acknowledge his or her "power to refuse," that is to refrain from making demands or inflicting anything unwelcome without receiving consent. But in this case the notion of justice is not *derived* from that of consent. The argument is that it is only from the point of view of justice that we can understand what consent is: roughly because we have to employ conceptions of justice in determining what does and what does not require a person's consent and also in discerning whether consent can truly be said to have been given in a particular case.

I have given above the merest sketch of one of the most important themes in Simone Weil's later writings, and I shall discuss aspects of it in subsequent chapters. My present concern is with the earlier "Reflections Concerning the Causes of Liberty and Social Oppression." Here, as I said, equilibrium between human beings is discussed in terms of a conception of human beings as essentially *active* creatures and activity is thought of as something which can be understood in the first instance independently of an individual's participation in a social life.

I have already in previous chapters discussed many aspects of Simone Weil's conception of an individual's "activity" at about the time of this essay. The essay concentrates at first on a description of the harshness of the environment that an individual faces in a primitive economy: an economy, that is, with little social coordination and organization in which each individual is mainly dependent on his or her own efforts for survival. In such an economy a human life will be largely dependent on the natural rhythms of the environment: day and night, the seasons, the movements of animals, and so on. One point which gets a good deal of emphasis is that a person's own needs are equally subject to natural rhythms (for example hunger, the need for sleep, sexual drives) and are as much factors to which he or she has to respond as are the things in the environment. If the environment is seen as a network of necessities in which the individual is caught, then inner needs also belong to that network. Or, to put the same point in another way, the individual person is predominantly *passive* in relation to these inner needs as to the outer environment.

This is another point which may be thrown into relief by a contrast with Simone Weil's later way of thinking. In the very late *The Need for Roots* the concept of "the needs of the soul" is paramount.[3] These "needs" however are not treated as something with which the individual merely has to *contend,* as it were, but as actually constitutive of the individual's nature. Or: they characterize his or her perspective on the world. They spring from the fact that "human beings have an eternal destiny," and this in its turn is made possible by the fact that what is most fundamental in such beings is "the desire for good." The word "good" here does not designate any particular state of affairs; it conveys rather that the desires we have for particular objects, such as food, clothing, a sexual partner, are embodiments of the desire for good from which springs our eternal destiny. This desire for good finds its expression only in and through the character of people's desires for such particular objects. It is only through their relation to the desire for good that such particular desires constitute genuine needs. On this view it is in the character of such desires that an individual's perspective on the world is to be discerned. In *Oppression and Liberty,* on the contrary, needs are part of the world on which an individual has a perspective. I think it is plausible to see, in this conception, remnants of Simone Weil's early quasi-Cartesian conception of "I" as pure activity, not characterizable in any other way, whereas on the later view I have an essential direction or posture: I am by nature oriented towards good.

It is to be expected that such a change in emphasis in the account of human nature will bring with it a corresponding change in the conception of what constitutes equilibrium between human beings. The nature of this change will occupy much of the discussion from Chapter 9 onwards. In the present chapter and in the next, however, I wish to explore the consequences of the picture of the relation between activity and equilibrium on which *Oppression and Liberty* is based.

To return to this then: because, in a primitive economy, a person is exposed directly, qua individual, to the necessities of the natural world – the cushioning effect of the natural family group does not get much emphasis here – there will only be extremely limited opportunity for planning ahead and making provision against future contingencies. All energies will be expended on a hand-to-mouth exploitation of the immediate situation.

This is obviously an extremely general and *a priori* picture, not based on historical or anthropological researches so much as being a result of the exigencies of a particular way of thinking: an important aspect of which is the generalizing tendency of Simone Weil's thinking about "necessity" that I have referred to earlier. A very natural objection would be, for example, to point out that not all human environments are of a piece; some are harsh, some mild; resources are sometimes scarce, sometimes plentiful. She concedes this, but does not think it makes much difference:

> It is true that nature is milder or harsher towards human needs according to climate, and perhaps depending on the period; but to look expectantly for the miraculous invention that would make her mild everywhere, and once and for all, is about as reasonable as the hopes formerly placed in the year 1000.[4]

This response, of course, however apposite against certain kinds of utopian dream, does not address the objection against her own over-generalizing tendencies. But she goes on to make another point which is much more interesting and which in fact exploits the resources of that very general philosophical schema which the objection attacks. She draws on the idea that human needs themselves belong to the "nature" with which human beings have to contend and argues that, if the pressure of external circumstances is removed, a person will become increasingly enslaved to internal forces:

> There is no self-mastery without discipline, and there is no other source of discipline for man than the effort demanded in overcoming external obstacles.[5]

And again:

> The human body can in no case cease to depend on the mighty universe in which it is encased; even if man were to cease being subjected to material things and to his fellows by needs and dangers, he would only be more completely delivered into their hands by the emotions which would stir him continually to the depths of his soul, and against which no regular occupation would any longer protect him.[6]

But in fact there is more than meets the eye even to the anti-utopian gibe about the "miraculous invention." The point is not merely that there is no reason to expect technology to produce an invention that will make nature "mild everywhere." It is rather that all the achievements of technology are necessarily bought at a price and that there is a confusion involved in picturing technological advance as a progressive liberation of human beings from natural necessities. There is no such thing as a liberation from, or even mitigation of, natural necessity. What sometimes may *look* like that is really a change in the form of that necessity.

A large part of what makes new technology work as a mitigation of the hand-to-mouth relationship between individuals and their natural environment described above is the fact that it makes possible – indeed necessitates – a division of labour. They are no longer engaged simply in satisfying their own immediate needs in the face of natural rhythms which have to be accepted as brute facts. They can now initiate rhythms of existence of their own, based on foresight and protection against contingencies. This goes hand in hand, of course, with much more manipulation and control of the environment than was previously possible. People can now lay up stocks for future use, build walls, dam rivers, construct bridges, and so on, and thereby model the environment to suit their needs.

The central point at this stage of Simone Weil's argument might be expressed by saying that the word "they" is being used in two different ways in that previous paragraph. In the description of the primitive economy (before the division of labour) we could, instead of talking about "people," speak of "each individual person." We can no longer do that when speaking of an economy based on the division of labour. We are now talking about a particular organization of society in which different individuals play different roles.

But to talk about an organization of society is again to talk about *necessities*. Considered as individuals, people are just as much subject to the social necessities imposed by the division of labour as they were previously to the necessities of the natural environment. What is more, what are politely called "social necessities" in the preceding sentence take the form of subjection to other individuals (who of course acquire their power from the social organization under which all live).

> In short, man seems to pass by stages, with respect to nature, from servitude to dominion. At the same time nature gradually loses her divine character, and divinity more and more takes on human shape. Unfortunately, this emancipation is only a flattering semblance. In reality, at these higher stages, human action continues, as a whole, to be nothing but pure obedience to the brutal spur of an immediate necessity; only, instead of being harried by nature, man is henceforth harried by man. However, it is still the same pressure exerted by nature that continues to make itself felt, although indirectly; for oppression is exercised by force, and in the long run all force originates in nature.[7]

Here I think we have to distinguish between the aptness of the description which is being given of the transformation from a primitive economy to one based on the division of labour and, on the other hand, the metaphysical picture that lies behind it: a picture Simone Weil's attachment to which I have already drawn attention to. It is the picture of an all-pervading necessity which forms, as it were, the fabric of the natural world. I think there is no doubt that in the present instance, as a matter of intellectual history or biography, that picture played a considerable part in giving her description of the social transformation in question the form it has. But the metaphysical picture is not, so to speak, logically required by the description; if we do not realize that, the sketch of early economic history we are being offered may seem to require us to accept more theoretical baggage than is necessary.

Let us consider the last passage from *Oppression and Liberty* that I quoted: in particular the insistence that "human action continues, as a whole, to be nothing but pure obedience to the brutal spur of an immediate necessity"; that "it is still the same pressure exerted by nature that continues to make itself felt"; and other similar remarks. These *may* be taken as simply an emphatic insistence that it would be mistaken to think that the change from a primitive to a more complex economy represents pure liberation for the human beings involved; and that is all right. However, there is certainly a metaphysical emphasis here on the notion of *"the same* pressure exerted by nature." That is clear from the immediate context, but also from the general metaphysical picture to which Simone Weil again and again seems to appeal in her writings. So it is not merely pedantic to ask questions. What more is said than in the description of the economic transformation? By what criteria do we decide that two instances of pressure are instances of "the same pressure"; and if we do say that, what other possibility are we distinguishing it from?

I turn now to the distinction between liberty and oppression. As has already been implied, Simone Weil does not regard subjection to discipline as such as oppressive. On the contrary, her view is that to be completely "free" of the discipline imposed by having to cope with external circumstances would be to subject oneself to an anarchy of imperious and not understood inner drives. Freedom, she says, is a relation between thought and action: that is, it goes with the discipline of methodical procedures involved in thinking. But it must be self-imposed discipline, whereas the discipline involved in the division of labour is, as far as the individual is concerned, "heteronomous" – the Kantian language is mine – partly because it is not something that most people are able either to take or leave, but something that imposes itself on them; partly, and more important, because it will generally involve a division between entrepreneurial and executive functions. And for this last reason the relation between thought and action which characterizes freedom is absent.[8] Those who execute do things dictated by the thoughts of other people; but also: those who initiate action do not themselves carry out the action. Freedom, therefore, is ruptured on all sides.

Now, the "relation between thought and action" which is here said to constitute freedom is something that I have discussed extensively in earlier chapters and something which is one of the great themes of Simone Weil's *Lectures on Philosophy*. But here, in *Oppression and Liberty*, there is a different emphasis. The absolutely free man, she writes, would be

> he whose every action proceeded from a preliminary judgment concerning the end which he set himself and the sequence of means suitable for attaining the end.[9]

The central place of *judgment* in this conception distinguishes it
from mere arbitrariness, since it pertains to judgment to bear on
an objective set of circumstances "and consequently upon a warp
and woof of necessities." Liberty, then, is only possible when
someone does not have constantly to respond to the pressure of
immediate circumstances, since such a response involves no judgment concerning those circumstances. (Here we can see the distinction between "constraint" and "necessity" developed in *Lectures* applied to the distinction between a primitive and a more
advanced economy.) "Blindly submitting to the spur with which
necessity pricks him on from outside" is "servitude" (N.B.: *not*
"oppression"). Liberty, by contrast, is "adapting himself to the
inner representation of it [sc. necessity] that he forms in his own
mind."

This conception is contrasted with that according to which freedom is a relation between a desire and its satisfaction. One of the
most important points made by the contrast is that it does not
make freedom depend on the success or failure, or the ease or
painfulness, of whatever is done. What is important is that there
is no *humiliation* involved in a person's failure to achieve what is
wanted, "as long as it is he himself who disposes of his own capacity for action."

It is worth spelling out the thought behind this, since there is a
difficulty about it which goes right to the root of the conception
of social life developed in *Oppression and Liberty*. The contrast
between the two conceptions of free action can be expressed by
saying that each of them takes a different view of the point, or
value, of acting freely. According to the desire–satisfaction model,
the point of acting freely is that you get what you want; with the
corollary that if you *don't* get what you want your action fails to
have that point. The point of the action depends on its outcome.
This is not true of the thought–action model, according to which
the point of free action lies in the character of the action itself,
the manner in which it is performed, whatever its outcome may
happen to be.

Now it is clear that for Simone Weil the superiority of the
thought–action account lies in the fact that it links freedom with
human dignity. If you have disposed of your own capacity for
action as best you can, you are not humiliated by not getting what
you wanted, even if you are disappointed. This is an important
idea which I certainly do not want to denigrate. But the question

I want to ask is whether it is an idea to which Simone Weil is actually entitled in the context of her argument. Where, we must ask, does the idea of "humiliation" come from? It is an idea that has its place and its importance against the background of a certain sort of communal life in which people are bound to each other by attitudes of mutual regard which are important to them and which are fragile. I do not want to say that only a person who is conscious of the ill opinion of others can feel humiliated – that would not be true; but I do want to say that the cases in which it is not true are only intelligible against a backcloth of concern for the good opinion of others. Without that, there is nothing about failure to attain what one wants which could be thought of as humiliating.

But this is a background that Simone Weil *cannot* presuppose. The whole emphasis in her account of freedom at this time is that it is to be found in a direct confrontation between the individual and nature: *without* the intervention of other human beings. In her early notebook she quotes Goethe's *Faust* in dealing with the same point:

> Stünd' ich, Natur, vor dir ein Mann allein
> Dann wär's der Mühe wert, ein Mensch zu sein![10]

The point is not that she just *happens* to have provided no account of a social background against which this talk of humiliation would make sense; it is rather that she is trying to *construct* an account of what a community would look like in which there was room for the dignity of individuals, and therefore, too, room for humiliation. The conception of free action as involving only the individual in direct confrontation with nature is an essential feature, indeed *the* essential feature, of that construction.

But the situation is worse than this, as I must now try to show. In presenting Simone Weil's account of free action in *Oppression and Liberty* I remarked the continuity with her account of necessity in *Lectures* but at the same time said there was a difference of emphasis. In *Lectures* it was important that an individual's activity should be understood from "the materialist point of view," from the point of view, that is, of an observer; it consisted in the following of methodical procedures which are objectively describable.

In *Oppression and Liberty* on the other hand free action requires an "inner representation" and a "preliminary judgment." The implication is that the relation between thought and action is one that is apparent only to the agent, since the inner representation and the judgment are not apparent to the observer. And it is an implication that Simone Weil herself stresses and which plays a crucial role in her account of oppression. Because thought is, in this sense, hidden, she argues, the principles of action which lie behind and are responsible for people's actions are inaccessible to an observer. Hence people are essentially "mysterious" to each other. But this means that there is no possibility of people treating each other in a rational, methodical way. Hence, since free action requires such rational methodical action it is impossible to be free in one's dealings with other human beings.

What are we to make of this? Are we to regard this talk about "inner representations" and so on as a backsliding to the Cartesianism from which she seemed to be liberating herself in *Lectures*? There are times at which it almost seems so. But I think a more fruitful way to look at it is to trace the difficulty to an internal deficiency in the account in *Lectures* itself. Whereas a great deal is said there about the character of the human reactions to natural phenomena from which springs the conception of those phenomena as belonging to a coherent natural order, very little is said about the character of the human reactions *to other human beings,* from which springs the conception of human beings (including myself) as belonging to a community. What sort of relation to another human being is involved, for instance, in my *understanding what the other says?* Here we encounter the kinds of difficulty involved in such a conception as "the rule by which he proceeds" that Wittgenstein discussed so extensively in his mature works. In fact the obstacles Simone Weil sees in *Oppression and Liberty* to one person's understanding the thought processes of another could be put in similar terms. Wittgenstein states the difficulty as follows:

> This was our paradox: no course of action could be determined by a rule, because every course of action can be made out to accord with the rule.[11]

A course of action is "determined by" a rule if the agent himself or herself is following that rule; that a spectator can formulate a rule with which the course of action is consistent is no guarantee that the agent is in fact following that rule. It is no good for the spectator to *ask* the agent what rule is being followed, because the agent's response will be just another piece of behaviour which the spectator will have to interpret, concerning which, therefore, he or she will be in the same quandary. There seems to be no way, therefore, by which a spectator can get beyond a piece of observable behaviour to the reality of the agent from whom it issues.

I have chosen that last way of putting the problem in order to bring out its connection with the notion of equilibrium. Equilibrium, I said earlier, is a stable relation between things of a sort which involves no violation of the reality of any of the things related. Two active human beings, therefore, could be in equilibrium with each other only in so far as the actions of each respected the reality of the other. But the account of the relation between thought and action with which Simone Weil was working at this time seemed to make no room for two such agents to *know* the reality of the other, let alone respect it. Wittgenstein dissolved his "paradox" by pointing out (later in the passage just quoted) that "there is a way of grasping a rule which is *not* an *interpretation,* but which is exhibited in what we call 'obeying the rule' and 'going against it' in actual cases"; and he backed this up with detailed descriptions of the kinds of behaviour that exemplify what we call "obeying a rule" and *also* of the kinds of behaviour in which what we call "grasping the rule that someone else is following" is exemplified. There is a similar development, though executed in a very different style and leading in a rather different direction, in Simone Weil's later work: a development involving much more attention to the actual character of people's reactions *to each other* than one finds in *Oppression and Liberty.* This development will be the subject of my later chapters.

At the stage of her thinking we are now examining, however, the conception of human beings as essentially mysterious to each other has the consequence that no intelligible way can be described in which people can come to agree on a common way of life, since no one has any sure way of assessing what others really have in mind. So the presence of another human being will always be an essential threat to one's realization of one's own projects; and the only way to avert that threat is to dominate the other. Naturally, not everyone can achieve a dominating position, so human relations will always be between those who dominate and those who submit; but since the essential reality of a human being is to be active, such relations will never constitute an equilibrium. Somebody's nature will always be violated.

This picture is, of course, strongly reminiscent of the "natural condition of mankind" described in Hobbes's *Leviathan.* In both cases, moreover, the leading idea is a certain account of the relation between thought and action from which is derived the impossibility of any genuine mutual trust. There is one important respect in which Simone Weil's account has a different emphasis from that of Hobbes. For him, there is a clear distinction between the one who dominates and the one who submits: and such a clear distinction is crucially required by the notion of "sovereignty," his recipe for mitigating the solitary, poor, nasty, brutish, and short character of human life in such a situation. But this is not so unambiguously so in Simone Weil's account. Drawing on ideas in Hegel and Marx (amongst other writers at least as far back as Plato) she points out that domination itself characteristically involves an element of submission, though this fact may be hidden even from the one who thinks to occupy the dominating position. We saw, in Chapter 5, how in *Lectures* she quoted Bacon: "Homo naturae non nisi parendo imperat." In *Oppression and Liberty* she argues that the same holds good for people's domination of their fellows. The power necessary for such domination does not come from them alone; they draw it from their environment. That environment is in very large measure a human, social environment. So their power comes, in large, probably pre-eminent, measure from the society in which they exercise their domination. They can dominate some human beings only in so far as, one way or another, they have the support of others. They *depend* on that support. They will continue to receive it only in so far as it seems worthwhile to others to give it. So somehow or other they have to induce them to give it. That means flattering their expectations, which is a form of servility or submission even if – perhaps even especially if – the flattery is a deceitful one. In *Oppression and Liberty* Simone Weil fills out this general account with a trenchant description of competition in industrial society. Her chief criticism of Marx is directed against the idea that industrial society could ever itself evolve conditions in which things were fundamentally different.

It would not be much of an exaggeration to say that the whole of Simone Weil's life work was directed at finding a description of the human condition which would make a genuine equilibrium between human beings at least conceivable. She was always realistically pessimistic about the possibility of ever bringing such an equilibrium about as a lasting state of affairs. This, however, would not destroy the value of such a description, which would provide us with a perspective from which we could attain a better understanding of life as it actually is. – I think one sees this aspiration most clearly and most beautifully expressed in the essay on *The Iliad* which I have already mentioned and to which I shall be returning.

At the time she composed "Reflections Concerning the Causes of Liberty and Social Oppression" an intelligible conception of human equilibrium was inaccessible to her because of certain confusions which continued to infect her understanding of the nature of "activity" in the life of a human being. I shall try to make good this claim in the next chapter.

8

"COMPLETELY FREE ACTION"

The obstacles to a genuine "equilibrium" between human beings seem to lie in the very nature of the human condition as pictured in "Reflections Concerning the Causes of Liberty and Social Oppression," the centrepiece of *Oppression and Liberty*. That condition is characterized as a living together of beings whose most essential feature is activity. The argument is that the moment such beings become mutually dependent, as they do when their attempts to assert their active natures in the face of a hostile nature lead to a division of labour, the active independence of some, and perhaps of all, is inevitably threatened. Because such active independence is essential to human nature, this state of affairs is not a true equilibrium. The problem, therefore, is to work out what form of association could possibly constitute such an equilibrium. Needless to say, the form of the problem's *solution* will be determined by the considerations which first generated the problem.

Those considerations arise out of the way Simone Weil conceives *activity*. I have already discussed at some length the problems which this concept created in "Science et perception dans Descartes" and the way in which she tried to deal with those problems in *Lectures on Philosophy*. "Reflections Concerning the Causes of Liberty and Social Oppression" shows that the concept is still causing her serious difficulties. The difficulties are of two sorts. Some of them are due to her not having completely worked through and taken to heart the main line of thinking in *Lectures*. Some of them are due to deficiencies still involved in that line of thinking itself.

One set of difficulties is generated by the conception of thought as something separate from, and causally related to, bodily activity. Now, that conception is of course *attacked* in *Lectures* – the attack is precisely what characterizes the "materialist point of view." What becomes evident in *Oppression and Liberty* is that the implications of this attack have still not been fully taken to heart. The other set of difficulties comes from the conception of thought as *instrumental,* as concerned with means and ends. While *Lectures* certainly does not consistently stick to this conception, it is nevertheless, as I have tried to show, dominant in the account there given of concept formation. I shall come back to this second point at the end of the present chapter.

"True liberty," it will be remembered, is defined as "a relationship between thought and action" and

> the absolutely free man would be he whose every action proceeded from a preliminary judgment concerning the end which he set himself and the sequence of means suitable for attaining this end.

Simone Weil recognizes that this is an "ideal limit" which human life never reaches, like the opposite situation in which a person is "completely a slave" in the sense that "all his movements proceed[ed] from a source other than his mind." An abstract model of such "ideal liberty" she says is provided by "a properly solved problem in arithmetic or geometry," such that

> all the elements of the solution are given, and man can look for assistance only to his own judgment, alone capable of establishing between these elements the relationship which by itself constitutes the solution sought. The efforts and successes attending mathematics do not go beyond the compass of the piece of paper, the realm of signs and figures; a completely free life would be one wherein all real difficulties presented themselves as kinds of problems, wherein all successes were as solutions carried into action.[1]

What should we understand here by the last phrase, "solutions carried into action"? The phrase does of course have a perfectly good use. If I am planning to hang wallpaper in my home, I measure the dimensions of the walls, do some simple geometrical and arithmetical calculations, and buy materials from the shop in accordance with the calculations. Then I hang the paper.

But this sort of thing cannot be quite what Simone Weil means; at any rate it is not what the direction of her discussion suggests. For instance, she treats the fact that the natural world may always throw up unforeseen contingencies as itself an "impediment" to ideal freedom. It is clear that carrying the solution of a mathematical problem into action in the way I have just exemplified is of its nature *already* exposed to such contingencies. The shopkeeper may give me the wrong amount of paper, the paper may tear, and so on. What Simone Weil wants to be able to say is that, in the ideal case of a completely free action, the successful completion of the action would have the same relation to the thinking from which it issues as does the correct solution of a mathematical problem to the calculation from which *it* issues. Now the reason why this is unattainable is not just that it is an ideal limit. It embodies a confusion. "Actions" which were not subject to contingencies would not have any effects on anything either; which is as much as to say they would not be actions at all. Take the actions I perform in cutting the wallpaper for example: the relation of those actions to the environment in which they are performed which makes them apt to result in strips of paper of the desired length is precisely that relation which also makes it possible that the paper will tear and frustrate the purpose of the action.

Let us try to see what has gone wrong. Simone Weil writes that under the "ideal" conditions imagined "the performance of any work whatever would consist in as conscious and as methodical a combination of efforts as can be the combination of numbers by which the solution of a problem is brought about when this solution results from reflection." Now, the word "combination" is in fact being used in two quite different ways in the phrases "combination of efforts" and "combination of numbers." The formula $6 \times 8 = 48$ expresses, I suppose, a certain combination of numbers. Of course it makes no sense to say that something might happen to upset or dissolve this combination. That it makes no sense is a feature of the grammar according to which the word "combination" is here being used.[2] By contrast, suppose that I have to get forty-eight people on a bus; I arrange them into six groups of eight and then let them on the bus group by group. There will then be forty-eight people on the bus *provided everything has gone according to plan.* But if the people involved were British soccer fans, for instance, one can imagine all sorts of things.

It is true that many of Simone Weil's own discussions, particularly in *Lectures,* show that she is alive to and fascinated by this sort of distinction. But her discussions also show that she is not entirely clear about what sort of distinction is at issue. In fact, I believe that the example I have been discussing raises issues somewhat analogous to those she herself talks about in her discussion of the Pythagorean problem of incommensurables.[3] That is to say, there is a confusion about the relation between a mathematical and practical operation analogous to the confusion she pointed to there between an arithmetical and a geometrical operation. And the dangers inherent in the former confusion are in fact already foreshadowed in some of her remarks about mathematics and language in *Lectures*.

The important section on mathematical reasoning in *Lectures* brings together many of the points about language, order, and necessity I have already discussed. But it also makes some new points related to our present concern. She considers, on page 79, some questions about how mathematical reasoning is related to the real world.

> In geometry, even if we consider the matter as materialists, there is always language and order. The syllogism comes in once the demonstration has been made. How does one make the demonstration? With lines. Still, the lines do not exist in nature. How then can mathematics be used for the construction of machinery? for material things like railways, motor-cars?
>
> Where do lines get this magic power from – these faint marks on paper, on a blackboard? The king of the universe is the triangle, or rather, first of all, the straight line.
>
> Let us look for the general characteristics of straight lines, of geometrical figures. Why would one not use branches of a cedar tree to do geometry?
>
> We see then that geometrical figures are (a) manageable, (b) simple.
>
> A straight line is simpler than a curve because one can scan it more easily; a straight line is simpler than a surface because one can scan a straight line but not a surface.
>
> It is a mark of our greatness that we can reduce inaccessible things to things that are simple; it is a sign of our weakness that we cannot do this at once.
>
> Further these figures are (c) things that are fixed in nature and (d) symbols, which have no solidity, offer no resistance, have no weight, can be used without any chance of mishap.
>
> So it is just because these things hardly have any existence and are completely in our power that we can use them to gain dominion over the world. (Cf. language through which everything is at our disposal.)

That passage is very characteristic. It seems to me magnificently suggestive in many directions, but also dangerously so. The use she makes of the word *maniable* repays attention in this connection: "manageable," "controllable." It often signifies a simple contrast between things that are more or less easy to "handle" *in the same sense of that word.* We can handle matchsticks more easily than we can cedar branches; they are easier to get hold of, can be moved about more readily, and so on. Similarly, chalk marks on a blackboard can be controlled more easily than can matchsticks; they can be arranged and will stay in position without danger of being knocked askew, they can be erased very simply with no problems about where to put them when not in use, and so on. These are very familiar and obvious facts. But they are facts which are very important for the role mathematics plays in our lives and are easily overlooked in philosophical discussions about "the nature of mathematics." Think of the role of mathematics in building a bridge, for instance. We do not have to assemble girders and put them together by trial and error – no very complicated structure would get built in that way. Instead, we draw plans according to exact measurements, make calculations, and amend the plans according to the results of those calculations.

These are the kinds of "reminder" the importance of which for philosophy Wittgenstein repeatedly emphasized. Many of Simone Weil's remarks can be interpreted along those lines. For instance, it may be said of lines drawn on paper or on a blackboard that they "have no solidity, offer no resistance, have no weight, can be used without any chance of mishap." This would be a perfectly acceptable way of saying that the resistance, weight, chances of mishap, and so on are *negligible* and do not need to be taken into account when we are dealing with drawn diagrams in a way which would not be true if we were dealing with steel girders.

But although such factors may be negligible *in a given context,* it is not that there is no intelligible application for these concepts at all. There is, for example, an increase in the weight of a piece of paper when a line is drawn on it that is detectable within a certain technology. There are circumstances in which there may be a mishap: someone might inadvertently burn the piece of paper bearing the diagram. These are not possibilities that one takes into account in normal circumstances, or that one should or even could take into account in all circumstances. And so it is in order for us to say that there is "no solidity" and so on to the items we are dealing with here.

But it would be going rather far to express *that* sort of point by saying that "the lines do not exist in nature"; "these things hardly have any existence *(ces choses existent à peine)*." Simone Weil's use of the expression *à peine* is interesting here: it marks the uneasy ambiguity to which I want to draw attention. To say that the lines do not exist in nature is to say that, if we are taking as our paradigm of what it is for something to *exist* the application of this term to girders, heaps of cement, matchsticks, or, for that matter, pencil marks on paper, or chalk marks on a blackboard, we cannot speak of the "existence" of the geometrical figures the properties of which and the relations between which we are investigating. That is, we are drawing attention to the marked *grammatical* differences (to use an expression of Wittgenstein's that is not at all alien to Simone Weil's way of thinking) between the use of such words as "line," "point," "surface" *in geometry* and our use of words for physical things and properties.

It remains of course to give an account of how these different grammars are related to each other. Simone Weil does not do this in anything like the detail with which Wittgenstein describes similar matters. But she does make some interesting and valuable suggestions. In the passage I have quoted, for example, the remarks about lines as "symbols of movement" are quite reminiscent of Wittgenstein's discussion of "the machine as symbol."[4] And in other places in *Lectures* and elsewhere she makes some extremely interesting observations about the ways in which our concepts of regular geometrical shapes permeate our manual operations and, especially, the construction and use of tools. These observations develop the arresting remark that "one might say that geometry lies at the basis of a science of work."[5]

What I am arguing is that in "Reflections Concerning the Causes of Liberty and Social Oppression" the development of this idea is distorted by confusions concerning the relation between geometry and its application. These confusions are embodied in the conception of the absolutely "free" performance of a piece of work in which a "combination of efforts" is "as conscious and as methodical" as is the "combination of numbers" which effects the solution of a mathematical problem.

> Man is a limited being to whom it is not given to be, as in the case of the God of the theologians, the direct author of his own existence; but he would possess the human equivalent of that divine power if the material conditions that enable him to exist were exclu-

sively the work of his mind directing the effort of his muscles. This would be true liberty.[6]

Three quite different contrasts are involved here. (1) There is, to begin with, the quite common or garden contrast between a piece of work which is entirely under the worker's own control and one which is not. An example of the former would be a worker felling trees, working for his or her own gain, planning the execution of the job, familiar with the materials and tools of the job and understanding their properties and capabilities. The contrast here is with someone who, for instance, works on a production line and is charged with a constantly repeated mechanical operation. That worker does not understand the significance of the operation, does it only because he or she is paid to do so, knows nothing of how the work is related to the end product and little about the nature of the end product itself.

(2) Second, there is a contrast between a task like the example of felling trees and the task of solving a mathematical problem.

(3) But third, there is a contrast which is important to Simone Weil's argument, but which she seems not to notice. I am thinking of the contrast between what is involved in *solving* a mathematical problem: what, as it were, lies between first confronting the problem and finding a solution; and what actually *constitutes* a mathematical problem: the relation between the elements of the problem and its solution. When I say that she seems not to notice this contrast, I mean that she often seems to think that what she says applies to the first term of the contrast when in fact it only properly belongs to a characterization of the second.

Consider, for example, the expression used on page 87 of *Oppression and Liberty:* "He would forge the conditions of his existence by an act of mind" – a way of speaking that goes with what she says about "immunity from accidents." It might be said that a mathematical problem is what it is "by virtue of an act of mind." That is not a phrase I much like, but it would mean something like "by virtue of having been *set.*" Now, it belongs to the nature of a well-formed mathematical problem that the formulation of the problem completely determines the conditions for its solution. In other words, its solubility or insolubility can be seen from an examination of the problem as set; there is no sense, in *this* context, in speaking of some "accident" which makes a once soluble problem insoluble. "It" would then no longer be the same problem.

Such considerations *might* lead us to speak of the solution of a mathematical problem as being "completely open to one's own judgment without the possibility of any interference." This is unobjectionable as long as it is understood as making a *grammatical* or *conceptual* point. That is to say, we ought to be clear that we have not found some inviolable enclave of human activity, immune from accidents. We have simply specified a way of speaking in which talk of "accidents" is grammatically out of place.

This is clear if we now look at the other term of the contrast (3): what is involved in actually solving a mathematical problem. I mean this in the sense of a fully temporal process of which it makes sense to ask when it took place, how long it lasted, and so on. A process of this sort is as subject to accidents as any other: as building a bridge, for example. Illness, tiredness, stupidity, loss of one's notes, an accident with the ink bottle, a person from Porlock: there is no end to the possible contingencies that may hamper, prevent, or facilitate the solution to the problem.

This point is closely related to my earlier remarks on the ambiguities in Simone Weil's talk about the "manageability" of words and mathematical signs. The physical marks are certainly subject to accident in the sense that talk about the possibility of accidents is conceptually in order even if accidents are so rare that their likelihood can be and is treated as negligible.[7] But numbers and geometrical figures cannot be spoken of in that way: our concepts of them are determined by the fact that we do not countenance such talk.

The confusion comes to a focus in the use of the word "exclusively" in the remark (previously quoted) that a person would have "the human equivalent of that divine power [sc. be the direct author of his own existence] if the material conditions that enable him to exist were exclusively the work of his mind directing the effort of his muscles." The analogies on the basis of which this is said suggest the exclusiveness of the relation between the conditions and the solution of a mathematical problem. But the relation between "the work of the mind" and "the effort of the muscles" comes into quite a different category. We might, for instance, speak of such a relation when describing an athlete who beautifully paces herself so as to win a race. Nothing, as it were, comes between the decisions she makes on how fast to run and the movements of her limbs. But that is not to say that there are no conditions on which the maintenance of this relation depends. If she gets out of training, succumbs to a virus, and so on, the efforts of her muscles will no longer answer to the work of her mind.

The point of these remarks is not to proscribe the use of the word "exclusively" in such contexts. *In* those contexts it is unlikely to be misunderstood. But its use is complicated and ragged in a way which is inimical to a tidy philosophical account of action. Anyone wishing to give such an account will be under considerable pressure to misconstrue it. Simone Weil had already responded to such pressure earlier, in "Science et perception dans Descartes," when she claimed that somebody could not be purely active in respect of the movements of the body. Thoughtful muscular effort is indeed subject to temporal accident; but the possibility of such accident is already provided for in the grammar of our use of expressions like "exclusively," "completely within one's control," and so forth.

Does all this matter for Simone Weil's account of oppression? Yes, it does. As I have tried to bring out, the difficulties in the way she conceives geometry in relation to its application go together with the idea that in thinking about a geometrical problem the human mind is free in the sense that it is completely independent of all contingencies. But while geometrical figures are independent of contingencies, the mind that thinks about them is not. I believe that the picture of a person's mind as independent of contingencies contributes substantially to her idea of it as inaccessible to the awareness of others. She is thinking of it, as it were, as performing its essential functions independent of any vehicle of expression: since any such vehicle is going to be subject to contingencies. But in so far as completely free thinking has to be conceived as independent of all means of expression, it is *ex hypothesi* inaccessible to the understanding of other human beings. And *this* idea is central to her way of conceiving oppression in *Oppression and Liberty*.

> Matter can give the lie to expectations and ruin efforts, it remains none the less inert, made to be understood and handled from the outside; but the human mind can never be understood or handled from the outside. To the extent to which a man's fate is dependent on other men, his own life escapes not only out of his hands, but also out of the control of his intelligence; judgment and resolution no longer have anything to which to apply themselves; instead of contriving and acting, one has to stoop to pleading and threatening; and the soul is plunged into bottomless abysses of desire and fear,

for there are no bounds to the satisfactions and sufferings that a man can receive at the hands of other men.[8]

It might be thought that membership of an organized human society would give the individual intelligence something to grasp. On the contrary:

> Now, if there is one thing in the world which is completely abstract, wholly mysterious, inaccessible to the senses and to the mind, it is the collectivity; the individual who is a member of it cannot, it would seem, reach up to or lay hold of it by any artifice, bring his weight to bear on it by the use of any lever; with respect to it he feels himself to be something infinitely small. If an individual's caprices seem arbitrary to everybody else, the shocks produced by collective life seem to be so to the second power. Thus between man and this universe which is assigned to him by destiny as the sole matter of his thought and actions, the relation oppression–servitude permanently sets the impenetrable screen of human arbitrariness.[9]

Simone Weil retained this attitude to the "collectivity" throughout her life, but at other times it was qualified by the realization that human societies also have something positive and indispensable to offer to the spiritual life of human beings. In *The Need for Roots* for example she speaks of the collectivity as "food for a certain number of human souls" (p. 7). But even in very early writings, as we have already had occasion to note of the *Lectures,* she emphasizes the role of society in giving the individual access to language and culture. That seems to be almost forgotten in the main argument of *Oppression and Liberty.* The individual and his or her thinking are understood in uncompromisingly individualistic terms. Human society, so far from mediating the application of thought to the circumstances of an individual's life, is the main obstacle in the way of such an application.

The upshot of this part of the discussion is that the problem of equilibrium, in so far as it is seen as generated by the inaccessibility of an individual's thought processes to others, is impossible to solve. The very most that could be achieved would be a "solution" like that suggested by Hobbes: the imposition of a sort of stability by sheer force. But this could not count as a solution for Simone Weil, since it would entail violating the active natures of those involved and would thus not be a true equilibrium.

At the beginning of this chapter I said that there were two major difficulties arising from the manner in which practical reason is understood in *Oppression and Liberty,* the second being its instrumental character. I shall conclude the chapter with some remarks about this. The free person is the one who uses personal judgment to determine personal ends and the means of achieving them. The "image of a free community" is provided by

> a handful of workmen in the building trade, checked by some dif-
> ficulty, [who] ponder the problem each for himself, make various
> suggestions for dealing with it, and then apply unanimously the
> method conceived by one of them, who may or may not have any
> official authority over the remainder.[10]

It is of course no accident that the example concerns people *work-ing,* since Simone Weil avowedly regarded the concept of work as central to an understanding of human social life. And one of her main reasons for so regarding it was her idea that it is in work that a person as a thinking being confronts nature directly: and "directly," at this stage, meant "as an individual." I referred in Chapter 7 to her approving citation of Goethe's *Faust* on this point. But the example obscures a problem: perhaps the most important problem of all for her position at this stage. Workers on a building site are already engaged in a common enterprise: the problems they face, the discussions they take part in, and the solutions they agree on presuppose that as a framework. Simone Weil is hardly entitled to presuppose such a framework, and that for two reasons.

First, the account she has offered of free action makes the possibility of setting up such a framework a problem; it certainly cannot be presupposed in the solution to the problem. It is indeed rather extraordinary that, at this stage in her argument, with all the emphasis she has laid on the essential obscurity shrouding one person's thought processes from another, she can allow herself to say:

> There is but one single and identical reason for all men; they only
> become estranged from and impenetrable to each other when they
> depart from it; thus a society in which the whole of material exis-
> tence had as its necessary and sufficient condition that each individ-
> ual should exercise his reason could be absolutely clearly under-
> stood by each individual mind.[11]

This notion of a single common reason is one she shares with, amongst others, Descartes and Kant, by both of whom she was greatly influenced. But her own argument hardly licenses her to assume it here. It is the presupposition of a common enterprise on which all are engaged that encourages her to say such a thing: the enterprise of promoting the conditions of "material existence," which would, therefore, have to be understood by everyone in the same way.

Second, and in the end more important, social life cannot in any case be regarded as a common enterprise on the analogy of an industrial concern. No doubt there is something that unites fellow citizens, but it is not a set of common purposes. That is not to deny of course that fellow citizens may sometimes have common purposes; it is not even to deny that in certain circumstances (war, for instance) fellow-citizenship may require people to have common purposes. But that is not what constitutes their fellow-citizenship. The question what *does* constitute this is indeed not far removed from the question what constitutes equilibrium between human beings living their lives together: that is, precisely the question Simone Weil is trying to answer. And the presupposition of her way of approaching the question is that the free person would have to confront nature *as an individual,* not as someone who, by definition as it were, is regarded as engaged in a common enterprise with other individuals. I am free when I decide for myself, on the basis of my own judgment, what my enterprise shall be.

It is by this time clear that the problem of equilibrium is one to which there can be no solution in the terms in which it has been posed. The notion of *justice* has to be brought into the discussion at quite a different point, not as something negotiated between individuals each of whose real interest lies elsewhere, in the fulfilment of his or her own projects, but as itself constituting that interest and as an essential condition of any understanding whatever, whether of oneself, of one's relations with others, or of one's relations with the natural world. In the remainder of the book I shall discuss this new conception of the problem as it evolves in Simone Weil's later thinking.

9

THE POWER TO REFUSE

In the preceding chapters I have tried to show how the account of concept formation underlying Simone Weil's early thinking led her into difficulties when she tried to apply it to the conception human beings have of each other. Let me recapitulate the outlines of the argument.

Our concepts are formed as our primitive, unreflective reactions to our surroundings are transformed, refined,[1] into more ordered, methodical modes of behaviour. The order in which the steps constituting these procedures are carried out is a necessary one in the sense that observance of the order in the carrying out of the steps is a criterion of their constituting a given methodical procedure. In many cases certain abstract conceptual constructions are created, the necessary properties of, and relations between, which are derived from the necessary order of the procedural steps by which they are created. These concepts are given physical application in our dealings with our environment; they are used, for instance, in the description of various objects in such a way that the necessities involved in the concepts become criteria for the classification of those objects into determinate kinds. Objects of a certain kind are thereby themselves characterized as having certain necessary properties and relations.

Thus, for example, "we cannot construct a polygon before a triangle."[2] This necessary feature of our geometrical procedure helps to determine the concepts "polygon" and "triangle," in such a way that various sorts of polygon are related to the triangle in a necessary way. When we apply these concepts, say to physical diagrams, the description of those figures as, for instance, trian-

102

gles and squares will depend on their meeting the specifications imposed by those concepts. And if we then make physical constructions, like bridges, on the basis of those diagrams, we shall use the geometrical necessities in, for instance, our diagnoses of anything that has gone wrong in their manufacture.

> If the equilibrium of a balance did not agree with the theory of the lever, one would say that there is something wrong with it.[3]

But our concepts of human beings are not like that. Later Simone Weil was to argue that therefore a *different* sort of order is required in our dealings with them; but in "Reflections Concerning the Causes of Liberty and Social Oppression" she seemed to think that they are such as to rule out the possibility of *any* systematic or ordered treatment. Whereas the laws according to which *things* behave are a function of the descriptions we apply to them (descriptions involving conceptual requirements which *we* as methodical observers and experimenters have imposed), the behaviour of a human agent depends on that agent's own understanding of the nature of that behaviour. Since the agent's thought processes are inaccessible to third parties, these find themselves unable to respond to them in any systematic way. They may indeed succeed in imposing their own descriptions on the agent's behaviour, but that is not a case of *understanding* the behaviour of an autonomous agent; it is rather a domination and thereby a violation of the nature of a potentially autonomous agent. In this Simone Weil sees the oppressive nature of social prestige and of propaganda in time of war. The point is brought out beautifully in her essay on *The Iliad* (first published in 1940) and also in "The Power of Words"[4] (first published in 1937 under the title "Ne recommençons pas la guerre de Troie"). The trouble with her position at the earlier date of "Reflections Concerning the Causes of Liberty and Social Oppression" was that she found herself compelled to see this as a paradigm of *any* sort of interdependence between human beings.

There is another strand in this line of thinking that must be highlighted: a line of thinking close to a major theme in the (in other ways very different) philosophy being developed at about the same time by her contemporary at the École Normale, Jean-Paul Sartre. As we have seen, Simone Weil linked the formation of physical concepts with coming to regard objects as *obstacles*. This seemed to require that our dealings with our environments should be conceived instrumentally, that our methodical procedures should be thought of as directed towards the attainment of ends or the successful completion of projects – our own of course. Since, therefore, one's conceptual articulation of the environment is a function of one's methodical procedures, one's understanding of the world one lives in will necessarily be from the point of view of one's own projects. *Other people's* projects will have no reality for one except in so far as they enable one to predict how those others are going to behave relative to oneself. Thus the imposition of one's own descriptions on the behaviour of others is in a sense at the same time a subordination of others to one's own interests and projects. The situation is exacerbated by the fact that, as it is claimed, the thoughts and desires from which our actions proceed are hidden from each other's understanding. The result of *that* is that even one's efforts to understand others in relation to one's own desires and projects is doomed to failure. Nothing is left but to sacrifice any attempt to understand and either to try to protect one's interests as best one can by mastery of the other or to give up the struggle and subordinate oneself to the other.

I want to stress that I take these to be *dominant* strands in Simone Weil's early thinking. They exist alongside other, quite different, thoughts, later development of which helped her to overcome her difficulties. But, as I have tried to show, they were difficulties which had profound repercussions on her early diagnosis of the nature of social oppression.

In considering how her thought concerning these issues changed, I am going to rely heavily in the following chapters on five late essays of hers which seem to me to constitute some of her very best work. These are:

(1) "Human Personality" ("La personne et le sacré")
(2) "The *Iliad* or the Poem of Force" ("L'*Iliade*, poème de la force")
(3) "Are We Struggling for Justice?" ("Luttons-nous pour la justice?")
(4) "The Legitimacy of the Provisional Government" ("La légitimité du gouvernement provisoire")
(5) "Essai sur la notion de lecture" ("An Essay on the Notion of Reading")

I shall start with a quotation from the essay on *The Iliad* which links her later treatment of the concept of a human being with her early account of concept formation.

> Anybody who is in our vicinity exercises a certain power over us by his very presence, and a power that belongs to him alone, that is, the power of halting, repressing, modifying each movement that our body sketches out. If we step aside for a passer-by on the road, it is not the same thing as stepping aside to avoid a billboard; alone in our rooms, we get up, walk about, sit down again quite differently from the way we do when we have a visitor.[5]

Her approach is, in one major way, the same as that in *Lectures on Philosophy*. We do not act differently towards a person and a billboard because we believe different things about them. We just do react differently. The "dance" that constitutes our perception of the world has different steps here. In so far as beliefs colour our dealings with human beings – and of course it is not denied that they do – they are rooted in these primitive reactions, not vice versa.

The big departure from *Lectures* is her strong emphasis on the radical *difference* between our perception of a human being and of anything else, between the steps of the dance involved.[6] But she continues to put her point in terms of the notion of an "obstacle." This comes out most explicitly in "Are We Struggling for Justice?"; I want to quote from it at some length:

> In other words only obstacles set a rule or a limit for human action. These are the only realities with which it comes into contact. Matter imposes obstacles according to its own mechanisms. A man is capable of imposing obstacles by virtue of a power to refuse which he sometimes possesses, and sometimes not. When he does not possess it, he constitutes no obstacle, and hence no limit either. From the point of view of the action and agent he simply does not exist.
>
> Whenever there is action thought reaches right through to a goal. If there were no obstacles the goal would be attained the moment it was conceived. That is how it is sometimes. A child's mother has been away; he sees her from far off and is in her arms almost before realizing that he has seen her. But when immediate attainment is impossible, one's attention, which to begin with was fastened on the goal, is inevitably claimed by the obstacles.
>
> They are the only things that do claim it. Without them it is not brought up short. Anything within the field of action which does not constitute an obstacle – as, for instance, men deprived of the power to refuse – is transparent for thought in the way completely

clear glass is for sight. It has no power to stop, just as our eyes have no power to see the glass.

Someone who does not see a pane of glass is not aware of not seeing it. Someone else who, being in a different position, does see it, is not aware that the other person does not see it.

When our will finds expression externally to us, through actions carried out by others, we do not spend our time or our power of attention on investigating whether they have consented to this. That applies to us all. Our attention, being completely absorbed in the success of our project, is not claimed by them as long as they are compliant.

It has to be like this. Otherwise things would not get done and if things did not get done we should perish.

But the result is that action is defiled by sacrilege. For human consent is something sacred. It is what man grants to God. It is what God comes searching for as a beggar amongst men.

It is this very same thing that God continually beseeches each of us to grant him which other men despise.

Rape is a frightful caricature of love without consent. Next to rape oppression is the second horror of human existence. It is a frightful caricature of obedience. Consent is as essential to obedience as it is to love.[7]

This passage contains many striking thoughts of course, some of which I shall be returning to later. There is one point of great general significance for the assessment of Simone Weil's thinking that I must mention here. In the passages I have just quoted, in the text and in note 7, a quite general contrast is made between our reactions to human beings and our reactions to "matter," "things." The impression is given that the reactions within the two classes are all of a piece; so that, in an encounter with another human being there are only two choices: one reacts either as to a human being (that is, with respect for his or her "power to refuse") or as to a thing, in which case one does not recognize the reality of a human being's presence at all. In fact the dominance of this crude contrast seems to me a blemish on the otherwise extremely powerful essay on *The Iliad*. At other times she does not make this mistake but, on the contrary, emphasizes the mixed and even contradictory character of our reactions to human beings, for instance the way in which the reaction of compassion for the afflicted is often at war with an instinctive recoil, contempt, or even hostility. I shall leave this important issue there for the time being and try to say more about it later, especially in Chapter 12, "Incommensurability."

A feature of the quoted passages which is striking if we place it in the context of the difficulties to which I have drawn attention in Simone Weil's earlier position is the way in which the notion of *necessity* re-enters the picture. To recognize the existence of another human being is to acknowledge a certain sort of obstacle to some projected actions; that is to say, it is to acknowledge that there are some things one *must* do and some things one *cannot* do in dealings with the other which hence constitute a limit to the ways in which we can pursue our projects. Our recognition of these necessities is internally related to our grasp of the kind of being we are confronted with. In other words, Simone Weil is here introducing a concept of necessity, related to a concept of ordered action, at the precise point at which she had claimed it to be impossible in "Reflections Concerning the Causes of Liberty and Social Oppression": the point at which we have to deal with other human beings. And again, if we place the passage from "Are We Struggling for Justice?" alongside the preceding one from the essay on *The Iliad*, we see that in a certain respect the way in which the notion of necessity is introduced here is very similar to that in the *Lectures* in the discussion of the formation of concepts of physical things. In both cases an initial primitive, unreflective reaction is later refined into a mode of behaviour exhibiting a necessary order and involving the application of genuine concepts. At the beginning of the progression are reactions like the peculiar way I step out of the way of a passer-by. At the end is the insistence that I may involve another in the execution of my projects only if he or she has consented to be so involved. To establish *this* is to establish an order exhibited *in the other's behaviour* and it may demand a difficult inquiry, exhibiting very special conceptual features.

I want now to examine this a bit further. In the passage I quoted from the *Iliad* essay the emphasis is on the power exercised by the mere presence of a human to *inhibit* actions which one would otherwise be inclined to perform. In a striking phrase she speaks of "ce temps d'arrêt d'où seul procèdent nos égards envers nos semblables" – "that interval of hesitation, wherein lies all our consideration for our brothers in humanity," as Mary McCarthy finely translates it.[8]

I am emphasizing the immediate, unreflective character of this hesitation. Of course, hesitation in the presence of another human being is very often the result of thought, or is at least the *expression* of thought. In her discussion of *The Iliad*, for instance, Simone

Weil dwells on the moment when Achilles is moved by the sight
and words of "divine Priam" who has fallen on his knees before
him.

> He spoke. The other, remembering his own father, longed to
>   weep;
> Taking the old man's arm, he pushed him away.
> Both were remembering. Thinking of Hector, killer of men,
> Priam wept, abased at the feet of Achilles.
> But Achilles wept, now for his father,
> Now for Patroclus. And their sobs resounded through the house.

In the same essay she speaks of such a moment of hesitation as
"between the impulse and the act, the tiny interval that is reflection." I do not think we should take this as meaning that there is
always reflection where there is hesitation between impulse and
act. The point is rather that the tendency to hesitate in certain
circumstances is the seed out of which grow certain kinds of thinking about our fellow human beings.

The concept that is central to those kinds of thinking is that of
consent. Suppose, for example, that walking along the street I find
myself on a collision course with another man. The "moment of
hesitation" consists here perhaps in an inclination to step out of
his way. If he steps out of my way, that can be interpreted as his
expression of consent that I should continue my course unde-
flected. If he, not seeing me perhaps, continues on his course, I
may or may not yield to my original impulse. If I do, that can be
interpreted as a rudimentary expression of a determination not to
deflect him from his course without his consent. This does not
mean that I have actually to think such a thought. But expressing
the matter in the way I have gains its sense from the analogy
between this case and other, more complex ones, in which I do
have to make a decision, based on reflection, on whether or not to
impose my own wishes on someone else who is affected by them
and who does not consent to my realizing them.

That analogy makes sense, of course, only in so far as what I am
reacting to in this way is *another human being;* and what is important about a human being in this connection is, according to
Simone Weil, "a power to refuse, which he sometimes possesses
and sometimes does not." What she is saying here is more complicated than may appear at first sight and I shall proceed slowly.

If someone is on a collision course, not with another human
being, but with a driverless vehicle, behaviour such as I imagined

above would make no sense. Of course we can easily imagine someone mimicking such behaviour, but this is the sort of visual *joke* that Charlie Chaplin specialized in. What makes it a joke is that the vehicle has no "power to refuse" in the sense that it is not capable of the kind of behaviour that we should read as an "expression of consent." But this *also* means that, in such a case, nothing one might do would *count* as "respecting the power to refuse" of whatever it is one is confronted with. (Of course one may be mistaken about what one is confronted with, but in the present context that is an uninteresting qualification.) The importance of this is that it brings out the *reciprocal connection* between the orders characterizing the behaviours of the two parties involved. A's behaviour can only be described as a case of "respecting B's power to refuse" if B is (at least believed by A to be) capable of behaviour expressing a power of refusal. What sort of behaviour is that? Roughly, the power to choose, make decisions, exercise practical reason. The possibility of describing behaviour in these terms, furthermore, exists only in a context where one characteristic sort of response that it elicits is the response we are describing as "respecting" the other's power to refuse.

As we have seen, Simone Weil speaks of a human being as sometimes having such a power to refuse and sometimes not. The contrast here is not that between a being that possesses rational faculties and one that does not. She means something like this, perhaps: that sometimes one is in a position where one's refusal is seriously taken notice of by others and sometimes not. Thus Priam, because defeated and completely in the power of the Greeks, no longer has the power to refuse. That means that nobody is going to take any notice of anything he says. But it *also* means – and this is important to Simone Weil's discussion – that he himself will no longer attempt either to give or withhold consent. His falling on his knees is not an expression of consent; it is an acknowledgement of the fact that he is no longer in a position to give or withhold it.

This points to another reciprocal connection between being capable of behaviour that can be read as an expression of consent and living amongst other beings who will in fact read one's behaviour in that way. Simone Weil lays much emphasis in the essays I have listed on the fact that, in the normal course of events, that sort of equilibrium between human beings exists only where there is a balance of *power,* of "force," such that people's power to refuse can be *enforced.* (She does not deny that there may be recognition of someone's power to refuse even where it is unenforceable; but where this happens, she claims, we have something "supernatural." But I shall defer discussion of this to a later chapter.)

At present I want mainly to bring out the connection between these points and what was said about *necessity* earlier in this chapter. When we recognize another's power to refuse we recognize certain necessities to be observed in our dealings with the other. This may mean simply that we recognize that we shall get into trouble, shall not be able to realize our wishes and projects, if we do not acknowledge the other's power to refuse, in so far as the other is in a position to enforce his or her own wishes – either by personal strength or with the help of others or by calling on the powers of enforcement of the state. Simone Weil seems here to be regarding this as a case of treating the other as a purely material obstacle. But although the readiness to acknowledge another's power to refuse is a tender plant and is not likely to survive for long in an environment where it cannot be enforced, it remains the case that people do, in many cases, acknowledge it without thinking about whether it can be enforced or not and even where they know it cannot. This acknowledgement is the thought that there are certain things they *must* (or must not) do without the other's consent; and they are responding here to a necessity of a different sort.[9] It is what Simone Weil is speaking of when, in "Human Personality," she *contrasts* the "restraint upon our will" imposed by "material necessity" with the restraint imposed by "the existence of other human beings around us."[10]

The word "restraint" is used in two different ways here. If I want to get to a place on the other side of a river over which there is no passage, the river is a restraint, an obstacle, in the sense that nothing I can attempt is actually going to get me to the place I want to go to. We might say that the restraint is not so much on my will as on the possibility of realizing what I will. If I give up my attempt (and thus, in a sense, my volition) I do so because it is futile. Compare this with the case described by Nathan to King David:

> There were two men in one city; the one rich, and the other poor.
> The rich man had exceeding many flocks and herds:

But the poor man had nothing, save one little ewe lamb, which
he had bought and nourished up: and it grew up together with him,
and with his children; it did eat of his own meat, and drank of his
own cup, and lay in his bosom and was to him as a daughter.

And there came a traveller unto the rich man, and he spared to
take of his own flock and of his own herd, to dress for the wayfaring
man that was come unto him; but took the poor man's lamb, and
dressed it for the man that was come to him.

And David's anger was greatly kindled against the man; and he
said to Nathan, As the Lord liveth, the man that hath done this
thing shall surely die:

And he shall restore the lamb fourfold, because he did this thing
and because he had no pity.[11]

The pitilessness of the rich man consisted in his not observing
the restraint on his will represented by the existence of the poor
man. Contrast *this* "restraint" with that imposed by King David in
his wrath. If the rich man had refrained from taking the lamb out
of fear of that wrath, it would not have been the existence of the
poor man that restrained him so much as the expectation of unacceptable consequences to himself. From the perspective of the
rich man's project the restraint exercised by King David's power
is something to be circumvented if possible, whereas the poor man
is not, for one who has pity, an obstacle to be circumvented. However, the difference between the cases cannot be given watertight
expression in a general formula; and the significance of any general formula will in any case be apparent only in its application.
The force of the difference is shown in the example itself and
through our ability to see other cases as analogous. That is
brought out by the marvellous way in which Nathan uses the story
to bring home to David the enormity of his own conduct in send-
ing his lieutenant Uriah to his death in order to satisfy his lust for
Uriah's wife.

And Nathan said to David, Thou art the man.[. . .]

Wherefore hast thou despised the commandment of the Lord, to
do evil in his sight? thou hast killed Uriah the Hittite with the sword,
and hast taken his wife to be thy wife, and hast slain him with the
sword of the children of Ammon.

Nathan's story illustrates another point that it is important to be
clear about. King David reacts by imposing sanctions on the rich
man who has oppressed his poor neighbour: "the man that hath
done this thing shall surely die: And he shall restore the lamb fourfold." We might say: he restores the poor man's power to refuse,

which has been violated, through the imposition of force. Within the context thus created, respect for someone's power to refuse will not be "pure," it will be mixed with desire to avoid King David's sanctions. But it would obviously be a mistake to conclude that in such a case there is nothing more in a power to refuse than fear of sanctions. That would ignore what lies behind the imposition of sanctions: the fact that the rich man "had no pity." That is, the sanctions are imposed in deference to the thought that such "pity" is *due*, that it *must* be accorded in such cases. This latter "must" cannot itself be explicated in terms of fear of sanctions.[12] It is the sort of necessity to which Simone Weil is alluding in the opening paragraphs of "Human Personality," and which she expresses in terms of the "sacredness" of the human being. Recognition of this sacredness is expressed in the fact that "not without infinite scruple would I touch anything of his."

Perhaps it is tempting to try to express the distinction in terms of the "factual" and the "normative." In the story of Nathan and David, the king resolved to impose "factual" restraints because "normative" restraints had been ignored. And some such distinction as this might even be thought to be suggested, for instance, by the way Simone Weil writes in the long passage which I quoted from "Are We Struggling for Justice?" about the fact that the urgencies of everyday living constantly lead us to ignore other people's power to refuse so that "action is defiled by sacrilege." The suggestion is clearly that the sense in which the power to refuse pertains to human beings as such is that our behaviour towards them is to be judged against it as a standard, irrespective of whether we as a matter of fact respect it. So to say that the power to refuse characterizes the peculiar reality of human beings is not simply to describe how they behave towards each other; as often as not – perhaps even more often than not – their actual behaviour does *not* conform to such a standard.

However, though all this may be true enough, matters cannot be left there. We need to remind ourselves again at this point of one of the most striking features of Simone Weil's account of the concept of a human being and of the way in which this is formed: namely that its roots lie in ways in which human beings *do as a matter of fact* react to each other. When in "Human Personality" she says, "Not without infinite scruple would I touch anything of his," she is in some sense making a factual statement. She does not say: that is something I ought not to do, or even: that is something

which, as a matter of fact, I think I ought not to do; she says: I
would not do it. Similarly, in the passage that I quoted from "The
Iliad or the Poem of Force," she talks about the difference
between the ways we do in fact behave towards a human being and
towards a billboard. There is no mention of anything "normative"
there, just description of certain familiar facts. I am sure it would
distort, and even emasculate, her thinking if one were to say: We
behave like this because we see, or think, that we ought to. All the
same, there is on the one hand a case for saying that in this behaviour there is already a recognition of something normative; and
on the other hand, it is clear that Simone Weil's descriptions of
our behaviour towards each other are offered from the point of
view of the standard or norm implicit in the behaviour which
respects another's power to refuse. That being the case, it is of
course particularly important for us to be aware that such behaviour is in competition and conflict with *other* tendencies in our
relations with each other which seem to have an equal right to be
called "primitive."

As all this suggests, the relation between the notions of the factual and the normative is a tangled one. Simone Weil addresses
herself in a striking way to some of the problems it gives rise to in
another essay, published posthumously in 1946 and, as far as I
know, not reprinted or translated into English. It is called "Essai
sur la notion de lecture"[13] ("An Essay on the Concept of
Reading").

In this essay she points out that the effect of reading something
(in a quite ordinary sense of "reading," say in a letter or newspa-
per) can be as immediate as a sensation:

> Everyone has experienced in some measure the effect of bad news
> read in a letter or a newspaper; you feel gripped, bowled over as if
> by a blow, without realizing what it's all about, and later, even the
> sight of the letter remains painful. Sometimes, when time has dead-
> ened the pain a little, if, among papers you are handling, the letter
> suddenly reappears, a sharper pain arises, unexpected and as sharp
> as physical pain, gripping you as if it came from the outside, as if it
> inhabited this piece of paper, as burning inhabits fire. Each of two
> women receives a letter announcing that her son is dead; the first,
> on just glancing at the letter, faints, and never again until she dies
> will her eyes, her mouth, her movements be the same as they were.
> The second woman remains untouched, her appearance, her atti-
> tude do not change; she cannot read. What has taken hold of the
> first woman is not a sensation, but meaning, going straight to her

mind, cruelly, without any participation on her side, in just the way sensations take hold of one. It is as if the sorrow lay in the letter and leapt out of it into the face of the reader. As for the sensations themselves, of the colour of the paper or of the ink for example – these are not even apprehended. What is visually given is grief.

She goes on to use the word "reading" in a more extended way, but one that is by no means idiosyncratic:

The sky, the sea, the sun, the stars, all the things around us are, in the same way, something we read. What is called a corrected perceptual illusion is, similarly, a modified reading. If, at night on a lonely path, I think I see a man lying in wait, what imposes itself on me is not a tree, but a threatening human presence and, as in the case of the letter, it makes me tremble before I even know why. I get nearer, and suddenly everything changes, I no longer tremble, I read a tree and not a man. What we have here is not an appearance plus an interpretation; a human presence had penetrated my soul through my eyes and now, suddenly, it is the presence of a tree. If I hate a man, there is not the man on one side and my hatred on the other; when he approaches me something hateful approaches me; and the perversity of his soul strikes me more immediately than the colour of his hair. If he is blond, moreover, it is a hateful blondness; if he has brown hair, it is a hateful brownness. Esther, approaching Ahasuerus, isn't approaching a man who she knows can put her to death; she is approaching majesty itself, which reaches into her soul through her eyes, and that is why the effort of walking makes her falter.[14] Indeed she says so herself, that what she contemplates with fear is not the face of Ahasuerus but the majesty that is written there, which she can read on it. In such cases we commonly speak of the effect of imagination; but perhaps the word "reading" would be better. The word implies that we are concerned with effects produced by appearances which are not apparent, or hardly so. It is something else that is apparent, something that is to the appearances as a sentence is to letters; but it gives the impression of an appearance, suddenly, cruelly coming from outside and almost irrefutable in the face of evidence.[15]

I want to consider here the relevance of this essay for the distinction between fact and value and for the difficulties about that distinction which arise for us in trying to understand some of Simone Weil's points about a person's "power to refuse."

There is a tradition of thinking in philosophy which spans many different schools of thought and which goes something like this: The consciousness of human beings starts with sensations; on the basis of these they construct a picture of a world of objects. They themselves have certain innate desires and tendencies which are developed into evaluative attitudes towards these objects; these evaluative attitudes direct their actions. – There are of course very important differences in the detailed working out of such an account in various writers, but I am not directly concerned with those differences here.

As I tried to bring out in earlier chapters Simone Weil had already at an early stage attacked the most fundamental feature of such accounts: their attempt to derive our picture of the world from sensation. In the alternative account sketched in her *Lectures* activity and the practical attitudes and values without which activity is unintelligible come at the *beginning* of the story, at the point where concepts are first formed, and not at the end of it, as above. It is this same line of thinking that is being developed in a rather new direction in "Essai sur la notion de lecture." Because of the way concepts are formed and applied, and because of their connection with action and the aspirations and values that go with action, the world of which we are aware is one that is impregnated with values. That is to say, our concepts, which give this world its shape, are unintelligible except as concepts exercised by beings whose common life exhibits certain aspirations and values.[16]

Let me apply this thought to the concept of a fellow human being as one who has the power to refuse. As I have said, Simone Weil connects this concept with a kind of "hesitation" characteristic of our dealings with each other. This hesitation is primitive in that it is not based on any prior reflection. One direction in which this primitive hesitation may develop in the course of our dealings with each other is towards the idea of various kinds of restraints on our will which we (sometimes) observe, and also in the application of various kinds of criticism (both of others and of ourselves) when those restraints are not observed. That is to say, the initial hesitation develops into a set of attitudes which can be described as the observance of a norm. The observance of norms goes to characterize our understanding of the beings with whom we are dealing. ⟨"She is approaching majesty itself."⟩ So, the concept of a fellow human being thus formed *is* the concept of one to whom a certain consideration, or respect, is *due*. We cannot, as it were, prize that away from the other's nature; take it away and we have a different concept.

However, we do not all, or all the time, observe the *same* norms in our dealings with each other; and it is one of the main purposes of the essay on "reading" to deal with this fact.

> If someone, looking at the same newspaper, at the same spot, seriously insisted over and over again, that he read not 14 June but 15 June, that would worry me; I would not understand. If someone doesn't hate, doesn't fear, doesn't despise, as I do, that worries me. What? He sees these people – or, if they are far away, the indirect manifestation of their existence – and he doesn't read hatefulness, danger, contemptibility, love? That's not possible; he is dishonest, he is lying, he is mad.

As that last passage brings out, the concept of "reading" is not introduced in order to explain anything, but to highlight certain *problems*. People's readings of each other are not uniform; they may come into conflict; they are subject to change and may be manipulated. Simone Weil clearly regards this situation as a sort of *disorder* in the ways they read each other, as a lack of proper equilibrium between them. In a sense the whole essay is an attempt to understand the situation in a way which will justify this point of view.

> In times of peace the idea of causing the death of a human being, if it comes from within one, cannot be read in appearances; on the contrary, one reads in the appearances a prohibition on acting in such a way. But in a civil war, when it is a question of a certain category of human beings, it is the idea of sparing life which is anomalous, which comes from within, which cannot be read in appearances: it crosses the mind without translating itself into action. There is no possible process of transition from one state to the other. The transformation happens in a flash. Each of the two readings, while present, seems to be the only real and possible one, and the other seems purely imaginary. These are extreme examples; but our whole life is made of this same fabric, of meanings which impose themselves on us one after the other, each one of which, when it appears and reaches into us through our senses, reduces to phantoms all the ideas which might oppose it.[17]

I have already mentioned her emphasis on the power of prestige in the mechanism of oppression and the related power of propaganda in wartime. The concept of reading, as the passage above suggests, is one of her main instruments for analysing such phenomena. It highlights a problem. Is there such a thing as a *right* way to read situations, and in particular a right way to read other people; or can we do no more than point to the fact that people do as a matter of fact read each other *differently*? To imagine such an absolutely "correct" reading, she notes, is to imagine a reading

from the point of view of God; but the notion of reading is inap-
plicable to God and anyway, a more immediately relevant point,
imagining such a thing would hardly help *us* in reaching correct
readings. She suggests that, though this problem may seem intract-
able, thinking about "problems of value" in this way has the
advantage of making them *concrete* and brings together the issue
of a possible criterion of correctness with that of motivation. This
is because of the way the notion of reading is tied, from the beginning, to the practical attitudes of the one who reads.

> A man tempted not to repay a loan will not refrain from this sim-
> ply because he has read *The Critique of Practical Reason*. He will
> abstain, perhaps it will even seem in spite of himself, if the loan
> presents him with such an aspect that it seems to cry out to be
> repaid. Everyone has had similar experiences: when he would like
> to do something wrong but cannot. There are other occasions when
> he would like to behave well but cannot. An inquiry into whether
> the reading of someone who, contemplating the loan, reads it in the
> way described is better than that of another person, who reads in
> what he contemplates all the desires he could satisfy by holding on
> to the money: that is a more concrete problem than that of deter-
> mining which is of greater value, appropriating or repaying a loan.[18]

Reading the loan as "something which seems to cry out to be
repaid" involves seeing it not merely as something which can play
a role in my achieving my aims, not merely, that is, in its relation
to myself, but in its relation (for instance) to the lender. Clarity
about the nature of the loan is clarity about the relation between
myself and the lender: a kind of clarity which requires that I attend
to the reality of the lender's position and thereby also see my own
position from a different point of view. Attention of this sort is a
development of the primitive reaction of hesitation which is characteristic of the encounters of human beings with each other. This
was not brought into the picture of our relations with each other
in "Reflections Concerning the Causes of Liberty and Social
Oppression"; and that is the reason for the pessimism about the
possibilities of mutual human understanding which, as we saw,
runs through that essay.

What is now needed is an account of what the development of
this kind of understanding consists in. It involves what Simone
Weil describes as the construction of a "geometry." A sense of the

scope of this notion, as she conceived it, is suggested by the following passage from her notebooks:

> Importance of geometry in space, perspectives, projections, etc.
> – for purification in the Platonic manner.
> A centre from which may be seen the different possible readings
> – and their relationship – and our own only as one among them.
> Several readings – not through sentiment alone. The little shepherdess cries when her favourite lamb is taken to the butcher's, but continues to rear lambs for the butcher. The followers of Cortés wept because of the Emperor's humiliation. The Romans and Carthage. Vain and impure pity – it is not without its delights. It contains a justification.
> No, we should transport ourselves to that centre of thought from which the other person reads values; contemplate the values destroyed by what we are going to do.[19]

Alongside that we might put the following passage:

> We should have with each person the relationship of one conception of the universe to another conception of the universe. A man standing ten paces from me is something separated from me by a distance (ten paces), but also another point of view from which all things appear.[20]

In Chapter 4 I discussed the "dance" of perception as it is described in *Lectures on Philosophy;* I mentioned there Simone Weil's idea that there is an elementary geometry (in the primary, purely spatial sense of that word) involved in perception, not based on any thought, but involved in the body's immediate responses. This chapter has been, in a way, a counterpart to that in the sphere of our relations with other human beings. The phrase I quoted from the essay on *The Iliad:* "that interval of hesitation, wherein lies all our consideration for our brothers in humanity," expresses the possible growth of a "geometry" of human life out of certain of our primitive, unreflective reactions to each other. These reactions are the basis of a possible "geometry" of human relations. Spatial geometry develops out of the primitive geometry embodied in our bodies' movements and, once developed, makes it possible for us to correct the distortions to which perceptions from a limited point of view are otherwise susceptible. Simone Weil's underlying thought is that out of the characteristic "hesitations" involved in our dealings with each other can be developed a geometry which will enable us to recognize the ways in which we otherwise read each other as partial and distorted and to correct ourselves. Of course, the phrase "partial and distorted" already belongs to such a geometry and presupposes the standards of judgment inherent in it. It is not altogether clear how consistently alive Simone Weil is to the significance of this fact.

10

"THE VOID"

Waiting for God contains a section called "Love of the Order of the World" (which is one of the "forms of the implicit love of God").[1] It describes those features of the human condition which give rise to the problems discussed in the essay on "reading" in the following terms.

> Just as God, being outside the universe, is at the same time the centre, so each man imagines he is situated in the centre of the world. The illusion of perspective places him at the centre of space; an illusion of the same kind falsifies his idea of time; and yet another kindred illusion arranges a whole hierarchy of values around him. This illusion is extended even to our sense of existence, on account of the intimate connection between our sense of value and our sense of being; being seems to us less and less concentrated the further it is removed from us.

With one extremely important exception that passage might be an exposition of Spinoza's position. I want to spend some time exploring the comparison with Spinoza in the belief that this will help to articulate Simone Weil's point. In Chapter 9 I quoted a passage from "Essai sur la notion de lecture" in which she claimed that it is better to pose questions about the relative value of one form of action as compared with another in the concrete terms provided by the notion of "reading" than in the abstract terms used by Kant, partly because it combines questions about the "correctness" of valuations with questions about possible motivations for acting. What she says is reminiscent of Spinoza's contention that an abstract "knowledge of good and evil" can have no influence on the conduct of a person subject to emotion. According to

Spinoza, people are inevitably subject to emotions because of their finitude and the distortions arising out of the limited perspectives from which they are compelled to view things. In fact, for him, being subject to emotions and viewing things from a limited perspective amounted to much the same; and the behaviour which he thought inevitably resulted would necessarily bring people into conflict. An emotion could only be overcome by another emotion, not by any purely abstract thinking. That is to say, if a mode of acting springs from a person's perspective, it will be changed only if that perspective is changed. But a perspective is *not* an abstract way of thinking; it *is* a particular relation to the environment; it is the actual impact of the environment on someone. Indeed, any abstract "knowledge of good and evil" is necessarily confused just because it is divorced from the concrete world in which the agent exists. Clarity consists in seeing the world as it is and is achieved not by a retreat into generalities but, on the contrary, by making one's awareness of one's own position in the world more and more concrete.

Simone Weil's observation that "each man imagines he is situated in the centre of the world" might have been written by Spinoza. But he could never have preceded it, as she did, with the phrase "Just as God, being outside the universe, is at the same time its centre . . . " This marks the crucial difference between them. One major difficulty about Spinoza is to see how any *criticism* of the perspective on the world one happens to have is possible, or even conceivable. In theoretical terms the difficulty is to see what can be meant by phrases like "the perspective of eternity," given that the whole thrust of Part One of Spinoza's *Ethics* is directed at showing the senselessness of any such phrase as "outside the world." How, on his terms, can there be any point of view on the world except from within it and how can any point of view within it be freed from the forces to which its environment subjects it, given that, in a sense, any point of view is defined by its relation to such forces? His treatment of this question in Part One is the foundation of his account of human "bondage" in Part Four and is, at the same time, a formidable obstacle to the belief that human beings could achieve even the kind of "freedom" he attempts to describe in Part Five. The conception of the universe as a plenum is the metaphysical dimension of that bondage. We are, in all aspects of our thinking, feeling, and acting, caught up in a network of causal relations which contains no gap and within which, therefore, it seems there could be no room for any free play. Human action is always to be explained by antecedent causes: *existent* antecedent causes of course, since we cannot explain what exists by what does not exist. An object of desire does not exist prior to the action which attempts to bring it about, and it may never come into existence. Equally – indeed this could almost be regarded as another way of putting the same point – it makes no sense to speak of anything "outside the world," outside this causal plenum, by attending to which one could develop the clarity of mind and the strength to change one's relation to the environment. In particular, action and desire cannot be explained in terms of the notion of "good"; and we do not therefore free ourselves from the bondage of desire by reflecting on the good:

> We neither strive for, nor will, neither want, nor desire anything because we judge it to be good; on the contrary, we judge something to be good because we strive for it, will it, want it, desire it.[2]

It is, therefore, extremely hard to understand what it would be, in Spinoza's terms, to free oneself from the bondage of desire through which the forces in one's environment make themselves felt, since on his view not merely is one's attention necessarily claimed by the objects of one's desires, but there is nothing that can seriously compete with them. An emotion, as he says, can only be overcome by another and stronger emotion. A person can act only in so far as he or she draws energy from what the environment makes available, that is from the *return* which the environment offers for the expenditure of energy required for action. The rationale of someone's action cannot be such as to exclude any prospect of return;[3] that would be, in Spinoza's idiom, to explain existence in terms of non-existence.

Simone Weil is of course parting company with Spinoza when, in the passage I have already quoted from *Waiting for God*, she says: "To discern that all parts of the world are equally centres and that the true centre is outside the world, this is to consent to the rule of mechanical necessity in matter and of free choice at the centre of each soul." In a notebook she insists on the need for "a representation of the world including a void, so that the world may have need of God."[4] She does not mention Spinoza by name at that point, but it sounds like a very deliberate rejection of his view.

These passages are important and their interpretation raises a difficulty crucial to understanding the general character of her thinking. The difficulty may be brought out by attending to the move from saying that "all parts of the world are equally centres" to saying that "the true centre is outside the world." A *geometry* makes it possible to say the former but does not license the latter. A geometry in fact can say nothing about where the centre of the world is to be found, since, in a sense, it says nothing at all; it is a language providing certain *possibilities* of expression. It becomes unclear here whether Simone Weil is still speaking as a philosopher or is assuming another role. This ambiguity is well caught by Gustave Thibon:

> Between Simone Weil and a purely speculative philosopher there is the same difference as there is between a guide and a geographer. The geographer studies a region objectively: he describes its structures, assesses its resources, etc. The guide on the other hand leads one by the shortest route to a given destination. From his point of view everything which is conducive to this end is good, everything which hinders it is bad. Now Simone Weil is before all else a guide to the road between the soul and God, and many of her dicta gain from being interpreted, not as a description of the countryside through which we are passing, but as *pieces of advice to travellers.*[5]

I shall return to the difficulties of interpretation raised by this point in my last chapter. There is another difficulty too, discussion of which belongs here. The main concern of the passage from *Waiting for God* that I have been considering is of course to undermine my conception of *myself* as "the centre of the universe." But the alternatives expressed by saying that all persons are equally centres and saying that the true centre lies outside the universe are importantly different. The first form of expression concentrates one's attention on the particularity of other people's conceptions of the world in a way that the second does not. Indeed the second form of expression *could* be taken to suggest not merely that my own conception of the world has no particular importance in relation to those of others, but that no conception of the world of any individual has any particular importance since the truth is to be found somewhere else altogether.

In order to discuss this difficult matter I have to examine further the precise way in which Simone Weil parts company with Spinoza by introducing the conception of "the void" into her account of the nature of desire and its relation to action.

Spinoza rejects final causes, as I have noted, because to suppose that an action might require, as part of its explanation, reference to a future object of desire would be to suppose that *something* can be caused by *nothing:* and this again would be to treat nothing as a sort of something. But this applies to *all* objects of desire: what is desired is the possession of something; and one can only be said to "desire" to possess something as long as one does not already possess it. If we do speak sometimes of a desire for something we already possess we can only mean that we desire to continue to possess it. If, then, the object of desire is necessarily something non-existent it can never play a genuine role in the production of action. In so far as people *think* that their actions have "final causes" they are confused as a result of their ignorance of the true, efficient, causes.

Now I believe that Simone Weil did think that this account applies to a great deal of human conduct, perhaps most of it. There is an extended discussion headed "The search for Good in Plato" in a notebook, probably from the early 1940s,[6] in which she argues that we are for the most part confused about what it is we desire "for want of a proper understanding of and ability to apply the notion of relationship, or relativity." We want bread, for instance, only so long as we are hungry; it is only as long as we see a good for ourselves in bread that we want it; and that good does not lie in bread considered in itself "but in the appropriate relation existing between the bread and my hunger." If this means that my act of seeking the bread is caused by my need, Spinoza could easily agree. But he could not agree with what follows: that to be clear about what I want is to be clear about the nature of the good that I am seeking; and that "what we really want is always and only the good." The role of this last "purely grammatical statement" (as she calls it) is to prompt us to ask questions about precisely what good we expect from this or that object we are striving for. We do not always ask the necessary questions. She illustrates this with such pathological cases as Molière's miser, Harpagon, who imagines that it is gold in itself that he wants, forgetting that the good in gold resides in its relation to other things, its role as purchasing power in the market for instance. In this way, she says, gold becomes a "necessity" for him, something without which he cannot live, rather than a genuine good. But she thinks that the same confusion is present, less obviously, in countless non-pathological cases. Normal people differ from Harpagon in that their desires presuppose a far wider network of relationships than does his desire for gold; an entrepreneur may, for instance, seek money in order to further the success of a complex enterprise. But it is perfectly possible for such a person, by no means "abnormal" or "pathological," to be identified with the success of business as exclusively as was Harpagon with his gold. For that person too the business has become a "necessity" in the sense that its continued success is for him or her a condition for seeing any sense in life.

Simone Weil repeatedly argues that *all* "attachment" of this sort, which consists in seeing the point of one's existence as depending on particular objects, aims, or persons, is mistaking the necessary for the good. In fact, I think, she sees it as the kind of "bondage" of which Spinoza wrote. But she differs from him about the alternative. A pure aspiration towards the good[7] requires one to "detach" one's desires from any particular objects, though (like Diotima in Plato's *Symposium*) she also insists that one can only bring the good into focus by way of desire for particulars; there is no possibility of a direct relation between a human being and the good which bypasses the discipline of purifying desires from attachment to particulars. This indeed is what she means when she speaks of the necessity for "a void." It is the fact that there is something about desires for particulars which can never be satisfied that creates the void; and because the good in itself is not to be found among existing things, a void among existing things is necessary if our attention is to be focussed on the good: on the "negative sovereign good" which has no existence in the world.

> The world manifests God and conceals God. "Thou art indeed the hidden God." And yet: "They were able to know God through the world which makes him manifest."[8]

There is an important distinction of grammar between expressions of desire for particulars and the aspiration for the good. Whereas the former is satisfied in the attaining or preservation of some specifiable state of affairs, the latter is not and cannot be, since the good is not something to be found "in the world." But this creates a difficulty: to specify someone's desire is to specify its object, what would satisfy it if attained or preserved. So how could there be anything analogous to a desire the object of which cannot intelligibly be said to be attained or possessed by anybody, as is the case with the good? This is another form of the difficulty about what is to be understood by "a representation of the world containing a void."

To deal with the difficulty we need to consider more closely the notion of "satisfying" a desire. It is true – and it is something emphasized by Simone Weil – that over a large range of typical cases, to desire something is to desire to bring it into some specifiable relation with oneself. *What* kind of relation is in question will depend largely, though not exclusively, on the nature of the desired object. To want money is to want to have it at one's disposal to spend, or as an insurance against a rainy day, and so on. To want food is to want to be in a position to eat it. To want someone as one's friend is to want that person to stand in certain sorts of relation to oneself.

Do all desires exhibit this pattern? *Prima facie* there are cases which do not. Suppose there has been an earthquake in an area that is being visited by my friend. My desire is that my friend shall have escaped unhurt. It may be that there is no opportunity for me to involve myself in the situation in any way, for example by joining a rescue team.

Some have argued that such cases should be described differently: that what I desire in this situation is to *know* that my friend has escaped unharmed. In that case the object of my desire would of course still include a relation to me and its attainment would satisfy me. Now, of course, a desire thus characterized is a perfectly good possibility. It is even plausible to think that a desire of the sort originally described would normally be accompanied by such a desire for knowledge of its fulfilment. But it remains the case that a desire of the first sort is perfectly conceivable standing on its own.

Confusion about such cases is encouraged by an ambiguity in the term "satisfaction" as applied to desires. In one sense, a desire is satisfied by that state of affairs which is described as the object of the desire. Thus if I desire that my friend should escape the disaster, then the friend's escaping it is the satisfaction of my desire. This is a purely grammatical notion of satisfaction; it is a special case of the notion involved in saying that something satisfies a certain description, where no question of desire need arise at all. But there is another sense in which we speak of the "satisfaction" of the person whose desire is thus (grammatically) satisfied. I am hungry and eat, and my desire for food is satisfied; but

I am satisfied too. This might be called the "psychological" sense of satisfaction.

That the two notions are closely connected is obvious. It is easy to confuse them. But the story of King Midas, whose desire that everything he touched should turn to gold was satisfied, shows that they are not identical.

This distinction goes part of the way towards meeting the objection to Simone Weil that I was considering: that since the whole point of her conception of a "negative sovereign good" is that it will make no sense to speak of an agent as gaining possession of it, it cannot be a possible object of desire. But the kind of example I have discussed still falls far short of the detachment of desire from *any* particular objects that her conception requires. The desire for my friend's safety is fulfilled if and only if a particular state of affairs obtains, whereas she wants to speak of the desire for the good as one that has in a certain sense become quite independent of all that may happen or not happen.

This background helps to explain the importance of the notion of *absence* in Simone Weil's writings and her insistence that the reality of something is revealed just as much in its absence as in its presence. One of the most striking expressions and applications of this thought is to be found in *Waiting for God*. Love, or friendship, she writes, has two forms which belong necessarily together: meeting and separation.

> For when two beings who are not friends are near each other there is no meeting; when they are far apart there is no separation.

Hence lovers or friends have two desires.

> One is to love so much that each enters the other in such a way that they form but one being. The other is to love so much that even with half the earth between them their union is in no way diminished.[9]

Love of this sort exists only when the reality of the relationship for the participants does not depend on any expectation of return from it; or, as one may equally well say, when the reality which the lover sees in the beloved is not filtered through the expectation of any return from the relationship. Can we go further and say that the good that is sought in the love is independent of anything at all that may happen?

In her notebooks she develops this thought in a discussion of the relation between the concepts of *desire* and of *reality*, a discus-

sion that takes further her thoughts on the "relativity" of the
objects of desire.

> If we go down into ourselves we find that we possess exactly what
> we desire.
> If we long for a certain being (who is dead), we desire a particular
> being, therefore a mortal; and we long for that special being "who"
> . . . , "whom" . . . , etc., in short, that being who died at such and
> such a time on such and such a day. And we have that being –
> dead. . . .
> In such cases suffering, emptiness is the mode of existence of the
> objects of our desire. We only have to draw aside the veil of unreal-
> ity and we shall see that they are given to us in this way.[10]

And a little later:

> – To lose somebody: we suffer at the thought that the dead one,
> the absent one should have become something imaginary, some-
> thing false. But the longing we have for him is not imaginary. We
> must go down into ourselves, where the desire which is not imagi-
> nary resides. Hunger; we imagine different foods; but the hunger
> itself is real; we must seize hold of the hunger.
> The loss of contact with reality – there lies evil, there lies sorrow.
> There are certain situations which bring about such a loss: depri-
> vation, suffering. The remedy is to use the loss itself as an inter-
> mediary for attaining reality. The presence of the dead one is imag-
> inary, but his absence is very real; it is henceforth his manner of
> appearing.[11]

What are we to make of the superficially absurd claim that in all
cases "we possess exactly what we desire"? It must of course be
interpreted in the light of the claim that the real object of all
desire is "good" rather than any particular object. To say as much
is not, however, to deal with the difficulty; it is simply to state what
is difficult in another way. It is clear from the context that what is
at issue is a distinction between what is real and what is "imaginary" in a want, a distinction closely related to that which
G. E. M. Anscombe, writing in a very different spirit, has called
the distinction between genuine wants and idle wishes. Her way of
marking that distinction is helpful here: namely in terms of what
one is able and prepared to do in order to attain or achieve something.[12] There are limits of different sorts to what one is able to
do in order to attain something. One important kind of limit
derives from the nature of the object desired. For instance there
are certain activities which can meaningfully be spoken of as
directed at the attaining of money, such as working for payment,

negotiating a loan, swindling, stealing; others not, such as lying in bed, going to the opera. Of course stories can be imagined in which these latter *could* be understood as directed towards obtaining money; but the shape such stories would have to take is itself limited by the fact that it is the obtaining of *money* that is in question. The point is succinctly stated by Wittgenstein:

> Certainly to seek something is an expression of expectation. That is to say: *How* one seeks somehow expresses what one is expecting.

and

> If the activity of expecting were not connected with reality, one could expect a nonsense.[13]

People may of course be confused about what they want and this confusion may infect the measures they take, or fail to take, to obtain it. Moreover, clarity about such things may be painful and hence shunned. This is illustrated in very different ways in W. W. Jacobs's gruesome one-act play *The Monkey's Paw* and in Dostoevsky's description in *Crime and Punishment* of Raskolnikov's state of mind before he commits the murders.

The distinction between wants and idle wishes is closely connected too with what one is *prepared* to do in order to attain an end. I want, let us suppose, a certain sum of money. I want it at a particular time and in a particular situation; in those circumstances, some of the ways in which money is in principle obtainable are available to me, others not. For instance, there is no prospect of an inheritance, no one from whom money may be borrowed; perhaps the only alternatives are embezzlement or a long period of self-denial in order to save the requisite sum. Confronted with these alternatives I have to make clear to myself what I really want. Do I want the money on condition of becoming a liar and a cheat? Do I want it on condition of enduring years of privation? Someone who chooses one of these alternatives may be said to want something different from someone who chooses the other. Of course I may *wish* that the money could be obtained innocently and without difficulty; but to dwell on that is to allow the play of my imagination to cloud my perception of the world as it really is; we are back with an idle wish. In the actual situation with which I am confronted, what I want is revealed in what I choose; and the choice is not adequately represented as one between having and not having money. If we are speaking of wants which have a relation to my actual circumstances then I *can* only want an alternative which those circumstances actually present. And *what* I want in those circumstances is shown in the choice I make between those alternatives.

I want, then, what I choose. But I *have* what I choose precisely in choosing it! This sounds perverse because it seems to leave out of account the obvious possibility that I may be thwarted by events over which I have no control: my detection, conviction, and imprisonment, for instance, or a stock market crash which renders my savings worthless. But such an objection overlooks the force of the condition that my real want is revealed only in so far as I am clear in my mind about the reality of the situation. And it is part of the reality of the situation that crimes may be punished and stock markets crash: all plans are subject to contingencies and may go astray. The particular risks inherent in the course of action I choose are part of what I choose.

> How reconcile ourselves to the contradiction between accepting in advance every possible thing, without exception, in the event of its taking place – and, at a given moment, in a given situation, going almost beyond the limit of what we are capable of in order to prevent some particular thing from taking place?
>
> The key is certainly to be found in the distinction between present and future. Real events move no faster than the stars in their courses. The duration which separates an event in the future from the present is real.
>
> We prepare ourselves to accept one day such and such a future woe when it shall have become the past, but we do not confuse it with the past.[14]

Not being clear about this might be said to be the source of Saint Peter's sin, which Simone Weil locates less in his denying Christ than in saying to him in advance: "I will not deny thee,"

> since it was to suppose the source of loyalty to be in oneself, and not in grace. Since he was of the elect, this denial fortunately became clear. But in other cases, people's boasts may come true and be confirmed, and they never understand.
>
> How grateful I ought to be that I was born incapable even of picking grapes without the help of grace![15]

This example draws our attention to another important aspect of Simone Weil's treatment of the relation between desire and good. It emphasizes that one is not merely not in a position absolutely to command the future; but also not in a position to judge infallibly what is good. The denial turned out "fortunately" for Peter, she says. That is to say, it turned out to be a good for himself and for others in ways which he was in no position to judge in advance. (This is a situation of far more frequent occurrence than anyone would gather from reading most Anglo-Saxon moral philosophy.) Hence, she writes:

> We must want the good solely and unconditionally, whatever it may be, that is to say, no particular object of any kind. We must only want particular objects subject to conditions. We must want life if it is to be for us a good, death if, etc. . . . , joy if, etc. . . . , pain if, etc. . . . ; and that while knowing all the time that we don't actually know what the good is.
>
> In all our acts of willing, whatever they may be, over and beyond the particular object, we must want gratuitously, want the void. For this good which we can neither visualize nor define represents for us a void. But this void means more to us than all plenitudes put together.
>
> If we manage to reach this point, we are out of trouble, for it is God who fills the void.[16]

However, it is one thing to say that we are often not (or even never) in a position to say in advance in what outcome the good would lie. It is quite another thing to say that the good will be realized in *whatever* happens. The first claim is one that it might be possible to give reasons for of a philosophical sort. The second could only be held as a matter of religious faith. I do not say that it is any the worse for that; only that it is a claim of quite a different sort, which is beyond the scope of the sort of argument I have been considering. This is important not merely in itself, but in its bearing on the philosophical issue towards which this whole discussion is directed.

That issue might be expressed as follows. What is the relation between wanting, particular things wanted, and the notion of the good? A position which Simone Weil seems to argue for is that we are deluded in supposing that we want particular things, that it is always and only the good that is wanted, because whereas particular things are only wanted subject to conditions, good is the only thing wanted unconditionally. An essential link in the reasoning for this conclusion is the claim that whereas one may be disappointed in so far as one's wants are directed towards particular things, one can never be disappointed if what one wants is simply the good, because *that* will be accomplished *whatever happens*. And this claim is presented as an analytical, quasi-grammatical truth which is involved in the very meaning of the key terms that are in question. It then appears like an analytical, quasi-grammatical truth that in all cases, if one is clear about what one wants, one will see that its realization is entirely independent of anything that may happen. It will then seem as though one is somehow failing to comprehend and accept the essential constitution of the universe if one does not accept as unqualifiedly good everything, no matter what, that happens.

She did in fact think that she was forced to this conclusion and was distressed by its implications. This is clear from a remarkable passage in a letter to Père Perrin in which she says that the certitude of God's love involved in such an acceptance of everything that may happen is threatened by one thing:

> There is only one time when I really know nothing of this certitude any longer. It is when I am in contact with the affliction of other people, those who are indifferent or unknown to me as much as the others, perhaps even more, including those of the most remote ages of antiquity. This contact causes me such atrocious pain and so utterly rends my soul that as a result the love of God becomes almost impossible for a while. It would take very little more to make me say impossible. So much so that I am uneasy about myself. I reassure myself by remembering that Christ wept on foreseeing the horrors of the destruction of Jerusalem. I hope he will forgive me my compassion.[17]

I shall leave to the next chapter further discussion of the weaknesses in Simone Weil's philosophical position which led her to this, surely unacceptable, point. Here I shall content myself with suggesting, without further argument, that the notion of "the love of God" is being introduced in the wrong place. It is something which presupposes compassion for the afflicted and cannot preclude it: as indeed the example of Christ weeping for the foreseen sack of Jerusalem shows. Within the context of the Christian religion the importance of this example is that it is what might be called a *revelation* of what the love of God consists in. That means that it can appear only as a matter of religious faith, not as a philosophical truth embedded in the grammar of our fundamental concepts.

11

GEOMETRY

The issues discussed in the last chapter concerned in the main what might be called the *practical* aspect of the conception of oneself as the centre of the universe. But the conception has of course also a theoretical, or epistemological, aspect which comes to a head in difficulties about solipsism. Simone Weil always thought of these aspects as essentially intertwined. The following striking remark is an entry in a notebook made at the very end of her life.

> Philosophy (including problems of cognition, etc.) is *exclusively* an affair of action and practice. That is why it is so difficult to write about it. Difficult in the same way as a treatise on tennis or running, but much more so.
>
> Subjectivist theories of cognition are a perfectly correct description of the condition of those who lack the faculty, which is extremely rare, of coming out of themselves.[1]

I had occasion to discuss solipsism – the most extreme form of a "subjectivist theory of cognition" – in Chapter 3. It will be remembered that as early as her treatment of it in *Lectures on Philosophy* she had emphasized the importance of action: the quasi-geometrical structure and order involved in even the most primitive form of bodily activity is required if anything – including one's very sensations themselves – is to be a possible object of knowledge. As I tried to show, however, the account of action she was working with at that time proved inadequate to elucidate the relation of one human being, one centre of consciousness, with another; and one of the major difficulties was the instrumental conception of action, the conception of it as directed towards realization of an agent's own projects.

This particular difficulty is removed by the later modified account of action that goes with her introduction of the concept of "the void." But it is removed only at the cost of generating other difficulties. Here is a passage from the beginning of her second 1941 notebook, the intoxicating boldness of which needs to be met with a cool head.

> One loves whatever it may be solely for oneself (the *I* is the only value). [Hence] the *I* cannot be finite, its dimension is that of the world.
>
> The *I* is as big as the world; all sounds meet in the ear, etc. (An orchestra, and single line of the gramophone; but the tympanum . . .)
>
> One should identify oneself with the universe itself. Everything that is less than the universe is subject to suffering [being partial and consequently exposed to outside forces].
>
> Even though I die, the universe continues. That does not console me if I am anything other than the universe. If, however, the universe is, as it were, another body to my soul, my death ceases to have any more importance for me than that of a stranger. The same is true of my sufferings.
>
> Let the whole universe be for me, in relation to my body, what the stick of a blind man is in relation to his hand. His sensibility really no longer resides in his hand, but at the end of the stick.[2]

I shall not attempt to discuss all the large issues raised by this passage. But there is one matter which is central to the relation between this chapter and the issues discussed in Chapters 9 and 10. The image of the blind man's stick, taken from Descartes, is one Simone Weil often uses in connection with her concept of "reading." As the blind man extends his sensibility beyond the confines of his disabled body through the use of his stick, so do we all extend our sensibilities by reading one situation through another. For instance if one is a student of ancient history one reads the significance of the discovery of Philip of Macedon's tomb through the network of historical scholarship and knowledge by reference to which – professionally at least – one identifies oneself. One is excited by the discovery and may feel that it is great good fortune *for oneself* that such a discovery should be made in one's lifetime. In such ways as this, what happens outside our bodies comes to have a significance for us as great as, or greater than, what happens to our bodies themselves. I can extend my sensibility in such a way that I no longer locate myself and my well-being in my (biological) body. Parents may, for instance, identify their well-being with that of their children, in such a way that their bodily privations are insignificant to them if their children flourish and in such a way that they will regard themselves as happy in dying if that is a condition of the children's flourishing. For such parents there are of course, however, circumstances with which they *cannot* in this way identify themselves: for instance, the suffering of their children. And this, as is noted in the passage I have quoted, will be true for anyone who identifies himself or herself with anything "less than the universe." To find one's identity in the universe itself will then, so it might seem, involve accepting *whatever happens* as good.

If I have reached this state, Simone Weil says, "my death ceases to have any more importance for me than that of a stranger." The self-effacement involved in such a state may sound admirable. But is has implications which look less acceptable: for instance that a stranger's death or suffering or, for that matter, my child's death or suffering will cease to have any more importance for me than anybody else's, including my own. This is of course the same difficulty as the one I noted at the end of the last chapter concerning compassion for the affliction of others. Its re-emergence in the present context draws attention to a major source of her difficulty: namely the way, the as it were promiscuous way, she talks of "the universe" when she sets it against "the I."[3] Whatever the expression "the universe" is being used to speak of, it is certainly not something that is all of a piece, to be thought of and treated in all its aspects in the same uniform way. In particular, another person is not another bit of "the universe" like any other to be used as my blind man's stick. Indeed, she makes this very point herself a few pages later in the same notebook:

> The relationship between *I* and the world. I am such and such a star, in the sense that, when I write, the pen is a part of my body, and in the sense that, when I press the fraise down on to the metal it is at their point of contact that the centre of my existence lies, and in the sense that, when I look at a picture, . . . and in other ways besides. But what of the relation between *I* and other men? I am he who sees this cube from a certain point of view, but also he who sees it from a certain other point of view (from which I do not see it). I am he who reads sensations according to one law, and also he who reads them according to some other law.
>
> To love our neighbour as ourselves does not mean that we should love all people equally, for I do not have an equal love for all the modes of existence of myself. Nor does it mean that we should

never make them suffer, for I do not refuse to make myself suffer. But we should have with each person the relationship of one conception of the universe to another conception of the universe, and not to a part of the universe. A man standing ten paces away from me is something separated from me by a distance (ten paces), but also another point of view under which all things appear. The relationship between me and another man can never be analogous to the relationship between the blind man and his stick, nor to the inverse relationship either; that is why slavery is contrary both to nature and reason.[4]

Echoing Socrates, we might say that both solipsism and also the rather Spinozistic[5] reaction to solipsism expressed in the passage quoted from page 19 of *Notebooks* "neglect geometry."

When Simone Weil speaks of a geometry of human relations she has in mind more than just an *analogy* with geometry as applied to space. This is clear, for instance, in the section "Love of the Order of the World" in *Waiting for God*. The "order" of the world (in which consists its beauty) is expressed in geometry. And "love of the order and beauty of the world is . . . the complement of the love of our neighbour."[6] Just as love of one's neighbour involves recognizing him or her as a limit to what one may do in the pursuit of one's own projects, so love of the beauty of the world involves a respect for its order, a recognition of a value (beauty) it exhibits which is independent of oneself and one's projects and which thereby constitutes a limit to them. To recognize order and beauty in the world, therefore, one must somehow transcend the perspective of one's own projects and see things from a centre which is not a particular place in the space of facts.[7]

> Just as God, being outside the universe, is at the same time the centre, so each man imagines he is situated in the centre of the world. The illusion of perspective places him at the centre of space; an illusion of the same kind falsifies his idea of time; and yet another kindred illusion arranges a whole hierarchy of values around him. This illusion is extended even to our sense of existence, on account of the intimate connection between our sense of value and our sense of being; being seems to us less and less concentrated the further it is removed from us.

Geometry, as conventionally understood, corrects "the spatial form of this illusion"; and we need a discipline to correct our illusions concerning "values and being" which will enable us to "give up our imaginary position as the centre." This will transform our whole sensibility, the ways we read things. To be so transformed, to discern that all parts of the world are equally centres and that the true centre is outside the world, this is to consent to the rule of mechanical necessity in matter and of free choice at the centre of each soul. Such consent is love. The face of this love which is turned towards thinking persons is the love of our neighbour; the face turned towards matter is love of the order of the world, or love of the beauty of the world which is the same thing.

We have already seen something of the importance of the notion of *consent* to Simone Weil's account of our relations with fellow human beings. To respect another's power to refuse is to accept a limit on one's valuation of one's own projects. Here we see the same notion introduced into our relations with matter: to understand that I am not the centre of the universe I have to achieve a certain independence of the network of necessities which characterizes my own position, my own perspective. This does not mean that I can *free myself from* those necessities. What I can do is to accept them in a certain way, accept that my own existence, being but one element in the order of nature, is essentially a *limited* existence.

In order to understand better the way Simone Weil speaks about "geometry" in such connections we must examine some of her ideas about the use of geometry in the realm of physics. I shall concentrate on parts of the very striking essay "Classical Science and After."[8]

> The relation between an aspiration of human thought and the effective conditions for its realization has been, in all countries and at all times, the object, the model, and the principle of the different ways of knowing the world; this relation is sought in the phenomena of the visible world and from it is constructed an image of the universe.[9]

I am not concerned here with the sweeping historical claim but with the suggestion of a fruitful point of view from which we may make comparisons between different forms of human inquiry. This is indeed the role it plays in Simone Weil's own essay. Her idea is that the most fundamental concepts in terms of which scientific theories are expressed are unintelligible apart from their connection with human practice; and that this in its turn is unintelligible apart from the aspirations that underlie it. From this point of view, then, what is interesting about a form, or an era, of science is not its ability "to accumulate experiments," but its character as an attempt "to find a way to represent the universe."[10]

Furthermore, the spiritual and cultural value of such a form of representation has to be seen in its relation to some "aspiration of human thought." And this means, I think, not merely that we must determine how far a form of representation in fact does satisfy a given aspiration; we must also ask ourselves questions about the value of the aspiration itself. We must not forget here that asking such questions, and being satisfied with some answers rather than others, will reflect certain aspirations of our own. That is very relevant to our understanding of Simone Weil's own procedure: she is clearly not simply describing what scientists do, but measuring what they do against a certain standard.[11] In this very important respect she parts company from Thomas Kuhn (in *The Structure of Scientific Revolutions*) between whose thinking and her own on these matters there are, in other respects, certain parallels.

It is easy to see a connection with the methodology of *Lectures* and of "Reflections Concerning the Causes of Liberty and Social Oppression." There the "aspiration" underlying our representations of the world was, we might say, the expression of free activity. The model of such activity was the *project;* and carrying out a project was understood as following a methodical sequence of steps one after the other.

Now it is true that she insisted at that time, and indeed with great emphasis, that such a procedure is to be understood in terms of a relation between thought and action, rather than a relation between a desire and its satisfaction. As I remarked, the point of this is to emphasize the importance for human dignity of self-determination rather than success in getting what one wants. It is also true that she spoke, in the same spirit, of the free individual as one who exercises his or her own judgment in setting an end as well as in deciding on the best sequence of means for attaining this end. But although, especially in *Lectures,* she says a great deal about the nature of the latter sort of judgment, there is rather little about what is involved in setting oneself an end. I commented earlier that this gap in her thinking is perhaps concealed from her by the way she thinks of communal life on the model of cooperative work in an industrial concern – in which the ends of action are in a sense given.

"Classical Science and After" makes contrasts between three eras: ancient Greek science, "classical" – that is, roughly Newtonian – science, and modern science dominated by quantum mechanics. I shall be concerned here with her comparison between Greek and classical science.

The representational model for classical science she takes to be

> work, or more exactly, the crude elementary form of work, into which practice, knowledge, skill and inspiration do not enter. In other words, manual labour.[12]

It is concerned with the conditions necessary for producing a certain result, but has nothing to say, does not try to say anything, about the desirability or otherwise of that result. As a result, the world is represented as "totally indifferent to our desires." Such a representation is certainly not without spiritual value: it is, she says, "a purification if rightly used," in that, in any attempt to read values in the physical universe itself,

> man may easily confuse the aspiration for the good with his own desires; this impure compound is precisely what sin is; so in the attempt to grasp the world of values instead of the world of necessity there is a risk of encouraging the most dubious elements in oneself.[13]

Nevertheless she thinks such a risk must be taken, since an "account of the universe" in such terms must necessarily be a partial one.

> The universe it describes is a slave's universe, and man, including slaves, is not wholly a slave. Man is indeed that creature who, if he sees an object on the floor and wants to see it on the table is obliged to lift it; but he is also, at the same time, something quite different. And the world is indeed that world which sets a distance, laborious to cross, between every desire and every accomplishment, but it too is at the same time something quite different. We know for certain that there is something different, without which we should not exist. It is true that the matter which constitutes the world is a tissue of blind necessities, absolutely indifferent to our desires; it is true, too, in a sense, that they are absolutely indifferent to spiritual aspirations, indifferent to the good; but also, in another sense, it is not true. For if there has ever been real sanctity in the world, even if only in one man and only for a single day, then in a sense sanctity is something of which matter is capable; since nothing exists except matter and what is inscribed in it. A man's body, and therefore in particular a saint's body, is nothing else but matter and is a piece of the world, of that same world which is a tissue of mechanical necessities. We are ruled by a double law: an obvious indifference and a mysterious complicity, as regards the good, on the part of the matter which composes the world; it is because it reminds us of this double law that the spectacle of beauty pierces the heart.[14]

I have just now been treating the development of Simone Weil's thinking after "Reflections Concerning the Causes of Liberty and Social Oppression" as one in which she paid more attention to the determination of ends. And, as we saw in Chapter 10, she did indeed for some time continue to speak as though our relation to good is one of desire, that is, it seems, a relation to an end. But the development of her thoughts about beauty increasingly involves a recognition that the relation between thought and action has to be conceived in other terms altogether. This is marked by her use of the word "aspiration" rather than "desire." We shall see more clearly later where this development eventually leads her.

Much in her criticism of classical science would apply equally to her own earlier writings. She does, it is true, describe the "work" on which she sees classical science as modelled as interpreted in terms of a relation between desire and its satisfaction; and it is true that, in *Oppression and Liberty,* she rejected that formula as a model of free human action. Nevertheless, as I have argued, she hardly says enough at that stage about the kind of thinking that goes into a determination of *ends* to prevent her conception from collapsing into the one she rejects. Moreover, the terms in which she expresses her criticism often bring uncomfortably to mind analogies between what she is criticizing and her own earlier views. She says for instance that the attempted, but incomplete, suppression of any representation of the ends of action by classical science explains why it

> bases itself on linear motion, which is the very image of the project and is the thought of every man who desires to go somewhere, for example, or to seize or hit something or somebody; and upon distance, which is a condition inherent in every desire of a creature subjected to time.[15]

But this emphasis on linear motion is very like the emphasis in her own earlier epistemology on arithmetic and counting in the formation of concepts. "L'acte s'ajoute à l'acte." Travelling in a linear motion is a matter of taking one step after another. What is required, according to this late essay (1941), is a model of action which recognizes limits and proportion; and hence geometry comes to be emphasized much more than arithmetic.

There is a case to be made, so it seems to me, for thinking that these criticisms of classical science apply much *more* directly to her own earlier epistemology than they do to science itself.

Let me explain. Allowing that classical science can be aptly described in the terms Simone Weil suggests, one might defend it by saying that it does not after all *deny* the possibility or desirability of an investigation into the reasons for desire or the nature of human aspirations and the relations between these and the good, and so on. It simply does not concern itself with them, but leaves them to a different form of inquiry. Of course, such a defence cannot be combined with the claim, not unknown amongst the champions of science, that no other form of thinking is to be taken seriously. There would, for instance, be much truth in the claim that certain popular philosophies of science (which can be grouped under the label "scientism") do make no room for serious questions about the relation of human beings to the good; but that of course is independent of whether science itself, or any particular form of science, can be said to make such a claim. It might of course be said that there is a danger of intellectual and cultural fragmentation in the development of different forms of inquiry to deal with different sorts of question (such fragmentation being a matter of great concern to Simone Weil). And it is true that many of these different questions are themselves created by the practices and successes of science. For instance, progress in physiology generates new difficulties about the relation between its own explanations of the workings and movements of the human body and explanations of action in terms of reasons, desires, aspirations. If intellectual culture is to maintain its seriousness, such questions cannot be ignored. But that still does not mean that it is the responsibility or province of *science* to take them up. The unity of intellectual culture is not the unity of a single theoretical system, and there is no reason why it should be placed uniquely on the shoulders of science.

Simone Weil's own philosophical enterprise could not be defended in the same way however. Her account of concept formation is not intended to apply only to the concepts of science, but is quite general. And the attempt to achieve such generality continued to characterize her work, which can, indeed, hardly be understood in any other way. If, then, her own (early) account of concept formation is subject to the criticisms she makes of classical science, they can be said to apply to it much more damagingly, since it is in danger of foreclosing on the possibility of asking certain kinds of question by making no conceptual room for them.

However that may be, the emphasis in "Classical Science and After" is strikingly different. According to it the aspiration behind the form of representation characteristic of Greek science is not "the project," but the longing of a thinking being to escape the "necessity of time and space" to which it is chained by pleasure, pain, and desire so as

> to dwell in eternity, to embrace and dominate time, to grasp the whole extended universe at all its points at once.[16]

In fact, as we can see, this aspiration is nothing other than the longing to escape from the limitation of having to read the universe from a particular point of view. The possibility of achieving this, so the essay argues, is suggested by the spectacle which the world constantly presents to us, of objects which are juxtaposed to each other in space and time and which change in regular patterns from moment to moment. Human beings respond to this spectacle by producing constructions based on "such conceptions as limit, order, harmony, proportion, regular recurrence." We find such constructions in literature, music, architecture, painting. We also find them in science, and Simone Weil's contention is that we find them above all in Greek science.

There is an aspect of her thinking about this which is particularly important, but also very easy to miss. It is not *merely* that Greek science is being said to seek a representation which will show the harmony and proportion between the elements with which it explicitly deals, as for instance:

> Archimedes saw a line along the surface of the floating body as the image of the ratio between its density and that of the fluid.[17]

Her thought is *also* that the whole enterprise reflects in itself the incommensurability between the limited spatio-temporal character of human beings and their urge to understand the nature of the universe in which they exist. This incommensurability is experienced most sharply in the perception of *beauty*, as for instance that of

> a human body and face which arouse not only desire but also and more strongly the fear of approaching because of the risk of spoiling them, whose decay we cannot imagine although vividly aware of their extreme fragility, and which, by almost wrenching our soul away, make it violently aware that it is nailed to a point in time and space.[18]

Art attempts to overcome this incommensurability by constructing
a bridge between us and the object that will bring us into harmony
with it, that will show us as related to it through a proportion: in
the way in which Greeks "sought solutions for equations of the
secondary degree" and showed that elements that are arithmeti-
cally incommensurable are nevertheless geometrically proportion-
ate. The "number" that underlies this form of representation is
not "the number which enumerates nor that which is formed by
continually repeated addition" – that is, not the number which
Prometheus was represented as bestowing on man in the poem –
but

> the number which applies to ratios, for a ratio between two integers
> . . . is at the same time a ratio between an infinity of other integers
> suitably selected and grouped in pairs.

In sum, the aspiration of Greek science is "to contemplate in sensible phenomena an image of the good,"[19] that is to say an image
of the hidden harmony between human beings and the universe in
which they exist.

The is what I meant when I said that, for Simone Weil, speaking
of a geometry of human relations is not just analogical. Geometry
is the general form of people's attempts to make their relation to
the world intelligible. Now, that world is one that contains other
human beings and, as we have already seen, there are special problems about the relation between one human being and another.
These problems arise from the fact that another human being is
also a perspective on the universe, whose attempt to come to terms
with that universe must necessarily differ from anybody else's since
it can only start from his or her own limited perspectival readings.
We have also seen that these differences are calculated to bring
human beings into conflict with each other.[20] The equilibrium I
am trying to achieve, then, is with a world of which conflict is
already a feature. My task is not so much to avoid conflict as to
come to terms with conflict itself.

The wonderful essay "The *Iliad* or the Poem of Force" is her
most sustained attempt to elucidate the nature of this task. It is an
essay which bases itself quite explicitly on the ideas about geometry we have been discussing. Consider, for instance, the following
striking paragraph, which is a reflection on the constantly changing fortunes of the two sides in the Trojan War, as depicted by
Homer.

This retribution, which has a geometrical rigour, which operates automatically to penalize the abuse of force, was the main subject of Greek thought. It is the soul of the epic. Under the name of Nemesis, it functions as the mainspring of Aeschylus's tragedies. To the Pythagoreans, to Socrates and Plato, it was the jumping-off point of speculation upon the nature of man and the universe. Wherever Hellenism has penetrated, we find the idea of it familiar. In Oriental countries which are steeped in Buddhism, it is perhaps this Greek idea that has lived on under the name of Kharma. The Occident, however, has lost it, and no longer even has a word to express it in any of its languages: conceptions of limit, measure, equilibrium, which ought to determine the conduct of life are, in the West, restricted to a servile function in the vocabulary of technics. We are only geometricians of matter; the Greeks were, first of all, geometricians in their apprenticeship to virtue.[21]

The poem depicts the warring parties as completely at the mercy of forces which they do not know how to control and of which they are hardly even aware. When temporarily in the ascendant they think their success due to their own superiority over the vanquished, whom they treat as hardly human, as "things": that is to say, they acknowledge in them no "power to refuse." The vanquished in their turn are consumed by fear and despair; they are incapable of acting according to any rational plan, but abandon themselves to the whims of the victors, whom they regard almost as members of a different, superior species. The situation in fact has very much the form which Simone Weil had described as the inevitable form of human relationships in "Reflections Concerning the Causes of Liberty and Social Oppression."

The man who is the possessor of force seems to walk through a non-resistant element; in the human substance that surrounds him nothing has the power to interpose, between the impulse and the act, the tiny interval that is reflection. Where there is no room for reflection, there is none either for justice or prudence. Hence we see men in arms behaving harshly and madly. . . .

. . . At the time their own destruction seems impossible to them. For they do not see that the force in their possession is only a limited quantity; nor do they see their relations with other human beings as a kind of balance between unequal amounts of force. Since other people do not impose on their movements that halt, that interval of hesitation, wherein lies all our consideration for our brothers in humanity, they conclude that destiny has given complete licence to them, and none at all to their inferiors. And at this point they exceed the measure of the force that is actually at their disposal. Inevitably they exceed it, since they are not aware that it is limited. And now we see them committed irretrievably to chance;

suddenly things cease to obey them. Sometimes chance is kind to them, sometimes cruel. But in any case there they are, exposed, open to misfortune; gone is the armour of power that formerly protected their naked souls; nothing, no shield, stands between them and tears.[22]

Though *The Iliad* describes an extreme situation and although at the time Simone Weil wrote the essay (1939–40) it had a particular relevance to the contemporary state of Europe, she certainly thought of the truths she saw in the poem as applying quite universally to the human condition. She writes of Hector, whose wife is preparing a hot bath for him at the very time his body is being dragged in the dust behind Achilles' chariot:

> Far from hot baths he was indeed, poor man. And not he alone. Nearly all the *Iliad* takes place far from hot baths. Nearly all of human life, then and now, takes place far from hot baths.[23]

If, at any particular time, we happen not to be exposed to the extreme affliction of the Greeks and the Trojans, that is no more than good fortune. And of course overt war is not the only form affliction may take. As we have already seen, another of Simone Weil's great themes, for example, was the misery endemic to modern industrial society.

So far, then, "geometry" is involved in *The Iliad*'s description of the Trojan War in so far as it reveals, what is concealed from the participants, that their force is a limited quantity, that "their relations with other human beings are a kind of balance between unequal amounts of force." But this has a deeper aspect, to bring out which we might remind ourselves of a remark in the passage from a notebook which I quoted in the last chapter. The application of geometry to human affairs will enable us, she says, "to transport ourselves to that centre of thought from which the other person reads values; contemplate the values destroyed by what we are going to do."

Recognition that human action can destroy values is a central theme in Simone Weil's thinking. A moving example is her treatment of the destruction of the civilization of the Languedoc by the Albigensian "crusade" in the thirteenth century.[24] In the essay on *The Iliad* she expresses the point by speaking of the power of the force which rules human life to turn anybody who is subjected to it "into a *thing*." This is in some ways an unfortunate way of speaking and I will discuss it further in the next chapter. For the present it will suffice to note that she means, first, the power to kill – to turn a living human being into a corpse; but also, second, the power to rob a human being of what is distinctively human about him or her: ability to consent, or power to refuse. There is something else as well. Force may damage the human capacities not merely of the one who is at the receiving end but also of the one who, for the present, wields it. The conqueror's exhilaration may lead to behaviour that would be found unthinkable under other circumstances and which will be bitterly regretted when the exhilaration is past.

> Force is as pitiless to the man who possesses it, or thinks he does, as it is to his victims; the second it crushes, the first it intoxicates. The truth is nobody really possesses it. The human race is not divided up, in the *Iliad,* into conquered persons, slaves, suppliants, on the one hand, and conquerors and chiefs on the other.[25]

A theme which runs through Simone Weil's treatment of these matters is a certain "incommensurability" between force and the kinds of effect it can have. This indeed is what she is drawing attention to when she speaks of force "turning men into things." We have to try to understand her thoughts about this in order to see the full force of her emphasis on geometry as what is required in the study of human affairs. I shall discuss it in the next chapter.

12

INCOMMENSURABILITY

The way in which, in "The *Iliad* or the Poem of Force," Simone Weil speaks of force as "turning a man into a thing" is rhetorically very effective in its context; but there is something unfortunate about it, because it seems to class together very different sorts of case and is thereby likely to provoke doubts and objections which, though in a sense justified, are not in the end very relevant to what Simone Weil really wants to say. But because these difficulties *are* bound to arise, I must say something about them.

I have distinguished three aspects of "turning a man into a thing":

(1) killing
(2) robbing the victim of the power to refuse
(3) robbing the victor, or oppressor, of the power to act rationally, making him or her act brutally, and so on (There are of course further distinctions that could be made here.)

Number (1) is perhaps the least problematic kind of case. We find it quite natural to speak of a corpse as a "mere thing" in trying to express its categorical difference from a living human being. But even this case has a good deal more to it than that. For certainly we tend to act very differently towards human corpses from the way we do towards anything else; consider funeral rites, for example. And if we found someone, except in circumstances of dire necessity, treating a human corpse as we might the carcass of an animal, say, without any sign of being aware that something was amiss, we might indeed think there was a deficiency in that person's understanding. There are issues raised by this which are of considerable importance in some contexts,[1] but I do not think they affect the propriety of speaking as Simone Weil does of what happens when a human being is killed by force. It is indeed appropriate to speak of a categorical difference between a living human being and a human corpse and it is this, as we shall see, that is important.

Number (2) is more problematic. The victim is of course still in the natural sense a living human being. Is the victim being treated by the oppressor as though he or she were *not*? Simone Weil takes the description of Achilles with Priam ("Taking the old man's arm, he pushed him away") as a case of that.

> It was merely a question of his being as free in his attitudes and movements as if, clasping his knees, there were not a suppliant but an inert object.[2]

Well, perhaps. But not all the cases that she would include in this category can plausibly be described in those terms. The master who expects the slave to pander to every whim and imposes punishment if the slave does not is not treating him or her like an inert object. Nor is the slave who anxiously strives to anticipate the master's wishes behaving like one. We may think that the behaviour of neither is worthy of a human being, but that is a different matter. Such a thought is only intelligible concerning one who is recognized as a human being.

Something similar can be said of the cases that fall under (3). The reckless, obsessional behaviour of the warriors in the Trojan War is a saddening spectacle, because we think human beings are capable of something better. They are falling short of an important standard of human dignity and excellence. We may sometimes express this judgment as "They are not behaving like human beings." That *means* that they are falling short of a certain standard. It does not mean that they have actually ceased to be human beings. It does not even mean, regrettably, that they are behaving in ways untypical of human beings. Nor does Simone Weil think so. One of the main thrusts of her argument is precisely that such behaviour is characteristic of human beings under certain, by no means uncommon, circumstances. And that is a theme to which she constantly returns.

How damaging are such considerations? Not very, it seems to me. They affect her way of expressing herself rather than the serious point she is making. *Incommensurability* is the notion that is most important to this point; and that is why she places so much emphasis on *geometry* as the appropriate method of discussing it.

There is an incommensurability between a living human being and a corpse. (That is another way of putting what I meant when I spoke of a "categorical" difference.) One can of course give a continuous account of the physiological processes of death, describe the functioning of the living body, how this functioning changes and passes over into the processes of decay, and so on. From the point of view of physiology, one might say, the processes in the living body are conceptually on a level with those in a dead body. The description of the death of the *person* is different, however. Think, for instance, of Tolstoy's story "The Death of Ivan Ilyich," of Plato's description of Socrates' death in the *Phaedo,* of the Gospel accounts of Christ's Passion, of George Eliot's description of the death of old Mr. Featherstone in *Middlemarch:* four very different cases. Mr. Featherstone is a particularly pertinent example. He is represented, before his death, as gloating at the unpleasant shock he is preparing (in the shape of his will) for his survivors.

> We are all of us imaginative in some form or other, for images are the brood of desire; and poor old Featherstone, who laughed much at the way others cajoled themselves, did not escape the fellowship of illusion. In writing the programme for his burial he certainly did not make clear to himself that his pleasure in the little drama of which it formed a part was confined to anticipation. In chuckling over the vexations he could inflict by the rigid clutch of his dead hand, he inevitably mixed his consciousness with that livid stagnant presence, and so far as he was preoccupied with a future life, it was with one of gratification inside his coffin.[3]

In a description of the death of a human being we expect to find, for instance, allusion to the sort of life the person has led ("life" in that context not expressing a physiological concept), relations with family and friends, work, aspirations, successes, and disappointments, the spirit in which he or she approaches death. These are the surroundings of the concept of "the life of a human being," surroundings that go to make it the concept it is. And precisely the same goes for the concept of "the *death* of a human being." It is connected with mourning and grief, with the ending of certain opportunities and the opening up of others, with settling the dead person's affairs, making new arrangements, and so

on. Our understanding of what it is for a person to die presupposes an understanding that things of this sort are involved. The
concept of death will have all the complexity of the concept of the
life of whatever being it is applied to. Ecclesiastes compares successive human beings with the life and death of grass. But the *point*
of the comparison lies in the fact that our concepts of "life and
death" here are so different. You cannot tell the sort of story
about the death of a blade of grass that you can tell about the
death of a human being. And the force of that "cannot" is not
weakened by the reflection that there can be anthropomorphic,
allegorical stories about the death of blades of grass. Those are *not*
"the same sort of story" – stories about the death of human beings
are not anthropomorphic and are seldom allegorical. The terms
"life" and "death" are, as Wittgenstein might have said, used with
a different grammar according to the kind of creature we are
speaking of.

The grammar is also different when we are talking about physiological death and about the death of the person. The dead man's
body lies in the grave. Does *he* lie in the grave? Yes, we may say so.
But that is not to say we make no distinction. His widow, for
instance, may visit his grave and address him. It is not the body
that lies in the grave that she is addressing, but him, her dead husband. It may, and rightly, be said that talking to a living human
being is not addressing his body either, not even his living body.
But "living human being" and "living human body" are also different concepts. Although it may be important to the widow that
she goes to the graveside to address him, it may not. If it *is* important to her, that will not be for the same reason as that which
makes it necessary for me to get within earshot of a living human
being to whom I wish to speak. The body does not play the same
role in the notion of "talking to him" in the case where the ad-
dressee is living as in the case where he is dead.

These are no more than a few random selections from the
immensely complex network of conceptual connections and distinctions involved in our talk about living people and about
corpses. Are we justified in talking about it in terms of
"incommensurability"?

The death of someone one knows is often experienced as a *mystery*. That is, that is a way those who experience it often want to
describe it; and one does not need to be a religious person in
order to feel this inclination. Perhaps this way of thinking, or feel-

ing, is more likely where there was a strong emotional attachment to (or aversion from) the dead person; but I am not sure that this is necessary. What is the mystery? That he or she is *not there* any more; and that is not the same as *that such and such has taken place in and to that body:* although of course there are obvious enough connections. I am not going to attempt to explain what the mystery consists in. In a sense the point of using the term "mystery" in this context is to express that one's unease (and I stress that it may be in part an *intellectual* unease) is not of a kind to be removed or alleviated by any *explanation.* Certainly a great deal more and a great deal better could be said about this experience, or the inclination to talk in this way, than I have said; but in the end I believe we shall have to accept the inclination as something like a primitive phenomenon. That does not lessen its importance for the nature of our understanding of each other and of ourselves, of what we take human life to be.

Perhaps we can say that to sense a mystery here is to respond to an incommensurability between what we can say of the death of the human body and what we understand by the death of the person. That is brought out marvellously, I think, by the dreadful play on the word "dearer" in one of the lines from *The Iliad* quoted by Simone Weil:

> But they on the ground
> Lay, dearer to the vultures than to their wives.

If we do speak in this way, we shall perhaps want to say that there is the same sort of incommensurability involved in the conception of the violent killing of someone by force. What is the relation between the plunging of the length of steel into a body and all those consequences that go with our understanding of "this person's death"? Or, to link the question with an earlier quotation, if I kill someone, what is the relation between the physical act and its physical consequences and "the values destroyed by what I do"?

Here I think we reach something of great importance in Simone Weil's thought that force can reduce people to things. The effects of physical force do not all belong to the same category. Physical force can, for instance, destroy not only human bodies but also human values; furthermore, it can do so on one and the same occasion of its exercise, the one, as it were, through the other.

> Everything that is subjected to the contact of force is defiled,
> whatever the contact. To strike or to be struck is one and the same
> defilement. The chill of steel is equally mortal at the hilt and at the
> point. Whatever is exposed to the contact of force is liable to
> degradation.[4]

Defilement, degradation: these are not physiological effects; but
they are just as genuinely effects of the contact of the steel with
the body. Again, in "A Medieval Epic Poem," Simone Weil emphasizes that the civilization of the Languedoc was virtually destroyed
by the Albigensian Crusade. It

> has left no traces except the poem itself, some troubadours' songs,
> a few texts concerning the Cathars, and some marvellous churches.
> The rest has vanished; we can only try to guess what this civilization
> was like – this civilization and all its works, which were destroyed by
> arms.[5]

It is tempting to say, in connection with examples like these, that
physical force does not have purely physical effects; but this does
not mean that alongside the physical effects there are others, analogously to the way in which alongside the motion produced by the
application of force to a body there are also changes in tempera-
ture. It means rather that not everything that we call an "effect"
of a physical force is to be described in physical terms – not at
least in a univocal sense of the word "physical." We could not say
what was destroyed in the Languedoc without making use of terms
belonging to religion, to art and literature, to architecture. Of
course these cultural formations have physical expression. The
Cathar religion was manifested in the lives and practices of its
believers; literature comes to us in written texts, architecture in
buildings. All these expressions are physical enough, in a perfectly
good sense of the word "physical." What could be more physical
than a church? Or than the burning of a Cathar heretic at the
stake? (We should not allow self-styled "physicalist" philosophers
to deprive us of this use of the word. Even less should we allow
them to persuade us that what can be described in the language
of physics constitutes "everything that really happens": they have
even less of a monopoly of the concept of what really happens
than they do in the use of the word "physical.") And so it is perhaps better *not* to yield to the temptation to say that in these cases
physical forces do not have merely physical effects. It is difficult to
find general terms which express the point satisfactorily, though I
think it is clear enough in relation to particular examples.

What Simone Weil is saying can be brought out by considering the following example. Zoé Oldenbourg's fine book on the Albigensian Crusade ends with a description of the *auto-da-fé* at Montségur.

> Once the flames had caught well, both executioners and soldiers perforce retired to some distance off, in order to avoid suffering from the smoke and heat that the vast pyre discharged. In a few hours' time the two hundred living torches heaped together inside the palisade were no more than a mass of raw, blackened, bleeding flesh, slowly burning to a cindered crisp, spreading a ghastly stench of burnt meat right down the valley, and up to the very walls of the fortress.[6]

What is striking about this passage is precisely its place at the end of the book: a book which has dealt with, amongst other things, the purity and heroism of the lives of many of the heretics, the immense cultural vigour of the region in which heresy flourished, and so on. And it ended in scenes like this! Even if we leave all that cultural significance aside for a moment, the scene as described is dreadful enough even considered in "purely physical" terms. But what makes it dreadful is that these are living human beings who are being burned; not just the dreadful stench of the smoke, but that the source of the smoke is what it is. Someone who did not understand this would hardly understand what was being said in the quoted passage. But the same can also be said of someone who did not understand that this was the culmination of the stamping out of the Cathar Church. And what goes into such understanding is of a totally different conceptual order from what goes into an understanding of the processes of combustion.

There is a simple, but striking, corollary. If, as I take to be the case, understanding a physical force (like fire) is in very large measure understanding the kinds of effects it can have in various kinds of circumstance, then we have *not* properly understood fire if we think of its possible consequences in narrowly "physical" terms. It pertains to fire, one might say, considered in the context of the world in which we live (and how else are we to consider it?) that it can destroy values as well as trees.

It is *also* important to a clear understanding of fire (for example) to realize that the word "destroy" is being used in two radically different ways in the preceding sentence. Spelling out what goes into the destruction of a value would be an enterprise of a totally different kind from that of spelling out what goes into the destruction of a tree. And that is another way of saying that there is an *incommensurability* between fire considered as a potential destroyer of trees (or of human bodies) and fire considered as a potential destroyer of values. Different concepts will be appropriate in the two cases. – For instance, whether or not one agrees with what Simone Weil says about the "defilement" produced by the application of force in human life, what she says clearly makes sense as it would not were she talking about the application of force in the clearing of rocks from a piece of waste ground. It is no objection that, within the context of a certain sort of story, room could be made for the use of the word "defilement" here too; consideration of the kind of story that would have to be told would reinforce my point.

There are parallel incommensurabilities in the other sorts of case I distinguished as falling under the general rubric "turning men into things." Compare Priam before and after force has overcome him. He has lost all his human, let alone kingly, self-respect and power of self-determination. What physical theory would give an account of that change? Perhaps it will be claimed that there could be a physiological story plotting the changes in Priam's central nervous system from the time the Greeks break into Troy to the time Achilles confronts him. Perhaps indeed there could be, though physiology as we now know it is, I am sure, very far from being in a position to offer any such account. But even if it did, where would the notions of Priam's humiliation and self-abasement come in? *Those* are not physiological concepts; and nothing physiology could say would convey what is conveyed in a description like that found in *The Iliad*. For someone to say – as some will – that physiology and kindred sciences provide descriptions of all that "really happens" here would simply be for him to bury his head in the sand.

My examples so far have concerned, roughly speaking, the relations between, on the one hand, human beings and the values expressed in the lives of human beings and, on the other hand, the environment. But equally important are those cases which reveal an incommensurability within human beings themselves, between different aspects of "human nature." Consider once more from this point of view the contrast between the moment when . . . "Achilles shuddered to see divine Priam" and wept at his words, and the moment that follows when he impatiently pushed him to the ground. The two sorts of behaviour are not merely in marked contrast to each other; they are mutually opposed, even inconsistent. How could one and the same man do both these things, one after the other? It is no answer to the puzzlement expressed in that question to say that, as is undoubtedly the case, people are undergoing transformations like this all the time. That is precisely what is puzzling.

Let us take an example from our own times. I have heard it said that when first reports of what was happening in the Nazi extermination camps reached even those leaders in the west whose concern it was to help the European Jews, they just did not believe them.[7] Perhaps there was a tendency to think that whereas people are certainly capable of all kinds of brutality, *that* could not lie in human nature. Now, strangely enough, that is a thought which may persist after it has been established quite beyond doubt that human beings *did* behave like that. Even more strangely, some may think (as I do) that it is good that such a thought *should* survive the discovery of the facts. That is, that we should retain the thought that what we acknowledge undoubtedly to have happened in those camps was nevertheless something impossible. It may be objected that this is merely a misleadingly hyperbolic way of expressing one's moral outrage. And it *is* of course an expression of moral outrage. But what is important in the present context is the link between the notion of moral outrage in certain cases and the notion of *understanding*. In saying it is "good" that such a thought should survive the discovery of the facts I do not mean merely, or even chiefly, that this will have salutary social or psychological effects. I mean that there is a sort of truth in the thought. I feel like saying – and I am not alone in this – "I do not understand how people could behave in such a way"; and the use of the word "understand" is important, I think irreplaceable, in this context. That may upset our tidy philosophical schemata, but is a fact to be recognized. What is more, the puzzlement expressed here is not one to be removed by any sort of explanation. Sociological, psychological, historical explanations, and so on may help us to understand a great many things; but I believe they will leave the kind of puzzlement I am concerned with untouched.

One may describe the puzzlement as directed at an "incommensurability" between aspects of human nature neither of which can be denied. Where there is this sort of incommensurability our difficulty is one of finding any perspective from which all the phenomena under consideration can be seen together as systematically interconnected. This is part of the reason why Simone Weil emphasizes the importance of geometry in such cases. Only a geometrical form of representation can deal with incommensurables.

Perhaps the incommensurability is more striking when experienced in the first person. On pages 148 to 150 of *First and Last Notebooks* there is a discussion of Ben Jonson's *Volpone* which brings this out and which I shall summarize. In the hope of inheriting a fortune from "a repulsive old man" someone prostitutes to him his "young, chaste, and beautiful" wife. Simone Weil's reflections concern the husband's attempt to come to terms with what he has done; they turn on the contrast between his understanding of his intended action before the event, when he is under the influence of a particular motivation, and his later understanding of the accomplished action, when that motivation is no longer present. In this particular example the agent discovers that he acted under a factual misapprehension: there was never any question of his gaining the inheritance. For this reason the motive from which he acted now has no reality for him. However, I think it is quite clear that Simone Weil's discussion is meant to have a much broader application than to cases involving factual mistakes of that sort. There are, for instance, the striking remarks about desire in *Notebooks,* pages 489 to 491, which I discussed in Chapter 10, where she argues that the good thought to reside in particular objects of desire becomes exhausted when the object is obtained. Bread is desired as a good only so long as one is hungry. "The good was not, therefore, in the bread, but in the appropriate relation existing between the bread and the hunger." This thought can be applied to the case of *Volpone:* the husband has a motive for prostituting his wife only for so long as the inheritance lies in the future.

> A man with a young, chaste, and beautiful wife, whom he loves, would not prostitute her to a repulsive old man without a reason. It is as impossible as a weight rising without being lifted.
>
> But if he has done it because he thought it would win him an inheritance and then discovers that there was never any question of his getting the inheritance, then it is just as if he had done it for no reason – as if the weight had risen by itself.
>
> So the soul lives in the impossibility and cannot escape from it, because it is an accomplished impossibility, a past impossibility.

This "impossibility" is closely connected with what I have been calling "incommensurability." How are we to understand it?

Someone who is deliberating what to do imagines various alternatives and considers what is to be said for and against them. There may be certain actions which would almost certainly bring about the desired goal, but concerning which the agent does *not* deliberate, because they are *impossible*, though in a sense open to him or her. Perhaps for instance what is desired could be achieved by means of a certain murder without danger of discovery. But if the thought occurs to the agent at all, it never gains such a foothold in his or her mind as to be seriously deliberated over. It is not seen as a possible alternative. This is not to say there are overwhelming reasons against it; the point is it never achieves the status of having reasons for or against it considered. It is rejected as intrinsically impossible; even deliberating concerning it is an impossibility: to rehearse "reasons for and against" would be an idle, and tasteless, game; nothing would gain foothold as a reason.

What appears impossible to us at one time may become a matter for serious deliberation at another; the cause of this may be some powerful motive to which we have become subject. This is the case of the husband in *Volpone*. His motive is greed. He does not of course offer greed as a *reason* for acting. His reasoning takes the form "If my wife sleeps with Volpone I shall inherit his money." That is, he sees the prospect of future riches as a reason for inducing his wife to prostitute herself. It is his greed that makes him think in this way. This is what is meant by calling greed his "motive." Calling greed a motive for action expresses our recognition that it may sometimes induce someone to deliberate, and even act, in a way which in the absence of greed would not even come into consideration. This was the condition of the husband in *Volpone* prior to acting.

After the action the whole sequence of events presents itself to him in an entirely different light. For one thing, of course, the questions he asks are different: he is no longer deliberating what to do, but seeking an explanation of what he has done. The need for an explanation springs from the fact that he now recognizes his action as catastrophic, not in its consequences so much as in itself. But what sort of explanation does he want? It is not that he needs to know what his *reasons* were for doing what he did; in a sense he knows that perfectly well already. He knows that he did it in order to enrich himself. His difficulty is that he does not now understand how *that* can have counted as a reason for him at all, let alone a sufficient reason, for doing such a thing. Nor is he in doubt about his *motive;* he knows quite well that he acted from greed. What puzzles and torments him, we might say, is not *why* he acted as he did, but *how he could* have. In general terms we are familiar with the fact that motives like greed can make actions seem possible that otherwise would be recognized as impossible; that does not mean that in the case of one's own past action one can see how the motive does the trick. It is only as long as one is in the grip of the motive that the world arranges itself for one in such a way as to make certain sorts of consideration intelligible as reasons.

Two remarks from a notebook of Wittgenstein's concern the same point.[8]

> Envy is a superficial thing – i.e. the colour characteristic of envy does not go down deep – further down passion has a different colour ⟨*Färbung*⟩. (*That,* of course, does not make envy any the less real.)

> Why is the soul moved by idle thoughts? – After all they are idle. Well, it *is* moved by them.
> (How can the wind move the tree when it's nothing but air? Well, it *does move* it; and don't forget it.)

We evaluate motives on different scales. On the one hand we assess them according to their place in our conception of life: according to their relation to what we value and think important and worthwhile. On the other hand we assess them according to their power to move people to action. But these scales are not independent of each other. Sometimes we think of a person as moved to action not merely by motives which happen to concern matters that are important and worthwhile; rather we think it is that very fact, their very importance and worthwhileness, which provides the decisive motivation. An example of this would be Socrates' acceptance of his condemnation by the Athenian court on the grounds of the importance in his own life of Athens and its laws, as set out in Plato's *Apology* and *Crito.* And for someone to suggest that some further consideration is necessary to explain Socrates' *motive* for acting according to those considerations would, I think, be to suggest that he did not really act from those considerations at all. That is to say, it is part of our conception of the depth of certain considerations that that is sufficient to make it intelligible that someone should act from them. But we also know that people sometimes act contrary to what is most important and valuable to them – even in their own eyes. This is the case of the husband in *Volpone*.

A remark of O. K. Bouwsma's nicely illustrates the way in which the very words "deep" and "shallow" may be used according to quite different scales of assessment. He is discussing the scene in Dostoevsky's *The Brothers Karamazow* in which Fyodor Karamazov tauntingly questions his sons, Ivan and Alyosha, about the existence of God and immortality. Bouwsma says of Fyodor: "We may describe him as a deep trifler. His depth is on the surface and far below he is shallow."[9] The questions Fyodor starts by asking have an appearance of seriousness and depth. But the more one listens to him, the more one realizes that he does not in fact take seriously the issues he seems to be raising. This frivolity in the face of what is serious "goes deep" in the sense that there is not much more to Fyodor than this; that is, his frivolity is not, as in some people, a cover for an underlying seriousness.

When Wittgenstein wrote that envy is a superficial thing, he was not denying, I think, that a man may be consumed by envy even to the extent that there is not much room for anything else in his life. He was not suggesting that it must always give way to something much more substantial when a man's character is probed. He was making a judgment: that, namely, to be envious is to mistake what is important and serious in life, and especially in one's own life. In another place, speaking of Newton's dispute with Leibniz over priority in the invention of the calculus – but also obviously addressing himself – Wittgenstein wrote:

> It's a question of *envy* of course. And everyone who experiences it ought to keep on telling himself: "It's a mistake! It's a mistake!"[10]

Of course, I may tell myself this with conviction and *yet* still be unable not to act enviously.

I began this chapter by remarking that it is an apparent objection to the way in which Simone Weil talks of force as "turning men into things" that it seems to class together very different sorts of case. Can I be said to have answered this objection? Have I not on the one hand merely substituted one phrase ("incommensurability") for another ("turning men into things"); and on the other hand made matters worse by introducing new cases different again from those discussed in the *Iliad* essay? It is true that my procedure has consisted in doing both these things. I think nevertheless that it has achieved something.

Talk about "turning men into things" sounds as though it belongs to a metaphysical account of the universe: as divided into two radically different realms, the realm of matter and the realm of spirit. And Simone Weil undeniably in some moods writes in this vein. She does so, for instance, when she speaks, in the way against which I protested in Chapter 6, of a single all-embracing necessity to which everything in nature – including mankind – is subject. To this belongs her distinction between "the necessary and the good," thought of as a single, mutually exclusive and exhaustive classification of the ways in which human action may be understood. If we emphasize this aspect of her writing we shall think of her as a sort of dualist metaphysician: that is encouraged by such a title for a selection of her writings as *Gravity and Grace*.

This is certainly not a merely imaginary aspect. But it does not stand alone and there are features of her work which count strongly against such an interpretation. We have for instance such by no means uncharacteristic remarks as:

> To say that what we really want is always and only the good is like saying that what we desire is the desired. It is a purely grammatical statement.[11]

There is also a striking intellectual honesty in her discussions of the details of particular cases, especially in her notebooks. She is seldom afraid to do full justice to a feature of an example which runs a coach and horses through general metaphysical views to which her more abstract reflections may seem to be leading her. And this is entirely in accord with the central place occupied in her methodology by the concept of "attention":

> Our thought should be in relation to all particular and already for-mulated thoughts, as a man on a mountain who, as he looks for-ward, sees also below him, without actually looking at them, a great many forests and plains. Above all our thought should be empty, waiting, not seeking anything, but ready to receive in its naked truth the object which is to penetrate it.[12]

The metaphysical interpretation also underestimates the extent to which her thinking was constantly *changing* in response to such particular truths. An example of such change which is of special importance to the present issue is a very late remark:

> Real love wants to have a real object, and to know the truth of it, and to love it in its truth as it really is.

> To talk about love of truth is an error; it should be a spirit of
> truth in love. This spirit is always present in real and pure love.[13]

That is in marked contrast to the Platonic strain of much of her –
not very much – earlier thinking.

It seems to me that talking about "incommensurability" in connection with the issues mainly discussed in the present chapter is
at once entirely in accord with one of Simone Weil's most important ideas and avoids the metaphysical overtones of "turning men
into things." What it does is to draw attention to analogies
between a number of different difficulties we face in trying to
make sense of human life. It need not imply that they are really all
different manifestations of the *same* difficulty any more than the
use of this term in mathematics implies that all mathematical
incommensurabilities are of the same sort. As she said in a passage
from her pre-war notebook which I quoted in Chapter 2, in mathematics and also in "speculation, even in its purest form,"

> there is no way of opening broad vistas which the mind can observe
> without entering them. One must enter the subject before one can
> see anything.[14]

Before concluding this chapter and in the light of these last
remarks I want to return to "The *Iliad* or the Poem of Force." I
said earlier that this essay insists that in order to understand the
forces which operate in human affairs we need a way of appreci-
ating what is *lost* through their operation. Capability of destroying
human values is an important attribute and we cannot grasp it
without grasping *what* is being destroyed. It is characteristic of fire
(at certain temperatures) that it can destroy wood but not stone:
this would mean nothing to us if we did not know what wood and
stone were. It is also characteristic of fire that it can destroy people and ideas (through the destruction of books, for example): this
too will mean nothing to us unless we understand what people are
and the kinds of ideas that may be thus destroyed. I emphasize that
we need such an understanding if we are to have an adequate
grasp of *fire*.

In a conflict like the Trojan War the opposing sides may embody
different and conflicting values. "Force" can blind the participants in such a conflict to the values represented by their oppo-
nents at the same time as it may encompass a destruction of values
on both sides. The old saw that the first casualty in war is the truth

expresses recognition of both these facts. Those who are in the ascendant may hardly perceive the human reality of those whom they are crushing, let alone the distinctive view of life and of the world which perhaps is theirs alone. (That would for instance be particularly true of the Albigensian Crusade.) And those who are crushed may equally regard themselves as by nature inferior to the godlike beings who have vanquished and enslaved them. In such a case *both* sides are subject to a misunderstanding about their own condition and about what is going on. Those who do not understand that the others are also people, with potentialities as well as limitations and vulnerabilities analogous to their own, do not properly understand even themselves, because they do not understand the *conditioned* nature of their potentialities and limitations. And they do not understand what is going on not merely because they do not understand what the forces that have been unleashed are effecting, but because they do not even understand properly the *modus operandi* of the forces. They cannot do so because their misunderstanding is itself precisely an essential part of the mechanism of war. This is the importance of what Simone Weil writes about *prestige,* both in this essay and elsewhere. The notion that one side or the other in the conflict consists of beings who are somehow superior is one of the main ingredients of the force that side wields:

> Prestige, from which force derives at least three-quarters of its strength, rests principally upon that marvellous indifference that the strong feel towards the weak, an indifference so contagious that it infects the very people who are the objects of it.[15]

The way she writes in this essay often suggests that it is a universal law of nature that people will react in the way described. This is not of course true; and elsewhere she recognizes that it is not. I shall discuss problems connected with these conflicting tendencies in Chapter 15.

What "geometry" has to provide is a point of view from which the values of both sides can find expression. This point of view is that of *justice:* the "extraordinary sense of equity which breathes through the *Iliad,*"[16] which is described in the following fine passage:

> However, such a heaping up of violent deeds would have a frigid effect, were it not for the note of incurable bitterness that continually makes itself heard, though often only a single word marks its

presence, often a mere stroke of the verse, or a run-on line. It is in this that the *Iliad* is absolutely unique, in this bitterness that proceeds from tenderness and that spreads over the whole human race, impartial as sunlight. Never does the tone lose its colouring of bitterness; yet never does the bitterness drop into lamentation. Justice and love, which hardly have any place in this study of extremes and of unjust acts of violence, nevertheless bathe the work in their light without ever becoming noticeable themselves, except as a kind of accent. Nothing precious is scorned, whether or not death is its destiny; everyone's unhappiness is laid bare without dissimulation or disdain; no man is set above or below the condition common to all men; whatever is destroyed is regretted. Victors and vanquished are brought equally near us; under the same head, both are seen as counterparts of the poet, and the listener as well. If there is any difference, it is that the enemy's misfortunes are possibly more sharply felt.[17]

Although that does not perhaps sound much like what one usually reads in books on the theory of knowledge, the passage does in fact make an *epistemological* point. People, their values and institutions, can only be understood for what they are from the point of view of justice. It is only from this point of view that other people's readings of themselves and of the world can be given proper weight in one's own reading of them. Any sort of domination of them, or servile submission to them, will involve a distortion of one's understanding.

I shall postpone till later consideration of what we are to understand by the point of view of justice in this context and what are the conditions under which it can be attained.

13

BEAUTY

I want to break off my consideration of justice at this point and reflect first on the role played by *beauty* in Simone Weil's thinking. As the following passage shows, she sees a very close connection between them.

> The love of the order and beauty of the world is thus the complement of the love of our neighbour.
> It proceeds from the same renunciation, the renunciation which is an image of the creative renunciation of God. God causes the universe to exist, but he consents not to command it, although he has the power to do so. Instead he leaves two other forces to rule in his place. On the one hand there is the blind necessity attaching to matter, including the psychic matter of the soul, and on the other hand the autonomy essential to thinking persons.
> By loving our neighbour we imitate the divine love which created us and all our fellows. By loving the order of the world we imitate the divine love which created this universe of which we are a part.[1]

I recognize the apparent absurdity of trying to reflect on these striking ideas in abstraction from their religious dimension, but this is what, for the present, I want to do. I shall try to say something in my concluding chapter about the relation between these reflections and that religious dimension.

In my discussion of that "love of our neighbour" the manifestation of which we have seen to require the notion of justice, I emphasized the importance of the difference between the primitive reaction which lies at its root (the "moment of hesitation") and the reactions which were given prominence in *Lectures on Philosophy* as the source of our understanding of the natural order. These latter reactions were organized under the general heading

of "the project" of which, as she says in "Classical Science and
After," the very image is the straight line, connecting the agent to
the place he wants to get to,[2] a straight line from which any "hesitation" is a deviation. I have so far represented that concept of
our fellow human beings which grows out of this hesitation, as an
exception to the general rule that our concepts have their roots in
our projects. But it appears from what Simone Weil is saying about
beauty that there is something analogous to this hesitation in our
reaction to the natural world also. The response to beauty does
not *replace* the response to objects as obstacles to our projects, but
qualifies and limits it. Of course some such qualification as this is
already implied by the very general application of the notion of
geometry, discussed in Chapter 11, according to which the conception of a *natural order* to which everything belongs involves recognizing that everything, including the realization of our own
projects, is subject to *limits*. As we shall see, to say that these
responses are "analogous" is too weak; Simone Weil thinks of
them as inseparably intertwined in a way which is quite central to
her whole way of thinking in the later writings.

I want to approach this by considering again the relation
between thought and action and by first going back, briefly, to the
account of this given in "Reflections Concerning the Causes of
Liberty and Social Oppression": an account, namely, based on the
concepts of means and ends. As I remarked in another context,
although free action is said to be based on judgments concerning
ends as well as means to ends, there is virtually no discussion of
the former. The emphasis is on the thoughtful ordering of steps
in a productive process. In this consists the dignity of the
workman.

Consider now the following passage from her very late work *The
Need for Roots*. I quote at length in order not to miss the important
connections between ideas.

> The popular school's job is to give more dignity to work by infus-
> ing it with thought, and not to make of the working man a thing
> divided into compartments, which sometimes works and sometimes
> thinks. Naturally, a peasant who is sowing has to be careful to cast
> the seed properly, and not to be thinking about lessons learned at
> school. But the object which engages our attention doesn't form the
> whole content of our thoughts. A happy young woman, expecting
> her first child, and busy sewing a layette, thinks about sewing it
> properly. But she never forgets for an instant the child she is car-
> rying inside her. At precisely the same moment, somewhere in a

prison workshop, a female convict is also sewing, thinking, too, about sewing properly, for she is afraid of being punished. One might imagine both women doing the same work at the same time, and having their attention absorbed by the same technical difficulties. And yet a whole gulf of difference lies between one occupation and the other. The whole social problem consists in making the workers pass from one to the other of these two occupational extremes.

What is required is that this world and the world beyond, in their double beauty, should be present and associated in the act of work, like the child to be born in the making of the layette. Such an association can be achieved by a mode of presenting thoughts which relates them directly to the movements and operations peculiar to each sort of work, by a process of assimilation sufficiently complete to enable them to penetrate into the very substance of the individual being, and by a habit impressed upon the mind and connecting these thoughts with the work movements.[3]

The difference in imagery, as compared with that in *Oppression and Liberty,* is striking from the first. Instead of judgment "preceding" movement, she now speaks of "infusing" work with thought ("de donner au travail davantage de dignité en y infusant de la pensée").[4] The phrase that follows, moreover, might have been specifically directed at that temporal separation of judgment and action: "not to make of the workingman a thing divided into compartments, which sometimes works and sometimes thinks."

A central point in the new account is that "the object which engages our attention doesn't form the whole content of our thoughts." That is a big departure; earlier, attention was focussed almost exclusively on the agent's immediate project with little attention to the context of his action. It was almost as though Simone Weil wanted to *construct* that context by bringing together a collection of autonomously acting individuals. But now that context is the starting point of the discussion. The question concerns the role of the *school* as an agency transmitting a *culture* against the background of which work may have some dignity. I am not suggesting that she was blind in her earlier writings to the importance of culture as something transmitted from one generation to another. It figures for instance in her discussion of language in *Lectures on Philosophy.* But, at least in the "Reflections Concerning the Causes of Liberty and Social Oppression," she does not sufficiently bring that discussion to bear on her account of "free action."

The Need for Roots discusses, amongst other things, what a culture would have to be like to reach individuals' lives and illuminate
them in the way suggested in my quotation. The book was written
in 1943 as a contribution to the post-war policy planning of General de Gaulle's French liberation movement in London. Her positive proposals, while often very striking and thought-provoking,
seem to me rather uneven in quality; and I do not intend to discuss
them in detail. Not surprisingly, more convincing than her positive
suggestions are her critical remarks about the poverty of contemporary culture as it existed when she wrote. (In putting it like that
I certainly do not mean to suggest that anything much has
improved in the relevant respects since her death.) But it will be
well to look at an example to see something of what she has in
mind.

She objects, then, to the way in which, in contemporary French
village life, no connection is made between religious teaching and
daily life.

> In just the same way as the sun and stars the school teacher talks
> about inhabit the textbooks and exercise books and have nothing to
> do with the sky, so the vine, the corn, the sheep to which reference
> is made in church on Sundays have nothing in common with the
> vine, the corn, and the sheep in the fields . . . to which every day
> one has to sacrifice a little part of one's life.[5]

Her point is not confined to religion. The glancing reference in
the passage above to the teaching of science has behind it a whole
array of writings on the impoverishment of culture involved in the
specialization and resultant fragmentation of contemporary science, making it more and more inaccessible to most people
(including scientists themselves outside their own particular spe-
cialty).[6] I think it is important to appreciate how rooted this criticism is in her epistemology. The concepts in terms of which scientific theories are, and must be, couched, theoretically rarefied
though they may be, find their application in the lives of those who
deploy them. There *is* no other possible point of application. The
following remark of Wittgenstein's is very similar in spirit:

> A curious analogy could be based on the fact that even the hugest
> telescope has to have an eyepiece no larger than the human eye.[7]

This remark at the same time links up with Wittgenstein's discussions of solipsism *and* is very reminiscent of some of those reflections of Simone Weil's on that subject to which I drew attention

in Chapter 11. I mention these analogies not in the interest of some half-baked "history of ideas," but to suggest the close connections between these issues belonging to the critique of culture and quite central problems in metaphysics and the theory of knowledge. I believe that neither Simone Weil's nor Wittgenstein's thinking can be properly appreciated if such connections are not noticed.

I said that the application of concepts is in the lives of those who deploy them. The nature of that application will then depend very much on the quality of the lives in question; that is to say, the kinds of interconnection between different realms of experience that are available will depend on that. The more fragmented culture becomes, the fewer resonances will be heard in the theories of scientists, and the less culturally significant science will have become.[8] – That of course if a "value judgment": it does not deny that such a science may have overwhelming *effects* on culture and society. The important point to appreciate in all this, and one that runs through Simone Weil's writing on the subject, is that the "internal" health and vigour of science cannot be separated from its role in the culture to which it belongs. So it would be a misunderstanding for a scientist to say that these questions have nothing to do with him or her as a scientist and have to do solely with pedagogy and politics.

It should be obvious from earlier chapters, especially 10 and 11, that when Simone Weil emphasizes the importance of *beauty* in her remarks on the relation between thought and action in *The Need for Roots* she is not merely expressing a predilection for aesthetic values.

> The aesthetes' point of view is sacrilegious, not only in matters of religion but even in those of art. It consists in amusing oneself with beauty by handling it and looking at it.[9]

The passage goes on to speak of beauty as a "food." I think this is only apparently inconsistent with her emphasis elsewhere, which I shall discuss shortly, on the distinction between the responses to something as beautiful and as something to be "eaten." In those contexts she is contrasting the acknowledgement of beauty with the urge to appropriate and dominate: the beauty of something only emerges in so far as such an urge is inhibited. Here, however, she is speaking of the general cultural and spiritual importance of beauty, *given* the responses which enable it to appear to us in the first place. The response to beauty is, in her view, the pivot around which turns any understanding of "the order of the world." I want to consider this further.

In the course of some reflections on the notion of creation, in connection with Plato's *Timaeus,* she remarks, like Hume, that the world does not exhibit the kind of "finality" that would justify comparing it to an artifact constructed for a purpose.[10] Indeed, it is obviously *not* like that ("Il est même manifeste qu'il n'est pas ainsi"). It does however exhibit finality in a different sense, of a sort which suggests a comparison with a work of art. The point is not to compare just "the act of creation," but the relation to God of the world as we experience it in its temporal flow ("Providence"), with "l'inspiration artistique." In a work of art there is finality without any representable end.

> In one sense the end is nothing but the ensemble of means employed; in another sense the end is something completely transcendent. It is exactly the same with the universe and the course of the universe, the end of which is absolutely (*éminemment*) transcendent and not representable.

This conception is elaborated in a splendid section of *Waiting for God,* "Love of the Order of the World."[11]

> A beautiful thing involves no good except itself, in its totality, as it appears to us. We are drawn toward it without knowing what to ask of it. It offers us its own existence. We do not desire anything else, we possess it, and yet we still desire something. We do not in the least know what it is. We want to get behind beauty, but it is only a surface. It is like a mirror that sends us back our own desire for goodness. It is a sphinx, an enigma, a mystery which is painfully tantalizing. We should like to feed upon it but it is merely something to look at; it appears only from a certain distance.

Beauty constitutes the *only* finality known to us, she argues, because everything else is an end only relatively. Beauty must therefore be present in all human pursuits, in that it "sheds a lustre upon them which colours them with finality." Her point, here, I think, is that the acts by which we try to obtain particular objects would have the character of mere reflexes if they did not form a sort of teleological system, in which the worthwhileness of doing something is measured against its cost to us.[12] This is possible, however, only if some ends are seen as having a value which they do not derive from their relation to something else. It is the things that we regard in that way that have genuine "finality." In the case of a miser like Molière's Harpagon "all the beauty of the world is enshrined in gold." For most people the finality of gold is *luxury,* which, for those who seek it, "provides surroundings through which they can feel in a vague fashion that the universe is beautiful." It is the hope of "forcing a certain circle into a pattern suggestive of universal beauty" that makes *power* attractive; the circle is a limited one "but the hope of increasing it indefinitely may often be present," and this unsatisfied appetite "is due precisely to a desire for contact with universal beauty, even though the circle we are organizing is not the universe." To see anything as beautiful is always to see it in its relation to the order of the universe; that is why beauty appears only to the attitude of *contemplation:* the universe is not something that can be manipulated or consumed.

That last remark is a conceptual, or grammatical, one. It makes no sense to speak of "manipulating" or "consuming" the universe – and if you think that the ability to blow up this planet disproves that, you should think again! It amounts to much the same to say that the universe cannot be an instrument to any further end. Because, therefore, the finality of beauty is precisely final in that sense, the universe may be thought of as peculiarly the seat of beauty. This is another way of expressing the idea that art may present us things *sub specie aeternitatis.* As Wittgenstein remarked in a notebook: "A work of art forces us – as one might say – to see it in the right perspective but in the absence of art it is just a fragment of nature like any other"; and in the same passage and the same spirit he speaks of "seeing [one's] life as a work of art created by God and, as such, it is certainly worth contemplating, as is every life and everything whatever."[13] Putting the matter in this way brings out the connection between this conception of beauty and the problem Simone Weil raised at the end of "Essai sur la notion de lecture" concerning the possibility of distinguishing some actions as having greater value than others and some readings as more correct than others; and in fact she does in that place explicitly connect that question with the notion of beauty:

> Furthermore, the problem of value, posed in terms of this concept of reading, is concerned with truth, and beauty, as well as with good, without its being possible to separate them.[14]

Our inclination to ascribe to art the power to show us something *sub specie aeternitatis* shows that there are indeed important connections between our idea of beauty and that of "the universe." Different people will, of course, have their own preferred examples: for me some of the paintings of Rembrandt, with their representation of age and aging, are peculiarly moving cases. I think here particularly of his wonderful series of self-portraits – seen especially from the perspective of the late one in the Frick Collection in New York; the way in which here the life of a human being can be seen as having an eternal significance, not in spite of, but with and *through* its temporal vulnerabilities, seems to me to lie very close to what Simone Weil is talking about.

There is, however, a strain in her intellectual character (which, if not due to, is certainly fostered by the influence of certain ideas of Plato's) which leads her into exaggeration and distortion, here and elsewhere. For instance:

> With the exception of God, nothing short of the universe as a whole can with complete accuracy *(avec une entière propriété de termes)* be called beautiful. All that is in the universe and is less than the universe can only be called beautiful if we extend the word beyond its strict limits *(au-delà de sa signification rigoureuse)* and apply it to things which share indirectly in beauty, things which are imitations of it.[15]

Use of expressions like "complete accuracy" and "beyond its strict limits" is of course whistling in the dark. She is on firmer ground when she notes that in some cases certain "seductive factors" may "cause the things in which they are present to be called beautiful through lack of discernment." That is to say, we may sometimes use the word in such a way as to show that we are not observing distinctions which are important to what we are trying to say; and the word "beautiful," just because its uses are so diverse, may lend itself peculiarly well to fuzzy thinking and lack of discernment. But the diagnosis implied in that way of putting the matter is antithetical to the idea that there is in fact some "strict" sense of the term from which we are constantly deviating. The implied *remedy* for this situation is also something different, namely to apply a more varied and discriminatory vocabulary in order to express these differences, rather than to try to evaluate everything against some single (and in fact non-existent) standard. Commitment to such a standard, moreover, is not necessary to what lies at the heart of Simone Weil's discussion here.

There are two connected points that do lie at the heart of her discussion. The first is that something which may with some justice be called "a reaction to beauty" is particularly important for the way we form concepts of things as belonging to an order of nature. The second is that the conception of beauty involved here is one which provides us with a sort of criterion through which we may distinguish more and less adequate, or correct, readings of situations. Here the words "adequate" and "correct" have their sense in the context of a particular outlook, one that may be called a religious outlook. I think that much of what she says about these things does not stand or fall with her claims about "true" beauty as being all of a piece. Consider again the passage:

> We want to get behind beauty, but it is only a surface. It is like a mirror that sends us back our own desire for goodness. It is a sphinx, an enigma, a mystery which is painfully tantalizing. We should like to feed upon it but it is merely something to look at, it appears only from a certain distance.

The phrase "a mirror that sends us back our own desire for goodness" deserves to be taken seriously. As we have already seen, Simone Weil distinguishes "the desire for goodness" from desires for particular objects: the latter depend on our having particular needs, and when these are satisfied, the object is no longer desired. The desire for goodness, on the other hand, may be said to provide us with a standard against which the satisfaction of these particular needs can be judged. The discussion of *Volpone* provides an example: the husband's desire for riches, and the action it leads to, are judged against the standard of the good embodied in his deeper relations with his wife: a good which does *not* derive from anything he expects to get from her but from his perception of what she is. His despair is at his defilement of what she is. His desire for good is expressed here in his wish *not* to do anything that would interfere with the purity of her nature, however much doing so would help him towards his particular objectives.

In general, what Simone Weil understands by "the desire for good" can be thought of as wanting to *refrain* from interfering with whatever has value of its own. This is what is "reflected back" by whatever it is we see beauty in. And that is evident from her conception of this particular response to beauty: one which necessarily implies looking at the object "from a certain distance," that is which is antithetical to trying to *appropriate* it.

Let us now ask the Kantian question: how is it *possible* for objects to present themselves to us in this way? An answer is suggested by a remark from "Classical Science and After" that I have already quoted in a different connection:

> We are ruled by a double law: an obvious indifference and a mysterious complicity, as regards the good, on the part of the matter which composes the world; it is because it reminds us of this double law that the spectacle of beauty pierces the heart.[16]

This complicity, it will be remembered, resides in the fact that human beings, those very beings who aspire to the good, are *material* beings. One's spiritual life does not inhere in an indestructible something quite distinct from one's material nature; no, it is an aspect of that material nature. In this indeed is to be found the source – or at least one of the sources – of the "incommensurabilities" discussed in Chapter 12. (It might be said to be Descartes's unwillingness to accept such incommensurabilities that led him to his dualism; and Spinoza's refusal to acknowledge them that led him to his monism.) Beauty itself is the locus of one such incommensurability: between fragility and a reality which can be called eternal. This is exemplified by the ephemerality of the blossom on the trees, the beauty of which *depends* on its being there for not much more than a moment, but which is also one of those things which, when seen in certain circumstances, may change one's whole conception of the universe. It is, I believe, central to Simone Weil's thinking that the world can present itself to us like this only because we too, being material elements in the natural order, share that fragility. The very conception of such a natural order is based on the image of "objects juxtapositioned in space and changing from moment to moment": which itself may be taken as an image of fragility. But we are also the beings who feel ourselves called "to dwell in eternity, to embrace and dominate time, to grasp the whole extended universe at all its points at once."[17] What is more, this vocation is not in despite of our materiality: we are not to fulfil it as free-floating intelligences, but precisely *through* the ability to intervene in natural processes (for instance in experimentation) in ways only conceivable for beings themselves having a material nature.[18] This is one aspect of what we are to understand by matter's "mysterious complicity as regards the good."

We saw earlier that it is also precisely this materiality, this rootedness in a particular corner, that stands in the way of our getting a clear view of the order of nature and of our own place within it.

It is the response to beauty that leads us out of the corner. How does it do this? On the one hand, the fact that my position in the order of nature is the centre from which I see everything creates the impression that my position *is* the centre of the natural order. This position of mine, furthermore, is predominantly the starting point of various projects. Accordingly, the initial understanding that I reach of my surroundings amounts to no more than seeing how those surroundings relate to my projects. But responses to beauty are of quite a different sort and are potentially opposed to my pursuit of projects, in that they involve treating objects not as obstacles to be overcome but as things whose own peculiar reality and value is to be acknowledged, contemplated, and respected. Often, I shall only be able to regard them in this way by giving up favourite projects of my own. An example of this would be giving up the project of building a motorway through an unspoilt natural landscape. The example shows how bitter such a conflict may be.

Simone Weil's central thought is that to respond in this way is already to take a step outside my own limited and limiting perspective. It involves seeing something as having a being and reality independent of my projects; more, it involves measuring the significance of my own projects against something else. It introduces, we might say, the conception of an equilibrium between things: the conception of things co-existing in a relationship such that the nature of none of the elements is violated. Most important of all, it introduces the conception of an equilibrium between *myself* and other things. It involves the thought of my nature as an essentially limited one, not just in the sense that there are certain things that I cannot as a matter of fact achieve, but in the sense rather that my own nature requires an equilibrium between myself and other things, that is that I violate my own nature in violating the nature of something else. That thought is prefigured in, and made possible by, the response to beauty: the response of *not wanting to change* the object of my response. It is the only way I can come by the conception of something as having independent reality: without it things are real only relative to my projects. Forming the concept of something other than myself as having reality is recognizing the limited nature of my own reality. The horror at what he has done of the husband in *Volpone* shows how it is possible for my violation of something precious to be at the same time a violation of myself.

I noted earlier that Simone Weil recognizes that, although some response to beauty is necessary if activities are to have any genuine "finality," people do differ considerably concerning *what* plays this role in their lives. Thus for Harpagon beauty, and hence finality, lies in gold; for others it lies in power. For many it is luxury "which provides surroundings through which they can feel in a vague fashion that the universe is beautiful"; whereas for a few, like Saint Francis, only poverty makes this possible.

> Either way would be equally legitimate if in each case the beauty of the world were experienced in an equally direct, pure and full manner; but happily God willed that it should not be so. Poverty has a privilege. That is a dispensation of Providence without which the love of the beauty of the world might easily come into conflict with the love of our neighbour.[19]

The foregoing discussion may help to show why there should be this distinction. Love of luxury is self-centred in the sense that it involves amassing the means to protect oneself against the ravages of the environment; thus, of its nature, it is based on a radical *distinction* between the value of one's own needs and desires and that of other things. That is why it may "easily come into conflict with the love of our neighbour." Commitment to a life of poverty, on the other hand, is, one might say, the very image of self-abnegation: of refraining from measuring the value of things by reference to one's own desires. – This point is not affected, I think, by the reflection that there may be pathological forms of the love of poverty, as of other human dispositions, in which it *does* constitute a disguised form of self-assertion. Zoé Oldenbourg's representation of Saint Dominick is an interesting case of this.[20] Dominick was tireless in his mission to the heretics, preaching summer and winter on the road and in villages, living on bread and water, sleeping on the bare earth, "making people marvel at his endurance and the fiery authority of his words." But after a few years he became impatient for results and, according to Étienne de Salagnac, a member of the order which he founded, dramatically changed his tone with these words:

> For several years now I have spoken words of peace to you. I have preached to you; I have besought you with tears. But as the common saying goes in Spain, Where a blessing fails, a good thick stick will succeed. Now we shall rouse princes and prelates against you; and they, alas, will in their turn assemble whole nations and peoples, and a mighty number will perish by the sword. Towers will fall, and

walls be razed to the ground, and you will all of you be reduced to servitude. Thus force will prevail where gentle persuasion has failed to do so.

As we know, Saint Dominick was not exaggerating.

The example brings out another important point, which Simone Weil frequently comes back to. Self-assertion is by no means always founded in desires and projects which are selfish or self-regarding. Indeed, perhaps it is at its most terrible in cases where the ends in view are fired by cosmic enthusiasm.

"Essai sur la notion de lecture" speaks of an inseparable connection between truth, beauty, and good. This connection has played a large role in the foregoing discussion. There is a passage in the notebooks which identifies the connecting thread as the attitude of "not wanting to change," and relates this to the ideal of an undistorted reading as one in which we do not read "what we fear or what we desire."

> The beautiful: that which we do not want to change. The good: not to want to change it, in fact (non-intervention). The true: not to want to change it in one's mind (by means of illusion).[21]

In the case of beauty, "not wanting to change it" means, predominantly, not wanting to "eat" it,[22] which can be taken as a metaphor for any sort of *appropriation* which violates the nature of the object appropriated. We have to remember, of course, that there is more than one way of "appropriating" something or someone, and more than one way in which something's or someone's nature can be violated, some less obvious than others.

In the case of truth, "not wanting to change" has to do with matters like not wanting to doctor the evidence, overlook inconvenient avenues of inquiry, and so on; that is, wanting to read the situation *honestly*, however distressing that may be. Most of the work in this formulation is of course done by the word "honestly," which at once introduces the conception of the *good*. And that surely must be right. The concept of truth, considered as the standard according to which an inquiry or a pronouncement is to be judged, as something which many have been prepared to suffer and die for, would make no sense unless it were tied to a concept like honesty. Someone who said he or she was willing to die for the truth, understood solely in the terms used to present it in western analytical philosophical theories, would strike most people as just crazy, rather than as admirable: and rightly so. I do not mean

by this that the matters dwelt on in such theories have no connection with what Simone Weil is talking about here; but that this cannot be elucidated solely in such terms. We cannot do without a
conception of the "intellectual *virtues*" which are involved in such
remarks of hers as: "not to read what we fear or what we desire";
"not to read the solution in the figure, but the difficulties?"; "to
read in outward aspects something which another person, differently situated, differently affected, is able to read – by making the
same effort."

The attitude Simone Weil emphasizes in what she says about
truth is that of what she calls "attention," and it is not difficult to
see an analogy between this and the attitude appropriate to
beauty. This analogy sometimes leads her to speak of beauty as a
criterion of truth. Perhaps that is a dangerous way to express what
she is saying, since it sounds as though what were in question is
something like accepting a theory on account of its aesthetic ele-
gance. I think her most important claims are, first, that the attitude of attention is so closely analogous to the response to beauty
that they might almost be regarded as different forms of the same
thing and, second, that one who has such an attitude of attention
will find beauty in what inquiry reveals *simply by reason of its truth*
as revealed to attention. This last claim should not be regarded as
an empirical hypothesis, but rather as a sort of conceptual determination. That is, such a person's finding this sort of beauty in
what inquiry reveals will be a criterion of the inquiry's *being an
honest one,* or of its being genuinely and wholeheartedly oriented
towards the truth.

How to apply the notion of "not wanting to change" in the case
of the good is more difficult, as is signalled by the hesitant tone of
the remark "The good – not to want to change what?"[23] The difficulty springs from the fact that good has a much closer connection with action than have truth and beauty. And to act is to
change something. And Simone Weil certainly did *not* want to say
that devotion to the good committed one to not wanting to change
anything. The answer which she gives to her own question ("not to
want to change what?") is:

> My place, my importance in the world, limited by my body and
> by the existence of other souls, my equals.
>   To return a deposit?
>   To expose oneself to death? . . .

Not to want to change. Desire: always to arrest or hasten the flow of time.

Music – time that one wants neither to arrest nor hasten.

Necessity.

To accept to be subjected to necessity and to act only by handling it. War. *Gîta.*

To fight while thinking equally of defeat or victory?

Balance. Sun.

To accept to suffer within Time and to act within Time – indirectly.

He who appropriates to himself a deposit wishes that this deposit were not a deposit. He has received it as such. He could not have received it otherwise, for it would not have been given to him.

One man reads therein a deposit, another man does not. We must reach a unity in the reading thereof.

To read in outward aspects something which another person, differently situated, differently affected, is able to read – by making the same effort.[24]

The passage throws light on the connection between the good and both the beautiful (in the reference to music) and the true (in the remarks about the deposit). As long as one sees everything from the point of view of one's own projects, time is (as it is commonly called) "the enemy." Music shows us that it is possible to regard time differently. In a war one naturally aims at victory; but whether time will bring victory or not cannot be solely a matter of one's own efforts (which is *of course* not to deny that one's own efforts may well be all-important); nor, what is just as important and more difficult to acknowledge, can one know whether time will show one's victory to have been a good. One will be acting in accordance with necessity, and accepting one's own position in time, if one fights "while thinking equally of defeat or victory" – of course the application of that phrase has to be properly understood. Again, if I contemplate misappropriating a deposit that has been entrusted to me I am failing or refusing to recognize the temporal conditions defining my present possession of the money: the past conditions under which it came into my hands and the resulting future conditions concerning my obligation to return it. These conditions define the necessity, the desire to respect which constitutes what Simone Weil means by the desire for good: it is those necessities that one does not wish to change. And this amounts to much the same as not wanting to change "my own importance in the world," which is "limited by other souls, my equals."

14

JUSTICE

One outcome of the discussion in Chapter 12 was that justice is to be considered not just as a moral or social ideal to be striven for, but as a point of view from which alone a certain sort of understanding of human life is possible: as an epistemological concept, therefore. One needs to be careful in saying this, however. The understanding that is in question is not independent of one's moral, social, religious viewpoint: not one therefore which can be used as a foundation for such a viewpoint. It is rather a mode of understanding that presupposes the viewpoint in question. It is not easy to be clear about these relationships and as we shall see, particularly in the next chapter, Simone Weil does not always speak with the same voice about them.

The context and the terms in which the concept of justice has so far been introduced, in "The *Iliad* or the Poem of Force" for example, show that what Simone Weil understands by it is not something that can be taken for granted; that is to say, it is not clear on the surface what the relation is between her use of the term and the uses to which we are most accustomed in discussions of moral, social, and political issues. Fortunately, she has left an essay, and one of her most impressive, which deals with just this issue: "La personne et le sacré," or "Human Personality."

It is at once clear from this essay that the intellectual configuration which mainly characterizes our present time will make it peculiarly difficult to come to terms with her position. The text that is generally regarded as canonical in this configuration is John Rawls's *A Theory of Justice*. This book is indeed now frequently cited as the main evidence of "the revival of political philosophy" in the twentieth century. The conception of justice that Rawls explores and develops, the conception of a position regarded as the outcome of a negotiated compromise between rational agents each of whom is thought of as pursuing his or her own interests, belongs to the category of notions which Simone Weil characterizes as follows. They

> are themselves entirely alien to the supernatural but nevertheless a little superior to brute force. All of them relate to the behaviour of the collective animal, to use Plato's language, while it exhibits a few traces of the training imposed on it by the supernatural working of grace. If they are not continually revived by a renewal of this working, if they are merely survivals of it, they become necessarily subject to the animal's caprice.[1]

The difficulty is not just that she is starting from a point of view which itself constitutes a criticism of an enterprise like Rawls's, but that the terms of the criticism (reference to the "supernatural") can hardly make any sense to one committed to such an enterprise. This creates a problem about how precisely Simone Weil's discussion is to be thought of as relating to concerns like those of Rawls. But the problem arises not just in relation to one who accepts Rawls's particular "theory": it concerns the whole language in which questions about justice are commonly raised, at least in the second half of the twentieth century: the language of "rights." Rawls's enterprise uses this language, or at least deals in the conceptions that it expresses; Simone Weil challenges it. According to her it is a language entirely alien to the conception of justice. It expresses "the shrill nagging of claims and counter-claims" and evokes a spirit of contention.

> To place the notion of rights at the centre of social conflicts is to inhibit any possible impulse of charity on both sides.
>   Relying almost exclusively on this notion, it becomes impossible to keep one's eyes on the real problem. If someone tries to browbeat a farmer to sell his eggs at a moderate price, the farmer can say: "I have the right to keep my eggs if I don't get a good enough price." But if a young girl is being forced into a brothel she will not talk about her rights. In such a situation the word would sound ludicrously inadequate.
>   Thus it is that the social drama, which corresponds to the latter situation, is falsely assimilated, by the use of the word "rights," to the former one.[2]

As is often the case with Simone Weil's most striking images, this one (of a young girl being forced into a brothel) is intended not

just as an image to be struck by, but as an analogy seriously to be
reflected on. The young girl is not merely getting a raw deal; her
whole nature is being violated. And this is the case too, so it is
being argued, with workers forced to work in the conditions of a
contemporary production line, conditions which preclude any
possibility of work's constituting (as sexual love too may, though
she does not say this here) "a certain contact with the reality, the
truth and the beauty of this universe and with the eternal wisdom
which is the order of it."[3] Discussions of workers' rights usually
concentrate on questions of wages. This is as though

> the devil were bargaining for the soul of some poor wretch and
> someone, moved by pity, should step in and say to the devil: "It is
> a shame for you to bid so low; the commodity is worth at least twice
> as much."

Although, as we see, she expresses herself strongly about the
language of rights, it is important to realize that she is not rejecting it as always inappropriate. I think her discussion does not even
rule out the possibility that injustice may, in some cases, actually
take the form of a violation of somebody's rights. That is not the
same as saying, though, that this is what the injustice *consists in,*
even in such cases. This is shown by the intelligibility of the question: is it just that so-and-so's rights should be enforced in these
circumstances?[4] I think that this sort of relation between questions
about justice and questions about rights is part of what is being
pointed to when she says, in a sentence I have already quoted, that
the notion of rights is one of those "which are themselves entirely
alien to the supernatural but nevertheless a little superior to brute
force." The *inspiration* for a demand for rights may well be a concern for justice; it may be that in some circumstances to struggle
for rights is the best way of struggling for justice. But that does
not mean that the struggle for justice is the same as the struggle
for rights; the one struggle may be successful and the other not –
maybe that is even more often than not the outcome. And if the
distinction is forgotten, there is the danger that a concern for
rights will take one farther and farther away from justice; or that
the quest for justice will be entirely submerged.

There are many hints in this essay that it is not so much the
particular words that are used that are important as the spirit
underlying what is said. This, for instance, is one dimension of her

insistence that the cry of one who believes that he or she is being harmed – in a sense of "harm" that implies injustice – is a "silent" cry. This cannot mean that it is a cry for which there is no possible expression; and that, not merely because it would be nonsense in itself, but because Simone Weil does herself give examples: such as the cry of Christ on the Cross, "My God, my God, why hast thou forsaken me?" I think we must take her to mean not merely that the cry may emanate from somebody who is incapable of expressing it in words, but that, even where words are used, they do not by themselves determine "what is being said" or guarantee that what *is* being said will be understood. None of this, of course, implies that it is unimportant to try to find the most appropriate words in which to express such things. The fact that education does not supply those most in need of it with the linguistic resources to express their sense of injustice is itself a potent source of injustice.

All the same, in order properly to discern the protest of someone who is being violated it is not enough to be familiar with the words, if any, that are being uttered. Of course, that much can be said not merely of protests at injustice but of any utterances whatever: they express, and are understood to express, a particular thought only in certain contexts. But there are special obstacles *in the soul of the reader* in the way of recognizing protests at real injustice. "Attention" is necessary; and the peculiar difficulty of my attending to someone in such a situation is that it requires me to understand that we are both equal members of a natural order which can at any time bring about such a violation of whoever it may be, including myself. That is, I cannot understand the other's affliction from the point of view of my own privileged position; I have rather to understand *myself* from the standpoint of *the other's* affliction, to understand that my privileged position is not part of my essential nature, but an accident of fate.

> To acknowledge the reality of affliction means saying to oneself: "I may lose at any moment, through the play of circumstances over which I have no control, anything whatsoever that I possess, including things that are so intimately mine that I consider them as myself. There is nothing that I might not lose. It could happen at any moment that what I am might be abolished and replaced by anything whatsoever of the filthiest and most contemptible sort."[5]

It may be easy enough to express verbal assent to this; it is not so easy actually to think it.

The "silence" of the protest at injustice, then, consists in large part in the fact that there is probably no one to hear it. The discussion of my preceding chapter should help to show the importance of the perception of beauty in overcoming this deafness. Beauty too

> has no language; she does not speak; she says nothing. But she has a voice to cry out. She cries out and points to truth and justice who are dumb, like a dog who barks to bring people to his master lying unconscious in the snow.[6]

In this lies much of the cultural and spiritual importance of those greatest works of art and literature in which (as in *The Iliad*) the beauty of affliction, when seen from the point of view of justice, is displayed. (Needless to say, "beauty" in this context means something as far removed as may be from prettification.)

Simone Weil says that "there is certainly injustice" *whenever* the cry "Why am I being hurt?" "arises from the depth of a human heart":

> For if, as often happens, it is only the result of a misunderstanding, then the injustice consists in the inadequacy of the explanation.[7]

I think there is an important issue concealed by that last remark about which I shall try to say something.

The underlying assumption is surely that which also underlies much of Socrates' arguments against Polus in Plato's *Gorgias:* namely that whatever is done justly to a person cannot *harm* that person. Indeed, at one point Simone Weil *characterizes* justice as "seeing that no harm is done to men."[8] It appears, then, from the quoted remark that it is not merely necessary that what is done to a person (for example, but only for example, by way of punishment) should *be* just; it must also be *understood* by him to be just. The thought is that which the common saying tries to express: that justice must not only be done, but must be seen to be done. Nevertheless that saying does not quite succeed in capturing the underlying thought; neither does my own formulation so far; and neither I think does the formulation I have quoted from "Human Personality": "If [. . .] it is only the result of a misunderstanding, then the injustice consists in the inadequacy of the explanation." There is a nagging logical worry about all these formulations: namely that they first talk as though there were a just course of action to be determined, which *then* has to be understood as such by the parties affected by it, and that until they *do* understand this, the course of action is not just at all. So the question is raised: what then *is* it that the affected parties have to understand, if it does not exist until they do indeed understand it?

This may seem to be merely a sophistical piece of logic-chopping; but I think there is more to it than that.

I believe we should not think of justice in this connection as a state of affairs which could in principle be worked out independent of a common understanding arrived at in a certain way by the affected parties. For this reason I think it is misleading for Simone Weil to speak of "the inadequacy of the explanation" as what constitutes the injustice in the cases she has in mind. "Explanation" (*l'explication*) suggests a gap between what a situation requires and what it is understood to require which must not be allowed to open up. Common understanding, because it is an integral part of what justice consists in, cannot be arrived at through instruction in known truths. It must be the result of a discussion (a "dialectical" outcome) within which all parties must be prepared to adjust their views in the light of what is said by the others.

In putting the matter in this way I have deliberately suggested an important motivation for contractarian conceptions of justice such as that of Rawls. The point of such conceptions is of course precisely to insist that justice is essentially an outcome *negotiated* by the affected parties. That sounds close to the conception of justice as a "dialectical outcome" of communication between the parties, as I just expressed Simone Weil's conception. Now I have already, at the beginning of this chapter, insisted on the radical opposition between Simone Weil's view and one like that of Rawls. I must now consider more carefully what that opposition consists in.

I must first note an important difference between their procedures. Rawls's "contract" is an entirely abstract construction, a theoretical device. Normally the point of saying that a common arrangement must be arrived at by "negotiation" is that one must wait on the result of the negotiation in order to know what the arrangement is going to be. One may, of course, make more or less well-founded and shrewd predictions about the likely outcome, but such predictions must await verification or falsification by events. There is room for surprises. Rawls, however, does not say: put the interested parties together, set suitable limits to the kinds of consideration to be deemed relevant to the negotiation, and then retire to see what happens. He *calculates* the result. In

other words the outcome is not a genuinely negotiated one at all:
the idea of a "negotiation" is nothing more than a logical device
for presenting a certain form of argument, the conclusion of
which can be appraised by anyone. This is of course connected
with the fact that Rawls's contracting parties are not human beings
at all, but rational constructions. And the notion of "reason" or
"rationality" that is deployed is a purely *a priori* one: not derived
from any serious examination of how such terms actually are used.

It is interesting and instructive to compare Rawls's depiction of
his "contract" with the way in which Simone Weil argues in "The
Legitimacy of the Provisional Government." The essay develops
suggestions concerning how General de Gaulle, at the time still in
exile in London, might conduct himself after the liberation of
France, in order to breathe a spirit of legitimacy into the government of the country. Legitimacy, she notes, "is not a primitive
notion. It is derived from justice."[9] In fact, it is clear that she
regards it as a particular application of the notion of justice to a
situation involving the exercise of political power: and this is, of
course, the very application of the notion in which Rawls is most
interested.

She is concerned in this essay with a fundamental constitutional
question. Although the discussion concerns the peculiar position
of de Gaulle in relation to the government of France, her interest
goes far beyond that to the question of what would be required
for France to evolve a spirit of legitimacy in government which
would survive him. What, that is to say, is necessary for the conception of justice to take proper root in this particular historical
situation? Rawls, of course, is not, at least not ostensibly, concerned with a question thus historically conditioned. And this
might be thought to vitiate the comparison. But I think that would
be a mistaken conclusion. It is clear from the way in which Simone
Weil argues, both in this essay and elsewhere (for instance in *The
Need for Roots*), that she would regard an investigation into justice
as necessarily bounded in this historical way. Legitimacy (and *a
fortiori* justice) cannot be defined through "forms of government."

> A king can be legitimate. So can a parliamentary head of govern-
> ment. A king can be illegitimate; so can a parliamentary head of
> government, no matter how regular the forms which have been
> observed.

Legitimacy involves a certain trust on the part of the people
towards their rulers and this trust needs forms of expression, a

language. Particular political institutions, such as democratic elections, constitute such a language. Good faith and trust have to be expressed in the particular historically conditioned language that happens to be available. In one way what is expressed is the important thing; but that does not mean that the forms of expression that are available in a given situation are irrelevant to the question of justice and legitimacy. Political institutions

> are analogous to love letters, exchanges of rings, and other tokens between lovers. In some circles a woman would not consider herself truly married if she did not wear a gold ring. Of course the conjugal bond does not consist in the ring. It is all the same needful for women who feel like this to wear a ring.[10]

If then the notion of democracy is one of the central symbols in political thinking at a particular time, a just equilibrium will have to be one that takes democratic forms. At another moment in history, on the other hand, democracy might have nothing to do with, or even be antithetical to, justice.

> The forms and the expressions of consent vary greatly in different traditions and milieux. Thus a society of men much freer than we are can, if it is very different from us, appear despotic to us in our ignorance. We do not realize that outside the realm of words there are differences of language and possibilities of misinterpretation.[11]

This insistence on historical relativity is entirely alien to Rawls's way of thinking.

> Democratic thought contains a serious error – it confuses consent with a certain form of consent, which is not the only one and which can easily, like any form, be mere form.[12]

On the other hand she also speaks of "a sort of *objective* legitimacy" (the emphasis is mine) recognized by the declarations in de Gaulle's favour which took place in occupied France. Such declarations, she insists, were not the *source* of that legitimacy. She compares the situation to that in which a child of deported parents is taken in and lovingly cared for by someone, without protest from the family's relations or friends: this is enough to make it "just that this man should have the provisional guardianship of the child."[13] The important feature of the comparison is that while justice here is only to be understood in terms of the particular historical circumstances, it is not simply created by the say-so of the protagonists. This point, I believe, is closely connected with Simone Weil's emphasis on the "impersonal," a notion which plays a particularly large part in the argument of "Human Personality."

She calls the cry of the afflicted: "Why am I being hurt?" impersonal. This distinguishes it from demands for rights which belong to the domain of "claims and counter-claims," which are, that is to say, demands made by some persons against others. In negotiations based on the assertion of rights one attempts to get the best possible deal for oneself, given that each of the others is attempting the same. "For oneself" in this context *means:* in contrast with and in (at least potential) opposition to others. The terrain I am here describing obviously has a great deal in common with the scene of Rawls's original contract. The question which all the participants in this contract want to have satisfactorily answered is "Why has somebody else got more than I have?" This is indeed the question to which a large part of *A Theory of Justice* is devoted to providing an answer. Simone Weil does not *reject* this question: where it is being pressed, where people are upset by inequalities and think in terms of their rights, they will be distracted from justice. Such complaints therefore need to be "hushed"

> with the help of a code of justice, regular tribunals, and the police. Minds capable of solving problems of this kind can be formed in a law school.[14]

But the damping of such preoccupations does not get us to the heart of the problem.

The conceptions of justice developed respectively by Rawls and Simone Weil have in common that they essentially involve the understanding, and even the consent, of the affected parties. Justice is seen by both as essentially arising *out of* a sort of communication between the affected parties; it is not something to be first determined, then communicated *to* them. But on Rawls's account I consent to an arrangement because I see that it is the best bargain I can strike; that is, it is an arrangement I can reasonably expect others to consent to, and their consent is necessary to me *if* I am to get what I seek. But on Simone Weil's account I do not seek others' consent as a condition of getting something else; it is, on the contrary, the main thing I seek. So I attend to what others are saying, or in some other way expressing, not in order to assess my chances of realizing my own projects. I do not attend to them *for* anything at all; my attention is an expression of my attempt to understand – to understand both them and myself, because, for reasons we have already discussed, I cannot understand myself except through my understanding of others. Again, not that I try to understand them *in order* to understand myself; rather that the sort of understanding I am seeking precludes that distinction between understanding others and understanding myself. That is the sense in which what is in question is something *impersonal*.

One way in which Simone Weil's conception of justice shows its distance from normal ways of thinking about it is that she calls it "mad," which I suppose is about as far from neo-Kantian rationalism as one can get. She also calls it "supernatural." In one way both these ways of speaking make the same point; but the use of the word "supernatural" brings together important connections with other ideas, and raises problems, which I clearly cannot ignore.

Some of these problems are particularly pressing for the kind of account I have been trying to give of Simone Weil's thinking in this book. I have throughout emphasized a particular *philosophical* theme concerning what I have called concept formation. And at more than one point I have treated ideas which quite obviously have a strong religious significance for her in a determinedly "secular" way. This has been, in a way, all the more absurd in that the frequently striking and beautiful character of these ideas is entirely due to the intensely religious attitude to the world which they express.

I freely admit the perversity of this procedure. It is justified only to the extent that I have succeeded in drawing attention to a series of links between different aspects of Simone Weil's thinking which are not usually noticed; and to the extent to which these links are interesting in themselves. There is also perhaps some interest precisely in the way this procedure brings to a head certain difficulties about the distinction and relation between philosophical and religious reflection. These difficulties go beyond the interpretation of any one particular writer.

In addition to the general difficulties raised by my interpretive procedure, the specific *content* of my interpretation generates rather special problems concerning Simone Weil's use of the term "supernatural." But I think these *are* genuine difficulties which anyone who wants to think seriously about her work should face.

I have taken as my starting point the way in which Simone Weil came to "the materialist point of view" of *Lectures on Philosophy*.

In this connection I quoted, in Chapter 4, a passage from her early notebook in which she wrote

> The behaviourist psychology is the only good one, on the express understanding that one does not believe it. Everything that can be thought about the human condition is expressible in terms of behaviour – even including freedom [*in the margin:* even free thought (problems), or the most generous feelings (Platonic love . . .). Try to describe all these things without ever mentioning soul, spirit, etc.] The only thing that escapes is that which, since it is thinking, cannot be thought.[15]

That of course is a programme of problems rather than a summary of solutions. Undoubtedly, too, her conception of what the problems were changed as the years passed, one of the chief sources of change being precisely the growing importance of the concept of the supernatural in her thinking. But the continuity in her way of thinking about the problems is also not to be missed; it is strikingly shown, for instance, in the following passage from her New York notebook of 1942:

> Religion and behaviourism.
> The supernatural is the difference between human and animal behaviour.
> This difference is something infinitely small.
> The pomegranate seed or grain of mustard.
> (Clement of Alexandria: the women of Athens believed the pomegranate came from the blood of Dionysus.)[16]

I think we should resist the temptation to ask questions here about the difference between human and *animal* behaviour. Simone Weil certainly does not explore this alleged difference at all seriously, and we do not need to do so either. What is important is the feature of *human* behaviour to which she is drawing attention. There is no doubt in my mind that its root is "that interval of hesitation, wherein lies all our consideration for our brothers in humanity," referred to in the essay on *The Iliad,* on which I have already placed so much emphasis; and also the closely related response to the beauty of the world, which involves a similar "interval of hesitation" in the execution of our projects. What I have not so far discussed is the assimilation of these to the New Testament "grain of mustard," or the Greek "pomegranate seed," which puts it into the dimension of the supernatural. On the basis of what I have so far said there seems little justification for speaking in this way. Such responses may indeed be surprising, and in particular surprisingly at odds with other tendencies in human beings towards the most efficient possible realization of their projects. But if they do exist in human behaviour, they are just as much a feature of human nature, and therefore just as natural, as all the rest. After all, few who have considered the matter seriously would want to deny that human nature is extremely complex and full of contradictions. What does that have to do with the supernatural?

Furthermore, one of the most striking and, to my mind, most valuable features of Simone Weil's philosophical procedure is to root the concepts which are most important to her in actual, very concrete, features of human life. Although she is no enemy of abstract theoretical considerations, she does not start with these, but with the circumstances of life which give rise to them. Her procedure is strongly reminiscent of Wittgenstein's characterization of his own procedure as the offering of "remarks on the natural history of mankind." We are shown certain concrete tendencies of human behaviour and offered suggestions about how these may serve as the sources of our concepts. One might say that our concepts are given a natural foundation. For instance, "Human Personality" roots the concept of the sacred, in its application to human beings, in certain natural reactions and forbearances characterizing our relations with each other. Nothing would induce me to put out the eyes of this passing stranger. That remark characterizes my nature; what is supernatural about it? Indeed, in terms of a discussion such as this what meaning can we attach to the statement that it concerns something supernatural?

15

"A SUPERNATURAL VIRTUE"?

What sort of concept *is* that of the supernatural? We are not of course here in the territory occupied by ghosts, poltergeists, hauntings, spiritualism, and other paranormal phenomena, whatever that territory may be and whatever may be its more or less distant connections with the territory we *are* in.[1] The phenomena to which Simone Weil does draw attention are not paranormal and the Society for Psychical Research would have no interest in them.

Are we then in the region of metaphysics? Does Simone Weil have a theory about the nature of the universe, as divided into two realms, the natural and the supernatural? I think the answer must be a qualified no. But the question is not an easy one and I want to spend more time exploring it.

Let us consider what she says about creation, which is certainly a subject which is often discussed and theorized about by metaphysicians. It cannot be denied that to think about creation is to think about the origin of the world, of the universe. What could be more metaphysical than that?

Well, we find many extremely different *kinds* of interest expressed in this way: as an interest in the origins of the universe. There is for instance the narrative of the Book of Genesis. There is also the sort of thing one hears from astrophysicists and cosmologists debating the rival merits of "the big bang" and "continuous creation," where the same *word* ("creation") is used as in Genesis. People are often led to wonder which, if any, of these accounts is "right." Scientific knights, like Sir Fred Hoyle and Sir Bernard Lovell, talk about modern astrophysics as "rewriting

191

Genesis" or solving the spiritual difficulties of our culture raised by Albert Schweitzer.

Something has gone badly wrong here,[2] of a sort to remind us that the fact that one and the same phrase ("the origin of the universe," "creation") is used in two different contexts is poor evidence that the same sort of discussion is going on. Let us bear this in mind in thinking about what Simone Weil writes about creation. If we think of her as concerned with the same sort of issue as are astrophysicists, the kinds of consideration she appeals to must appear quite astounding or, not to put too fine a point on it, crazy.

For instance, a crucial role is played in her thinking by a passage from Thucydides' great history of the Peloponnesian War, describing the exchange between the ambassadors from Athens and the leaders of the little island of Melos, whom they were trying to bully into joining their anti-Spartan "alliance"; in other words into submitting themselves to the Athenian imperium. The Athenians' reply to the Melians' protest at their overbearing tactics was:

> And we ask you on your side not to imagine that you will influence us by saying that you, though a colony of Sparta, have not joined Sparta in the war, or that you have never done us any harm. Instead we recommend that you should try to get what is possible for you to get, taking into consideration what we both really do think; since you know as well as we do that, when these matters are discussed by practical people, the standard of justice depends on the equality of power to compel and that in fact the strong do what they have the power to do and the weak accept what they have to accept.

And later:

> So far as the favour of the gods is concerned, we think we have as much right to that as you have. Our aims and our actions are perfectly consistent with the beliefs men hold about the gods and with the principles which govern their own conduct. Our opinion of the gods and our knowledge of men lead us to conclude that it is a general and necessary law of nature to rule wherever one can. This is not a law that we made ourselves, nor were we the first to act upon it when it was made. We found it already in existence, and we shall leave it to exist forever among those who come after us. We are merely acting in accordance with it, and we know that you or anybody else with the same power as ours would be acting in precisely the same way. And therefore, as far as the gods are concerned, we see no good reason why we should fear to be at a disadvantage.[3]

The Melians refused the Athenians' demands, whereupon they were attacked and, inevitably, defeated. All adult males were put to death. Women and children were enslaved.

Simone Weil was fascinated by the clarity and candour of the
Athenians' statement of their position.[4] She also thought that, at
a certain level, they were right about the dependence of justice on
equality of power between the parties. That is, after all, just what
she herself says in "Human Personality" about the conception of
justice that is linked to rights. But on the other hand she insists
that the way the Athenian ambassadors' view, in Thucydides' version, is represented already shows that the Greeks did not believe
it to be the only possible one.

> By [. . .] keeping up appearances one makes it impossible or
> difficult for one's opponents to draw upon the strength which
> comes from indignation, and yet one's own purpose is in no way
> weakened. But fully to achieve this it is necessary for one to be gen-
> uinely convinced that one is always in the right, and that one's right
> is not merely that of the stronger, but is intrinsically right – even
> when this is not at all the case. The Greeks were never able to do
> this; we see in Thucydides how clearly the Athenians, when they per-
> petrated cruel abuses of power, were aware that they were doing
> so.[5]

She believes that the existence of this other possibility shows something about the relation of the world to God, about what is
involved in creation. This undoubtedly has close connections with
her view of this other justice as a "supernatural virtue"; but we
are still a long way from seeing what these connections are.

One thing that is clear is that the notion of *power* is fundamental. And it is important to pay attention to the way the Athenians
phrase their case. They say: "Our opinion *of the gods* and our
knowledge of men lead us to conclude that it is *a general and necessary law of nature* to rule wherever one can. *This is not a law that
we made ourselves*[. . . .] *We found it already in existence.*" Their idea
is, then, that there is a necessity about acting as they do towards
the Melians, and one which is somehow rooted in the nature of
things.

It is the same idea expressed by Simone Weil herself in "Are We
Struggling for Justice?" when she speaks of our constant, unthink-
ing practice of using other people in the service of our own projects and "do not waste our time and power of attention in examining whether they have consented to this" and comments: "This
is necessary. If it were otherwise, things would not get done, and
if things did not get done, we would perish." That is as much as
to say that the necessity of exercising power in the way described

by the Athenians is rooted in the nature of human life. Perhaps that sounds extreme if we think of the particular application of it made by the Athenians. But we must remember here some of the points discussed in earlier chapters, relating to the ways in which, as in Homer's Trojan War, social forces may so control people's readings of situations as to make the sorts of restraint which the Melians urged on the Athenian ambassadors laughably unthinkable.

Now, one of Simone Weil's main concerns, as we have seen, is to show that something else *is* thinkable, and *how* it is thinkable. In the essay on *The Iliad* she points to the conception of justice expressed in the poet's own depiction of the terrible events; and she finds something similar in the manner in which Thucydides depicts the events of the Peloponnesian War.

She also points to the example of Christ:

> Who, being in the form of God, thought it not robbery to be equal with God:
> But made himself of no reputation, and took upon him the form of a servant, and was made in the likeness of men:
> And being found in fashion as a man, he humbled himself, and became obedient unto death, even the death of the cross.
> Wherefore God also hath highly exalted him, and given him a name which is above every name:
> That at the name of Jesus every knee should bow, of things in heaven, and things in earth, and things under the earth;
> And that every tongue should confess that Jesus Christ is Lord, to the Glory of God the Father.[6]

This goes further, of course, in saying that Jesus was being "equal with God" in accepting his Passion in the way he did. As Simone Weil remarks:

> These words could have been an answer to the Athenian murderers of Melos.

An answer, that is, to their contention that their mode of acting is prescribed *by the gods* as a necessary law of nature.

> The Christian faith is nothing but the cry affirming the contrary. The same is true of the ancient doctrines of China, India, Egypt and Greece.
> The act of Creation is not an act of power. It is an abdication. Through this act a kingdom was established other than the kingdom of God. The reality of this world is constituted by the mechanism of matter and the autonomy of rational creatures. It is a kingdom from

which God has withdrawn. God, having renounced being its king, can enter it only as a beggar. As for the cause of this abdication, Plato expresses it thus: "He was good."[7]

The question that exercises me here is: what is added by bringing in the notion of creation and of "the reality of this world" in such a way? Why not just point to the examples – examples like that of Jesus, Homer, Thucydides and leave it at that? Why not just say: another conception of justice *is* possible; here are examples; do what you will with these examples? – Now I do, as a matter of fact, have considerable sympathy with the scepticism expressed in this question. But I do not want to leave the matter there, because we are still very far from understanding *what* more Simone Weil is doing than this.

The reference to the reality of the world as consisting of "the mechanism of matter and the autonomy of rational creatures" is obviously bound up with what I have called Simone Weil's account of concept formation. I have emphasized the large part played in this by the idea that our understanding of the nature of things develops in our methodical attempts to overcome obstacles to our projects. In so far as this side of concept formation is stressed it is natural to think it a corollary that only by pressing our powers of action to their uttermost shall we be able to probe and form a conception of the necessities of nature. This is not merely an abstract epistemological fantasy, as can be seen from critical disputes in contemporary science concerning the limits to, for instance, scientific research on human embryos, vivisection, the protection of the environment in the face of technological development, and so on. It is an issue raised in even more horrifying form by the medical experiments on concentration camp prisoners under the Nazi regime and by recent allegations of similar experiments on convicts in the United States after the Second World War.

It is interesting that these issues are often expressed as a conflict between the scientific imperative to increase knowledge and understanding and distinct ethical imperatives. This is not universally the case. I take it that the emphasis on *ecology,* for instance, and the insistence that human beings co-exist in ecological equilibrium with their natural environment is in part an attempt to show that the imperative to understand is subject to certain *internal* limits.

This is certainly Simone Weil's view. Her discussions of beauty are designed to show that the conception of the beauty of the universe is a necessary ingredient in our conception of a natural order; that it presupposes a response on our part which is a hesitation, an inhibition of our pursuit of our projects. Similarly, her discussions of what is involved in understanding the reality of human beings emphasize the notion of the "sacred" as integral to such an understanding, and insist again that it is a notion only arising as a reflection of an inhibition of our insistence on pursuing our own projects to their natural limits. – It would of course be a misunderstanding to object that notions like beauty and the sacred are on that account "purely subjective," since it is part of the same account that those other "natural" properties normally thought of as the province of science are equally revealed only to a particular human attitude, or "aspiration."

Now, the Athenians, in their reply to the leaders of Melos, do not merely affirm their intention to have their own way at all costs; they do not even merely affirm that their conception of what is just is as valid as the Melians'; they say in addition that they, and they alone, are thinking and acting in accordance with nature, adding that the Melians would do just the same were their position vis-à-vis the Athenians to be reversed. In fact they are not merely *opposing* the Melian appeal to justice, they are characterizing it as an *illusion*. Their position is effectively that argued by Thrasymachus in Book I of Plato's *Republic*. It's true, they are saying, that people do talk of its being "just" in some circumstances to refrain from utilizing all the power that is at one's disposal in order to attain one's ends, but there is absolutely no reason why that way of speaking should be taken seriously. It is just a defence of the weak against the strong; and why should the strong give way to the weak?

It is as though the Melians were saying: "You can't treat innocent people like that"; and as though the Athenians were replying: "Can't we? Just you watch!" Of course such a "reply" is not a reply at all, but a sick joke. But the Athenians act and talk as though it *were* a genuine reply, in the sense, that is, of a logical rebuttal. They are claiming that there is no sense in the Melian use of "cannot"; it is nothing more than a rhetorical way of speaking, not expressive of any genuine impossibility. And do they not show, by their subsequent actions, that there is no such impossibility as the Melians allege?

In my last remarks I have tried to put the Athenian case in a form with which I think many philosophers in our own time would agree. (In fact, I know they would, because I have heard them say it.) Their agreement is expressive of the idea that language cannot – cannot be allowed to – look after itself.[8] It isn't enough, they think, to point to the fact that we do as a matter of fact speak in a certain way. Our ways of speaking, our grammar, have to be justified; it has to be shown that they correspond to something real. This is precisely the view, at least as applied to the concept of justice, of the Athenian ambassadors to Melos and of Thrasymachus: there is a justice which is "natural" and if we use the word in any other way we are either deluding ourselves or trying to delude others.[9]

One way of combating Thrasymachus and the Athenian ambassadors would be to insist that they are wrong about "nature": that the nature of things *does* provide a warrant for speaking as the Melians do. Simone Weil's emphasis on the essential role of notions like beauty and the sacred in the formation of our concepts of the natural order and of our own relation to it may be regarded as such an argument. It is of course part of this argument that a readiness on our part *not* to exercise our power to the fullest extent of which we are capable is essential to our forming such concepts. Such an argument does not show that the Melians are "right," and the Athenians "wrong," to conceive justice as they each respectively do; but it does show that the Athenians are wrong to argue that the Melians' position is "contrary to nature."

This sort of argument certainly does not provide any warrant for introducing the concept of the "supernatural," however. As I remarked before, our reactions to beauty, and to each other, are as much a part of human nature as our other reactions. Even if it could be shown that these reactions are comparatively rare in relation to other opposing reactions, we should be a long way from considering them as something supernatural. We might even want to say that the comparative rarity of this sort of response is itself a feature of human nature. This shows that the notion of the supernatural is never going to be given an application by arguments along these lines.

Let us go back to the notion of creation. Simone Weil's idea that creation must be thought of not as God's exercising his power but as his refraining from doing so is quite certainly closely connected with the points about concept formation. This suggests that we should look on the phrase "the creation of the world" not as expressing something analogous to a physical making, but rather as expressing something like the making possible of a certain conception, a certain sort of understanding. So much seems to me to be right.

But Simone Weil's God is not just "the God of the philosophers," a convenient device for expressing certain metaphysical and epistemological views; he is the God of the Gospels – a very different matter. If I fail to do justice to this I certainly bring myself under the withering fire of this sentence of Kierkegaard's: "For why do we have our philosophers, if not to make supernatural things trivial and commonplace?"; and I should like to avoid that if I can. The difficulty of course is to avoid it without giving up one's philosophical responsibilities.

I remarked that the epistemological argument about concept formation, while it counters the Thrasymachian argument about what is "natural," does not show that the Melians are "right" and the Athenians "wrong" to conceive justice as they respectively do. It provides no metaphysical "justification" of its own. Now, there is certainly a strong strand in Simone Weil's thinking according to which it is mistaken to suppose that there could be any such justification. I believe that we may get closer to her notion of the supernatural if we investigate this.

In *Waiting for God* she characterizes the conviction that it is better not to command wherever one has the power as "true faith," in that it "places the Good outside this world, where are all the sources of power."[10] To say that good lies outside the world is to agree with the Athenians that there is nothing in the world which justifies the conviction. But to say that there is nothing *in the world* which justifies it is to say that there is *nothing* which justifies it. Of course that is not the same as saying it is *un*justified; and that perhaps is what the Athenians cannot see. One might put that alongside an important passage in the notebooks:

> The Roman who dies to save his slaves from torture loved God.
> Every master who believes that his slaves are his equals knows and loves God. And reciprocally.
> A painter does not draw the spot where he is standing. But in looking at his picture I can deduce his position by relation to the things drawn.
> On the other hand, if he puts himself into his picture I know for certain that the place where he shows himself is not the place where he is.[. . .]

The Gospel contains a conception of human life, not a theology. If I light an electric torch at night out of doors I don't judge its power by looking at the bulb, but by seeing how many objects it lights up.

The brightness of a source of light is appreciated by the illumination it projects upon non-luminous objects.

The value of a religious or, more generally, a spiritual way of life is appreciated by the amount of illumination thrown upon the things of this world.

Earthly things are the criterion of spiritual things.

This is what we generally don't want to recognize, because we are frightened of a criterion.

The virtue of anything is manifested outside of the thing.[. . .]

If a man took my left-hand glove, passed it behind his back, and returned it to me as a right-hand glove, I should know that he had access to the 4th dimension. No other proof is possible.

In the same way, if a man gives bread to a beggar in a certain way or speaks in a certain way about a defeated army, I know that his thought has been outside this world and sat with Christ alongside the Father who is in Heaven.

If a man describes to me at the same time two opposite sides of a mountain, I know that his position is somewhat higher than the summit.

It is impossible to understand and love at the same time both the victors and the vanquished, as the *Iliad* does, except from the place, outside the world, where God's Wisdom dwells.[11]

The passage as a whole seems to show that the remark "The Gospel contains a conception of human life, not a theology," is intended to be the principle on which we are to interpret Simone Weil's own reflections. Her insistence that "earthly things are *the criterion* of spiritual things" shows that we are not being offered a "metaphysics of the spiritual," but a certain way of thinking about the earthly. Thus, the point of the remark quoted earlier, that the "supernatural" is "the difference between human and animal behaviour" is to be taken seriously; only, of course, it is a difference which itself will only appear to someone who looks at the behaviour from the appropriate point of view. Anyone, for example, who genuinely does think that the Melian arguments to the Athenian ambassadors are simply nonsensical will not grasp the difference. (But of course there are difficulties here about how to understand "genuinely.")[12]

Perhaps, though, the phrase "from the appropriate point of view" in my last paragraph is troublesome? What *is* this point of view? It is a point "outside this world . . . with Christ alongside the

Father who is in Heaven." If we take this seriously, are we not
committed after all to a sort of religious metaphysics? Well, that
depends on what "taking it seriously" comes to! Here another,
somewhat later, passage from the same New York notebook[13] is
illuminating. Simone Weil speaks here of refusing to accept the
things of this world as goods "because I judge them to be false by
comparison with the idea of the good." Suppose someone won-
ders whether this good exists; it does not matter, she replies; "the
things of this world exist, but they are not the good." It does not
even matter that one has no idea what this good is. All one needs
to know is how to use the word so as to express "the certainty that
the things of this world are not goods." In fact, she says, it makes
no sense to speak of the existence or non-existence of the good:
"The good certainly does not possess a reality to which the attribute 'good' is added." Thus anything that *does* have such a reality
is not the good. That is all that has to be recognized.

> The things of this world exist. Therefore I do not detach from
> them those of my faculties that are related to existence. But since
> the things of this world contain no good, I simply *detach from them
> the faculty which is related to the good, that is to say, the faculty of love.*

The phrase which I have italicized is the important one. It means
that to recognize that the good lies "outside this world" is neither
to make an existential judgment nor to comment on the where-
abouts of some existent: it is simply to redirect one's love. Thus
one whose thought lies "with Christ alongside the Father who is
in heaven" is simply one whose love has a certain orientation.

But there are still problems. Someone may want to object that
if this is all that is meant it would be better to say so, and leave all
that misleading metaphysical-sounding talk aside. I think this
objection would display a misunderstanding, but I shall defer further comment on it until later.

There is another difficulty, however, which I think is a genuine
one and led Simone Weil towards the end to a more satisfactory
formulation. The difficulty could be expressed in abstract terms
like this. – What would it be to withdraw one's love from *everything*? Wouldn't this mean that one loved *nothing*? And wouldn't
that mean that one did not love at all? If it is objected that one's
love is withdrawn only from "the things of this world," that sounds
as though we are, after all, relying on there being something else,

somewhere else. And in this case our conceptual progress was only apparent.

What I call the more satisfactory formulation comes towards the end of Simone Weil's life in her last London notebook:

> Real love wants to have a real object, and to know the truth of it, and to love it in its truth as it really is.
>
> To talk about love of truth is an error; it should be a spirit of truth in love. This spirit is always present in real and pure love.
>
> The Spirit of truth – the fiery breath of truth, the energy of truth – is at the same time Love.
>
> There is another love, which is false.
>
> Here below one can only love men and the universe, that is to say, justice and beauty. Therefore truth is something that qualifies the just and the beautiful.[14]

The difficulty which I expressed above abstractly comes out in more concrete form in Simone Weil's treatment of *friendship*,[15] by which she means a *preferential* love for a particular human being. I noted earlier how, in her treatment of justice in "Human Personality," she emphasizes the notion of the "impersonal" and *at the same time* insists on the identity of justice and love (in the sense of charity). These two ideas can be combined because, as she here says, "Charity does not discriminate."[16] There is, therefore, a problem about how there could be a preferential form of love which is acceptable. (There is perhaps an even deeper problem about what "acceptable" can mean here, if it is itself meant to express something more than personal predilection.)

Now, in my view the best way to go about dealing with both these problems would be to investigate examples of forms of preferential love that one *does* find acceptable and try to see how they differ from those which one does not. It would also be important to reflect on the fact that "one's" judgments will almost certainly not be universally endorsed. (Why do I say "almost"? They quite certainly will not be.) A related fact is that one's own judgments on these matters are quite likely to be equivocal and shifting. These facts are not contingent, in relation to the issue in hand. They help to make it the sort of issue it is.

That Simone Weil sees the matter very differently is signalled in her opening words where she speaks of a preferential human love enshrining "an intimation and a reflection of divine love" as constituting friendship *"provided we keep strictly to the true meaning of the word."*[17] It soon becomes apparent that this is something more than just an eccentric linguistic usage or a statement of personal preference. "When anyone wishes to put himself under a human being or consents to be subordinated to him, there is no trace of friendship." "All friendship is impure if even a trace of the wish to please or the contrary desire to dominate is found in it." "Pure friendship [. . .] has in it, at the same time as affection, something not unlike a complete indifference. Although it is a bond between two people it is in a sense impersonal. It leaves impartiality intact."[18]

These pronouncements are in part undoubtedly an expression of Simone Weil's own experience of, and difficulties with, close personal relationships. As such we may respect them and feel compassion for her. We may also recognize that relationships describable in the terms she uses *may* indeed have it in them to become something terrible in certain circumstances. She herself gives telling examples where this is so: Arnolphe in Molière's *l'école des femmes,* Racine's Phèdre. But she does not even consider the possibility of other cases in which, by the grace of God, these dangers are avoided. Nor does she consider whether the risk of such dangers is a price we have to pay for some of the greatest things in human life. Othello's love for Desdemona certainly became something terrible; but would the love in the days before his jealousy, as described by Desdemona, have had its peculiar quality of magnificence if it had not contained within itself the possibility of turning into something terrible? Or, to take an example which Simone Weil does indeed mention, but certainly not *attend to,* the love between husband and wife may "as a result of habit" (as she puts it) bring about a kind of dependence of one on the other such that the death of the one partner crushes the other; but would one wish for a world without such relationships? Can one really assimilate such cases (as she does) to the miser's dependence on gold or the drunkard's on alcohol?[19]

Apart from the difficulties of a personal sort which I have mentioned, which to some extent must surely have influenced her account of such "preferential" relations, a generalizing tendency such as we have encountered in other contexts is also surely at work here. What she tries to do here is to treat this sort of case in terms similar to those in which she discusses justice in "Human Personality" and also in earlier sections of *Waiting for God.* Consider, for example, her attempt to apply her ideas about geometry to this sort of case.

Friendship has something universal about it. It consists of loving a human being as we should like to be able to love each soul in particular of all those who go to make up the human race. As a geometrician looks at a particular figure in order to deduce the universal. The consent to preserve an autonomy within ourselves and in others is essentially of a universal order. As soon as we wish for this autonomy to be respected in more than just one single being we desire it for everyone, for we cease to arrange the order of the world in a circle whose centre is here below. We transport the centre of the circle beyond the heavens.[20]

My main concern here is not to evaluate the kind of attitude to people that Simone Weil is describing and indeed advocating. As a matter of autobiographical fact, as a *generalized* attitude I find it anything but admirable; and I should think that it is – God be praised! – hardly a *possible* stance for many people to take. But my main point here is that it has little to do with what we ordinarily understand by "friendship," or by special forms of personal love, such as between mother and child, husband and wife, lovers, and so on. The geometer is indeed not interested in the particular figure as such. Now, it cannot be said even of the person who shows charity to a stranger, like the Good Samaritan, that he or she is not interested in the one being helped as such, but only in the universal properties of humanity which this one happens to instantiate. As Simone Weil herself remarks in "Human Personality," it may be all right to say "Your person does not interest me" even "in an affectionate conversation between close friends, without jarring upon even the tenderest nerve of their friendship" (though I should think that in most cases it would be as well not to make the experiment), but no one can "without committing a cruelty and offending against justice" say to someone "You do not interest me." Certainly such words spoken seriously between erstwhile friends or lovers would probably herald the imminent end of the relationship.

It is true that the notion of respecting the other's autonomy is very often crucial to the way we evaluate a close personal relationship. But it is not always relevant in the same way and does not always take the same form; and sometimes the nature of the relationship may even be such as to speak against it. An example of the latter sort of case might be that between Mary Garth and Fred Vincy in George Eliot's *Middlemarch,* where Mary's love is hardly conceivable apart from her recognition of Fred's need for her: a need which Simone Weil would certainly find offensive. (In gen-

eral *Middlemarch* is a mine of different kinds of case into which the
notion of "respect for autonomy" enters in quite different ways.)

The passage from the New York notebook which stimulated
these reflections speaks of detaching "the faculty of love" from
"the things of this world." We have to remember, however, that
for Simone Weil love and attention are closely connected; perhaps
the latter is even a form of the first. That I think is precisely what
is lacking from her treatment of friendship. It is however what is
emphasized in the passage I also quoted from the London notebook, in the sentence, for instance, "Real love wants to have a real
object, and to know the truth of it, and to love it in its truth as it
really is." That is very far from "detaching" love from the things
of this world. And it has to include the possibility that recognizing,
for example, someone in her truth as she really is, is going to
involve recognizing one's dependence on her or hers on me: in
which case that dependence too will be something to be loved.

What I described as the "generalizing" tendency discernible in
the treatment of friendship in *Waiting for God* might also be
described as the succumbing to a temptation to take the language
of the supernatural in a metaphysical way. This does not merely
misconstrue such language; it turns its original thrust through 180
degrees. To speak in the terms of this language is, as she herself
says, to express faith. Faith does not consist in the holding of a
theory based on argument, in thinking that a certain view is justified; it involves thinking in a way to which one recognizes questions of justification to be irrelevant.

I think it has to be acknowledged that Simone Weil repeatedly
does write in ways which seem to go against this way of thinking.
For example, she often seems to be trying to show that the language of the supernatural is *required* for certain phenomena
because these fly in the face of what is "natural." For instance,
commenting on the words which Thucydides gives to the Athenian
ambassadors at Melos, she writes:

> Possibility and necessity are terms opposed to justice in these
> lines. Possible means all that the strong can impose upon the weak.
> It is reasonable to examine how far this possibility goes. Supposing
> it to be known, it is certain that the strong will accompany his pur-
> pose to the extreme limit of possibility. It is a mechanical necessity.
> *Otherwise it would be as though he willed and did not will simultaneously.*
> There is a necessity for the strong as well as the weak in this.[21]

This looks like an attempt to prove that, according to our "natural" understanding of things, the strong *must* act to the limits of their power. The last three sentences seem to treat the proposition that this is a "mechanical necessity" as a *conclusion,* the argument being that we should otherwise have a contradiction: "it would be as though he willed and did not will simultaneously."

The image behind the argument is of the will as a kind of force, the extent and direction of which can be represented as a vector. Given this, along with sufficient information about the countervailing forces in the environment, and so on, it will then be a simple calculation to determine what the agent will do. To suggest that the agent might not go as far as the calculation shows would be unintelligible, *if we conceive the matter in this way.*

But what is this way of conceiving it? It is, surely, conceiving the will and its operations as mechanical forces. The argument does not, as its phrasing might suggest, *prove* that they are; on the contrary, it depends on our assuming that. The assumption is fed by the idea that to exercise the will, to act, is to engage in a project with a more or less definite end in view. But not only is there no reason for us to accept that assumption, but Simone Weil herself does not do so, as we have seen. And precisely this is a very important point in her criticism of the Athenian ambassadors' argument.

> The first proof that they were in the wrong lies in the fact that, contrary to their assertion, it happens, although extremely rarely, that a man will forbear out of pure generosity to command where he has the power to do so.[22]

Should not the notion of the will *include* the possibility of these other forms of behaviour? We have been offered no reason for confining it to actions directed towards attaining an end; no reason, therefore, for not regarding actions of other sorts as perfectly "natural."

I think it must be clear that no argument is going to prove that certain forms of behaviour *must* be seen as supernatural. There is no "must" about it. What we need, in order to understand how the expression is being used, is some exhibition of its use; we need to be shown it in action and to ask ourselves whether or not certain things become clearer if thought of in terms of that use. The following remark of Wittgenstein's, written in 1948, is apposite:

> An honest religious thinker is like a tightrope walker. He almost looks as though he were walking on nothing but air. His support is

the slenderest imaginable. And yet it really is possible to walk on it.[23]

It is worth mentioning here another entry in Wittgenstein's notebook, this time from 1929, which expresses a thought strikingly akin to Simone Weil's and may help to show what is at issue.

> What is good is also divine. Queer as it sounds, that sums up my ethics. Only something supernatural can express the Supernatural.[24]

The last sentence seems to imply that the concept of the Supernatural can be understood only in so far as we see it applied to particular cases, see what is described *as* supernatural. In Simone Weil's words, quoted earlier, "earthly things are the criterion of spiritual things." But they only serve as such a criterion in so far as they are seen in a certain light. There is no such thing as a demonstrative proof that things must be, or even can be, seen in that light. One can only try to present them in such a way that they *will* be seen in that light. There is no way of proving to me that I can walk on a tightrope. One can only try to show me how it is done and then I must try. Of course I may fall off. That is why Simone Weil continues in the passage I just referred to by saying that we are *afraid* of a criterion. There is no direct, guaranteed route to the Supernatural.

> No man hath seen God at any time. If we love one another, God dwelleth in us, and his love is perfected in us.

> If a man say, I love God, and hateth his brother, he is a liar: for he that loveth not his brother whom he hath seen, how can he love God whom he hath not seen?[25]

Saint John is making conceptual or grammatical points throughout this Epistle. Anyone who thinks that to say this is to trivialize it has a trivialized conception of conceptual or grammatical issues. That is also a conceptual or grammatical point.

One general characterization of what is involved in describing human life in "supernatural" terms can perhaps be risked. It is to give a description which *rules out explanations in natural, or naturalistic, terms.* But the difficulty here is of course to understand that italicized phrase correctly. Consider an example:

> The sympathy of the weak for the strong is natural, for the weak in putting himself into the place of the other acquires an imaginary

strength. The sympathy of the strong for the weak, being in the opposite direction, is against nature.

That is why the sympathy of the weak for the strong is only pure if its sole object is the sympathy received from the other, when the other is truly generous. This is supernatural gratitude, which means gladness to be the recipient of supernatural compassion. It leaves self-respect absolutely intact. The preservation of true self-respect in affliction is also something supernatural. Gratitude which is pure, like pure compassion, is essentially the acceptance of affliction. The afflicted man and his benefactor, between whom diversity of fortune places an infinite distance, are united in this acceptance. There is friendship between them in the sense of the Pythagoreans, miraculous harmony and equality.[26]

The supernatural virtue of justice consists of behaving exactly as though there were equality when one is stronger in an unequal relationship.[27]

Where there is equality of power we can explain why the parties reach the position they do: it is because the power of each is limited by that of the other. In the "supernatural" case there is no such explanation of why one party voluntarily refrained from exploiting the other; why for instance the benefactor did not go on to "buy" the sufferer. There are of course other cases where there is some hidden explanation: where there is an advantage to be gained which is not immediately apparent. But there are also cases where we (some of us) are confident that there is no such explanation. We may say, perhaps, that the person in the position of strength desists on account of the justice of so doing. This certainly need not mean that one puts it to oneself in those terms. And even if one does, that is still no "explanation" in the sense in which that word was used in the other case, the case of equality of power. "Justice" here characterizes the action determined on: one does the just thing because it is just. Does that say more than that one does the just thing and that there is nothing more to be said about it?

To call this "supernatural" serves to emphasize what an importantly different kind of phenomenon this is from the other case which, superficially, it so resembles. It is to emphasize that seeking an explanation in the manner towards which the superficial resemblance tempts us is inappropriate and rests on a misconstrual of the kind of situation we are dealing with.

> A man who is suspended looks the same as one who is standing, but the interplay of forces within him is nevertheless quite different, so that he can act quite differently than can a standing man.[28]

Wittgenstein's striking image is used by Simone Weil herself somewhere to make the very same point.

It may be objected that while we may establish empirically that an explanation of a particular form (for example in terms of an equilibrium of power) is not applicable in a particular case, there cannot be an empirical proof that no explanation at all is available in such cases. There is something in that, but it misses the point, which is *not* that it can be shown empirically that no explanation is to be found. The point about the kind of situation Simone Weil is discussing is not just that we are unsuccessful in finding the kind of explanation we are used to finding in superficially similar cases, but also that our own relation to such cases is entirely different. That is, we do, characteristically, react to them quite differently: they make us wonder, in a way which no explanation is going to satisfy; it is not the sort of wonder which explanations are designed to allay. However much is explained, a residue of wonder remains.

Simone Weil sometimes puts her point in terms of the "source of energy" for actions. Where there is a natural equilibrium of power, or where the agent expects some advantage from an action (which can of course be of the most diverse sorts), we can point to the source of energy which makes possible the action (or, what may be just as important, the refraining from action); in the other case we cannot. In such a case she says that the source of power is "outside the world." That is quite different from locating the source in some definite place. It is to say that, in the sense in which, in the one case, there is a source of energy which makes action possible, there is none in the other case. Now it may be felt to be misleading, even obscurantist, to put this point by saying that there *is* a source of energy, but that it lies outside the world with God. It is misleading if construed in the wrong way. But it may be defended in so far as it prepares the way for the possibility of saying further things, of making further constructions, from the point of view of which we may articulate certain things more clearly, and perhaps raise questions which would otherwise hardly be possible.

An analogy might be the difference between saying that two parallel straight lines do not meet and saying that they meet "at infinity." Here too "infinity" does not designate a place at which the lines meet. The point of using the phrase is not to be read off, as it were, from the situation described; it is to be assessed according to its geometrical fertility: the new constructions, proofs, and theorems that would not be possible without it. Another way of putting this would be to say that the sense of the phrase is not *derived* from the phenomenon of parallel lines to which it is applied, but lies in the geometrical use to which it is put. Of course, a large part of the point of that use will lie in the extent to which it enables us to increase our understanding of the phenomenon of parallel straight lines by suggesting connections with other, superficially quite distinct, phenomena. Analogously, the sense of saying that the actions, say, of the Good Samaritan are an example of "supernatural" compassion, or of saying that the source of energy that makes such compassion possible is "outside the world," is not founded on some feature that we observe to belong to the actions so described. It will emerge only in the further ways of speaking this will make possible, in the connections with other phenomena of human life suggested by those ways of speaking, and in the enlarged understanding thus made available.

This leaves unanswered the question whether this enlarged understanding will take the form of having new sorts of *explanation* available. Or whether it is an understanding answering to an entirely different sort of interest. The distinction implied in this question is expressed in the following remark from a notebook of Wittgenstein's from 1950.

> If someone who believes in God looks round and asks "Where does everything I see come from?," "Where does all this come from?," he is not craving for a (causal) explanation; and his question gets its point from being the expression of a certain craving. He is, namely, expressing an attitude to all explanations. – But how is this manifested in his life?
>
> The attitude that's in question is that of taking a certain matter seriously and then, beyond a certain point, no longer regarding it as serious, but maintaining that something else is even more important.
>
> Someone may for instance say it's a very grave matter that such and such a man should have died before he could complete a certain piece of work; and yet, in another sense, this is not what matters. At this point one uses the words "in a deeper sense."
>
> Actually I should like to say that in this case too the *words* you utter or what you think as you utter them are not what matters, so much as the difference they make at various points in your life. How

do I know that two people mean the same when each says he believes in God? And just the same goes for belief in the Trinity. A theology which insists on the use of *certain particular* words and phrases, and outlaws others, does not make anything clearer (Karl Barth). It gesticulates with words, as one might say, because it wants to say something and does not know how to express it. *Practice* gives the words their sense.[29]

Does Simone Weil offer us another sort of explanation in terms of the supernatural? Or does this term express an interest of a different sort: that is, an interest in something other than explanation? This question is raised fairly clearly by the following passage:

This universe where we are living, and of which we form a tiny particle, is the distance put by Love between God and God. We are a point in this distance. Space, time and the mechanism that governs matter are the distance. Everything that we call evil is only this mechanism. God has provided that when his grace penetrates to the very centre of a man and from there illuminates all his being, he is able to walk on the water without violating any of the laws of nature. When, however, a man turns away from God, he simply gives himself up to the law of gravity. Then he thinks that he can decide and choose, but he is only a thing, a stone that falls. If we examine human society and souls closely and with real attention, we see that wherever the virtue of supernatural light is absent, everything is obedient to mechanical laws as blind and as exact as the laws of gravitation. To know this is profitable and necessary. Those whom we call criminals are only tiles blown off a roof by the wind and falling at random. Their only fault is the initial choice which made them into such tiles.[30]

What is "this universe where we are living" being contrasted with? This is not so easy to say. One might expect the contrast to be with another realm not subject to laws of the same sort; but this would be wrong. She says that a person illumined by God's grace can do things which, though extraordinary, *do not violate any of the laws of nature.* In that case they can presumably be understood and explained in terms of such laws as well as can anything else. This of course is not excluded by the point, discussed above, that actions which are superficially similar may not be explicable in at all the same way.

It is true that she writes a little later that someone who desires to be obedient to God is as subject to "mechanical necessity" as before, but is now subject in addition to a new necessity "constituted by laws belonging to supernatural things." This certainly sounds as though explanations in terms of natural necessity are to be at least supplemented by explanations of a different sort. And the impression is reinforced by remarks, both in this and other works, which insist that the laws in terms of which these latter explanations are couched are as strict and precise as those of mechanical nature. But let us discount these (as they seem to me) blemishes and ask to what use these forms of expression are actually being put. ("Practice gives the words their sense.")

It is important to remember the point, already noted, that one who is open to God's grace does not act *contrary* to the laws of nature. The natural and the supernatural are not, in that sense, in competition with each other. What is in question is, rather, a possible attitude to the necessity thought to govern events in the world we live in. From a certain point of view matter in its passivity can appear as *obedient* to God's will; to think of it in this way is to love it

> in the same way as a needle, handled by the beloved wife he has lost, is cherished by a lover. The beauty of the world gives us an intimation of its claim to a place in our heart. In the beauty of the world rude necessity becomes an object of love. What is more beautiful than the action of weight on the fugitive waves of the sea as they fall in ever-moving folds, or the almost eternal folds of the mountains?[31]

To be clear about the nature of this perspective it is important to recall, from Chapter 13, that beauty does not lie below the surface of things but is *a reflection of our own aspiration towards the good;* and also that this aspiration is itself characteristic of one who accepts in a spirit of *obedience* the necessities to which one, like everything and everyone else, is subject. That is, one sees nature as obedient in so far as that is what one aspires to be oneself.

Simone Weil characterizes the point of view articulated here as lying "beyond space and time . . . where our Father dwells." I believe the point of this sort of language is to provide a way of expressing the connections between various attitudes, interests, strivings, aspirations, which are all part of our "natural history." It is only *because* they are part of our natural history that we have any chance of making sense of the notion of the "supernatural."

NOTES

2. *The Cartesian background*

1. See J.-J. Rousseau, *Du contrat social,* bk. I, ch. 1, first sentence.
2. See *Sur la science,* pp. 111–15, translated by Richard Rees in *Seventy Letters,* pp. 3–5.
3. This essay is published in *Sur la science,* and references in the text are to that publication. Since this book was written, a translation has been published ("Science and Perception in Descartes") by Dorothy Tuck McFarland and Wilhelmina van Ness in their edition of Simone Weil's *Formative Writings 1929–1941.*
4. "The Love of God and Affliction," in *On Science, Necessity and the Love of God,* p. 187.
5. *First and Last Notebooks,* p. 24.
6. See J. L. Austin, *How To Do Things with Words,* ed. J. O. Urmson (Oxford: Oxford University Press, 1962), passim.
7. "[. . . .] all thoughts really have 'I' as subject." "All thought implies a relationship, and it is always the 'I' which makes the relationship." These remarks both come from the section "Self-Knowledge," pp. 190–4 of *Lectures on Philosophy.* This very interesting section belongs to the "Miscellaneous Topics and Essay Plans" appended to the lectures; it contains much material which adds significantly to the particular aspect of the topic that I am discussing in this chapter.
8. See Chapter 4.
9. There are of course contexts in which phrases like "I add" have a point. If, for instance, Elizabeth is teaching someone elementary arithmetic she may say, "Watch what I do. See, I add 9 to 5 and get 14 . . ." It is noteworthy that here she is, as it were, taking a third party's view of her own activity. My argument in the text is that it plays no essential role in the execution of that activity.

212

3. The sensations of the present moment

1. *Lectures on Philosophy*, p. 32. I have given Hugh Price's translation. The French reads: "Quand nous ferons naître la pensée, elle naîtra ainsi dans un univers déjà rangé" (*Leçons de philosophie*, p. 24). Perhaps: "We shall see that thought comes to birth in a universe that is already ordered."

2. I have substituted "impossible" for the misprinted "possible" in the official translation.

3. *Philosophical Remarks*, sect. v, §48.

4. Gottlob Frege, "Thoughts," in *Logical Investigations*, ed. P. T. Geach (Oxford: Blackwell Publisher, 1977).

5. In contemporary Anglo-Saxon discussions of the "theory of meaning" this point is often expressed in terms of an opposition between "assertion conditions" and "truth conditions." I hope that the way I have put it in the text will suggest why I think such an opposition misguided. I have discussed the matter at greater length in "Im Anfang war die Tat" and "Facts and Super-facts" in *Trying To Make Sense* (Oxford: Blackwell Publisher, 1987).

6. It would be wrong to treat the quotation as a statement of Wittgenstein's own position. *Philosophical Remarks* is very obviously a transitional, even provisional, work in which we can see Wittgenstein struggling to articulate exactly what is wrong with preconceptions that he already realizes to be seriously misleading. There is of course a sense in which something similar could be said of all Wittgenstein's post-*Tractatus* writings; but it seems to me that in a quite special way we can see *Philosophical Remarks* as a clearing of the decks for a new departure. The book starts off by reporting his abandonment of the ideal of a "primary," or "phenomenological," language. The passage under discussion here is part of the attempt to make explicit that ideal and the temptations leading to it and at the same time to show what is wrong with it.

7. The central relevance of this point to empiricist epistemology is highlighted by Hume's extraordinary recognition, and immediate dismissal, of the "missing shade of blue" as a difficulty in section ii of his *Enquiry Concerning Human Understanding*. I am grateful to Steven Burns for reminding me of this.

4. "La simple perception de la nature"

1. *First and Last Notebooks*, p. 5.

2. In this context the term "passive" is not of course to be understood in the sense in which Hume, e.g., thought of impressions as occurrences in relation to which one is entirely passive. Here the distinction between activity and passivity is rather to be thought of as a way of characterizing the different roles played by people in interacting, e.g. in a conversation.

3. The first of these two quotations from *Lectures on Philosophy* is on p. 67; the second, on p. 75.

4. The distinction is very important in some, especially ethical, contexts. See, e.g., Peter Winch, "The Universalizability of Moral Judgments," in *Ethics and Action* (London: Routledge & Kegan Paul, 1972).

5. *Leçons de philosophie*, p. 50. I have given my own translation rather than Hugh Price's on p. 52 of *Lectures on Philosophy*.

6. *Lectures on Philosophy*, pp. 30–1. The thought is sharpened in Wittgenstein's striking remark: "It is part of the grammar of the word 'chair' that *this* is what we call 'to sit on a chair.'" What Simone Weil says on this subject in these early lectures is strikingly developed into the very important concept of "reading" (which again may be compared with Wittgenstein's treatment of "seeing an aspect" in *Philosophical Investigations*, pt. II, sect. xi), discussed in "Essai sur la notion de lecture," and constituting an indispensable element in much of her mature thought. See Chapter 9.

7. *Lectures on Philosophy*, p. 31.

8. Ibid., p. 44.

9. *Leçons de philosophie*, pp. 49–50; *Lectures on Philosophy*, pp. 51–2. Her conception of "imagination" at this point owes a lot to Kant's *Critique of Pure Reason*.

10. "Classical Science and After," in *On Science, Necessity and the Love of God*, p. 39.

11. See Chapter 13.

5. Language

1. Simone Weil, *Poèmes*, p. 22. I apologetically append a "translation."

An animal wild in his solitariness,
Incessantly consumed by a gnawing in his belly,
Which keeps him on the move, shaking with weariness,
Trying to flee from hunger, which he will only escape in death;
Crossing dark forests in search of a living;
Blind when the darkness of the night spreads;
Struck with mortal cold in the hollow of the rocks;
Coupling only in chance encounters;
The prey of the gods, crying out under their onslaughts –
That, O men, is what you would be but for Prometheus.

Creative, destructive fire, flame, the artist!
Flame, you who inherit the glow of the setting sun!
Dawn breaks in the midst of the too sad evening;
The gentle hearth has joined their hands; the field
Has replaced the burnt undergrowth.
Hard metal flows into the castings,
Hot iron bends and obeys the hammer.
A clear light beneath a roof fulfils the soul.
Bread ripens like fruit in the fire.
How he loved you, to make you such a beautiful gift!

He gave you the wheel and the lever. What a miracle!
Fate bends under the puny weight of hands.
From afar, necessity fears the grip
Which controls the gears, mistress of the roads.
O sea winds, conquered by a canvas!
O earth, exposed to the ploughshare, bleeding unveiled!
Chasm into which a fragile light is lowered!
The iron speeds, bites, tears, stretches, and crushes,
Obedient and tough. Arms bear their booty,
The heavy universe that gives and drinks blood.

He was the inventor of rituals and of the temple,
A magic circle to keep back the gods
Far from this world; and in this way man,
Alone and silent, contemplates fate, death, the heavens.
He invented signs, languages.
Winged words travel between generations
Across mountains, valleys, to move hearts and limbs.
The soul talks to itself and tries to understand itself.
Heaven, earth, sea are silent so that they can hear
Two friends, two lovers talking under their breath.

The gift of numbers spread yet more light.
Phantoms, demons fade away.
The voice, counting, knew how to chase away the shadows.
Even the hurricane is calm and transparent.
Each star takes its place in the limitless sky,
And speaks truthfully to the sail.
One act is added to another; nothing stands alone;
Everything answers to everything else on the just balance.
Songs are born, pure as the silence.
There are times when the shroud opens halfway.

Through him the dawn is an immortal joy.
But a merciless fate holds him bent.
He is nailed to the rock with iron; his brow falters;
While he hangs there, crucified, cold pain enters him like a sword.
Hours, seasons, centuries gnaw his soul,
The passing days make his courage fail.
His body twists vainly beneath the constraint;
The fleeting instant scatters his groans in the winds;
Alone and nameless, his flesh delivered to affliction.

2. *First and Last Notebooks,* pp. 26–7. I shall quote the remainder of that
   entry here, as it gives a good idea of the ferment of apparently disparate and sometimes conflicting thoughts which was the context of
   the remarks quoted in the text:

   [It is impossible to be dependent upon human beings without aspiring to tyrannize over them.

This is the source of all cruelties, both private and public. (but no, there is still something else . . .)]
Mathematics: abstract universe within which I depend solely upon *myself*. Realm of justice, because in it all good will is rewarded. ("Seek ye first the Kingdom of God and its justice.")
Secondly, the world; chance enters in. Progress (to ascertain – *to accept existence*). ["That's the way it is"] But to conceive chance properly (not imagining any god in it . . .) one must have passed through mathematics. Boat . . .
There are intermediaries: e.g. factory . . .

3. *Lectures on Philosophy*, p. 68. The French reads: "Nous pouvons évoquer ainsi n'importe quoi grâce au langage, qui nous transforme ainsi en êtres actifs" (*Leçons de philosophie*, p. 70).
4. *Lectures on Philosophy*, pp. 68–9.
5. The French reads "qu'on regarde en rêvant" (*Leçons de philosophie*, p. 42). Hugh Price translates this as "[which] one sees in dreaming"; this sounds too much like: "sees *in a dream*," which certainly cannot be right. The quotation in the text (part of which I discussed earlier, in Chapter 3) comes from *Lectures on Philosophy*, pp. 46–7. I have corrected the misprint "possible" in its last sentence.
6. *Lectures on Philosophy*, pp. 88–9. I have confined myself in the text to the material in this passage most to my present purpose. But the remainder of the passage will give some indication of the bold connections Simone Weil is already making at this time:

> Unfortunately, it is different people who make abstract constructions and who make constructions in the world.
> Kant: "The dove, when in its free flight it strikes the air and feels resistance, might well believe that it would fly better in a void." (The dove – that is thought; air – that is the world.)
> Bacon: "Homo naturae non nisi parendo imperat." (Man has command over nature only by obeying it.)
> It is only those actions and thoughts which have a necessity about them that are truly human. Whenever one does not have to act, one must avoid those actions and thoughts which have no necessity about them. A thought without necessity is a prejudice. But one has to distinguish between those prejudices which we can do without and those which we cannot do without.

7. There is a connection here with some of the things Wittgenstein writes in "Cause and Effect: Intuitive Awareness" (ed. Rush Rhees, trans. Peter Winch, *Philosophia* 6, nos. 3–4 [September–December 1976]: 391–445). He speaks there of a "reaction towards the cause," which involves looking *away* from the event which has caught one's attention (a blow on the head maybe) towards *something else* (perhaps the brick lying in the roadway beside one). One could see that (as did Wittgenstein) as the seed from which fully developed causal investigation grows.

6. Necessity

1. *Lectures on Philosophy*, p. 79.
2. For instance the following from "Science et perception dans Descartes": "So, through movement, my will is, as it were, scattered in time. In this consists the share that I have in the world. It is this double nature of my action which is reflected in all order, for instance in the sequence of numbers. So I can say that the world is completely encapsulated between one and two, potentially in a sense. One, two – this constitutes a grip for getting hold of the world" (*Sur la science*, p. 81).
3. This long and important essay forms the major part of *Oppression and Liberty;* the quotation is from p. 78. It is worth noting the striking contrast between the despairing tone of this passage and the enthusiasm generated by a similar thought in "Prométhée."
4. See for instance *Philosophical Grammar*, pt. I, II.
5. *Lectures on Philosophy*, p. 88.
6. Ibid., p. 79.
7. Ibid., pp. 88–9.
8. Ibid., p. 70. The last sentence reads in French: "Le langage nous permet d'établir des rapports entièrement étrangers à nos besoins" (*Leçons de philosophie*, p. 74). Perhaps: "independent of our needs"?
9. My use of the word "observance" brings to my mind a striking remark of Wittgenstein's which seems to me to lie in the same area as Simone Weil's "Prométhée": "Kultur ist eine Ordensregel. Oder setzt doch eine Ordensregel voraus [Culture is an observance. Or at least it presupposes an observance]" (*Culture and Value*, p. 83). *Ordensregel* (observance) in this context of course has the sense of the observance of the rule of a religious order.
10. *First and Last Notebooks*, p. 88. I shall be concerned with some of the implications of "including human facts" later in this book.
11. The French reads: "L'imprévu, c'est ce qui est autre que ce qui était contenu dans le langage méthodique" (*Leçons de philosophie*, p. 75). I do not think the sense of this is caught by Hugh Price's "The unforeseen is what is other than what methodical language contains" (*Lectures on Philosophy*, p. 72).
    Cf. also the following remark from "Classical Science and After" (in *On Science, Necessity and the Love of God*, p. 39): "An accident is always in a sense something neglected, or at least excluded from one's project." The importance of the distinction between *hasard* and *accident* is in no way weakened by the fact that it is obviously not a *sharp* distinction.
12. In using this form of words I am deliberately echoing Wittgenstein's "There is in these cases the possibility of an error, or as I should rather put it: The possibility of an error has been provided for" (*The Blue and Brown Books*, p. 67).
13. *Lectures on Philosophy*, p. 111.

14. "Classical Science and After." This is a translation of "La science et nous" in *Sur la science*.
15. Ibid., p. 35 (my emphasis).
16. Cf. Wittgenstein, *Culture and Value*, p. 57:

> The mathematician too can wonder at the miracles (the crystal) of nature of course; but can he do so once a problem has arisen about *what* it actually is he is contemplating? Is it really possible as long as the object that he finds astonishing and gazes at with awe is *shrouded* in a philosophical fog?
>
> I could imagine somebody might admire not only real trees, but also the shadows and reflections that they cast, taking them too for trees. But once he has told himself that these are not really trees after all and has come to be puzzled at what they are, or at how they are related to trees, his admiration will have suffered a rupture that will need healing.

Notice that Wittgenstein does not deny that the admiration may survive the philosophical clarification.

7. Equilibrium

1. *First and Last Notebooks*, p. 18.
2. This is included in *Simone Weil: An Anthology*, ed. Siân Miles (London: Virago, 1986).
3. See especially the opening section of *The Need for Roots*.
4. *Oppression and Liberty*, p. 84.
5. Ibid., p. 84.
6. Ibid., p. 85.
7. Ibid., p. 63. A similar line of thought is explored in masterly detail in Karl Wittfogel's *Oriental Despotism* (New Haven: Yale University Press, 1959).
8. This is the point of the first sentence of the passage quoted from *Lectures on Philosophy* in note 16 to Chapter 5 above: "Unfortunately, it is different people who make abstract constructions and who make constructions in the world."
9. *Oppression and Liberty*, p. 85.
10. *First and Last Notebooks*, p. 22. The quotation is from *Faust*, Act V: Mitternacht: "If I stood before you, Nature, a man by myself, Then it would be worth the trouble of being a human being."
11. *Philosophical Investigations*, pt. 1, §201. It is striking, by the way, that Saul Kripke, who misunderstands what Wittgenstein says about his "paradox" and who shows that he is himself subject to the very misunderstanding which Wittgenstein is identifying, expresses the relation between thought and action in just the same misleading language as Simone Weil, speaking of an "internal mental representation" by which I "grasp" a rule and which determines my subsequent behaviour. See Saul A. Kripke, *Wittgenstein on Rules and Private Language*

(Oxford: Blackwell Publisher, 1982), p. 7. There is a discussion of Kripke's treatment of this matter in Winch, *Trying To Make Sense*, pp. 54–63.

8. *"Completely free action"*

1. *Oppression and Liberty*, p. 86.
2. I am assuming here that by "combination of numbers" she means the arithmetical relation between the numbers themselves rather than the relations between my thoughts about them – which *can* of course be upset by contingencies. I shall say more about this distinction shortly.
3. *Lectures on Philosophy*, p. 116. And see Chapter 5.
4. Wittgenstein, *Remarks on the Foundations of Mathematics*, pt. I, §122. The extended discussion in this book of the nature of mathematical calculation and its relation to experiment has fascinating parallels with and divergences from Simone Weil's treatment of the same issues. Unfortunately it would demand too much space to examine this comparison thoroughly here.
5. *Lectures on Philosophy*, p. 80.
6. Ibid., p. 87.
7. Simone Weil comes very close to recognizing the point I am making in a number of places. Consider for instance the following remark from *First and Last Notebooks*, p. 6: "A confrontation between the nature of mind and the nature of matter occurs *twice over* – first in the relation between thought and signs – and then in the relation between theory and its application."
8. *Oppression and Liberty*, p. 96. The following passage from *First and Last Notebooks*, p. 41, suggests how this thought was connected with (and exaggerated by?) tensions in Simone Weil's personal life:

> To be confronted with things is a liberation of the mind. To be confronted with men, if one is dependent on them, degrades it – and it is the same whether dependence takes the form of subordination or of command.
> Cf. Diderot: "to adopt postures" (Neveu de Rameau)
> Why these men standing between nature and me?
> *never be forced to take account of an unknown thought* . . . (because in that case one is at the mercy of chance)
> [provisional remedy: treat mankind as a spectacle, except where one is attached by fraternal links . . . and *never* seek for friendship . . . live among men as I did in that railway carriage between St. Etienne and Le Puy . . . above all, never allow oneself to dream of friendship: everything has to be paid for . . . "rely only upon yourself"]

9. *Oppression and Liberty*, p. 97.
10. Ibid., p. 101.
11. Ibid., p. 99.

9. The power to refuse

1. Cf. Wittgenstein, *Culture and Value*, p. 31[e]:

   The origin and the primitive form of the language game is a reaction; only from this can more complicated forms develop.
   Language – I want to say – is a refinement, "in the beginning was the deed."

2. *Lectures on Philosophy*, p. 80.
3. Ibid., p. 84.
4. In *Simone Weil: An Anthology*, p. 238.
5. Ibid., p. 187.
6. The parallel with Wittgenstein is again striking. Compare for instance what he says in *Philosophical Investigations* pt I, §§472–7, about the "belief in the uniformity of nature" and in I, §§287 and 310, and II sect. iv, about the "belief in other minds." I have discussed this at greater length in "Eine Einstellung zur Seele," in *Trying To Make Sense*, pp. 140–53.
7. "Are We Struggling for Justice?" pp. 2–3. Compare too the following from "Human Personality": "There are no other restraints upon our will than material necessity and the existence of other human beings around us. Any imaginary extension of these limits is seductive, so there is a seduction in whatever helps us to forget the reality of the obstacles. That is why upheavals like war and civil war are intoxicating; they empty human lives of their reality and seem to turn people into puppets. That is also why slavery is so pleasant to the masters" (*Simone Weil: An Anthology*, p. 72).
8. *La source grecque*, p. 22; and *Simone Weil: An Anthology*, p. 194.
9. It is this latter sort of necessity the existence of which the Athenian ambassadors contested in their dialogue with the Melians in Thucydides' *Peloponnesian War* v.7 (a passage which Simone Weil greatly admired). "Our opinion of the gods and our knowledge of men lead us to conclude that it is a general and necessary law of nature to rule wherever one can." See Chapter 15.
10. See note 7 above.
11. 2 Samuel 12; translation of the Authorized Version.
12. Perhaps this is the point the Athenian ambassadors to Melos were confused about. See Chapter 15.
13. *Études philosophiques*, N.S. 1 (January–March 1946).
14. Veronese's painting of the scene, in the Louvre, conveys Simone Weil's point marvellously; it is hard to imagine that she was not familiar with it.
15. There is a very striking parallel between parts of this passage and parts of Wittgenstein's discussion of "seeing as," or "seeing an aspect," in *Philosophical Investigations*, pt. II, sec. xi. Wittgenstein discusses in much greater detail the role of such phenomena in the concept of perception; but he does not make the explicit connection with questions of ethics found here.
16. The most sustained application of this thought is probably the essay "Classical Science and After," which I shall be discussing in Chapter 11.

17. "Essai sur la notion de lecture," p. 16.
18. Ibid., pp. 18–19.
19. *Notebooks,* vol. I, p. 47.
20. Ibid., p. 24 (written in 1941).

10. "The void"

1. *Waiting for God,* pp. 158ff.
2. Spinoza, *Ethics,* pt. III., prop. 9, Scholium (*The Collected Works of Spinoza,* vol. I, ed. and trans. Edwin Curley, Princeton University Press, 1985).
3. This view is still widely held. We are for instance assured by a contemporary anthropologist that "an act from which there is no practical advantage vis-à-vis some other is impossible" (David Riches in *The Anthropology of Violence,* ed. David Riches [Oxford: Blackwell Publisher, 1986], p. 7).
4. *Notebooks,* vol. I, p. 148.
5. J.-M. Perrin and Gustave Thibon, *Simone Weil telle que nous l'avons connue* (Paris: Fayard, 1967), p. 177. This is one of the points at which the direction of her interests diverges most sharply from Wittgenstein's. Contrast Thibon's description with the following:

> Turing thinks that he and I are using the word "experiment" in two different ways. But I want to show that this is wrong. That is to say, I think that if I could make myself quite clear, then Turing would give up saying that in mathematics we make experiments. If I could arrange in their proper order certain well-known facts, then it would become clear that Turing and I are not using the word "experiment" differently.
> You might say, "How is it possible that there should be a misunderstanding so very hard to remove?"
> It can be explained partly by a difference in education.
> Partly by a quotation from Hilbert: "No one is going to turn us out of the paradise which Cantor has created."
> I would say, "I wouldn't dream of trying to drive anyone out of this paradise." I would try to do something quite different: I would try to show you that it is not a paradise – so that you'll leave of your own accord. I would say, "You're welcome to this; just look about you." (*Wittgenstein's Lectures on the Foundations of Mathematics, Cambridge 1939,* ed. Cora Diamond [Brighton: Harvester, 1976], p. 103)

6. *Notebooks,* vol. II, pp. 489ff.
7. *First and Last Notebooks,* p. 161.
8. Simone Weil sometimes uses the phrase "the *aspiration* towards the good" as distinct from *"desire"* (for a particular object). But she also sometimes speaks of good as an object, indeed *the* object of "desire."
9. *Waiting for God,* p. 126.
10. *Notebooks,* vol. I, p. 20.
11. Ibid., p. 28.
12. G. E. M. Anscombe, *Intention* (Oxford: Blackwell Publisher, 1957).

13. *Philosophical Remarks,* pp. 70, 71.
14. *Notebooks,* vol. I, pp. 47–8.
15. *First and Last Notebooks,* p. 161. There is a slightly different version in *Notebooks,* vol. I, p. 148:

> . . . for it was supposing the source of faithfulness to be in himself and not in grace. Happily, as he was chosen, this denial became manifest to all and to himself. How many more there are who make similar boasts – and they never understand!
>
> (May all my denials become manifest. May they also be of rare occurrence.)

16. *Notebooks,* vol. II, p. 491.
17. *Waiting for God,* p. 91.

11. Geometry

1. *First and Last Notebooks,* p. 362.
2. *Notebooks,* vol. I, p. 19.
3. Notice that Wittgenstein's *Tractatus* (of which my last quotation from Simone Weil's *Notebooks* is in some ways so reminiscent) succumbs to much the same temptation. Cf. *Tractatus* 5.64: "Here it can be seen that solipsism, when its implications are followed out strictly, coincides with pure realism. The self of solipsism shrinks to a point without extension, and there remains the reality co-ordinated with it."
4. *Notebooks,* vol. I, pp. 23–4.
5. I have in mind Part V, Proposition 39 of Spinoza's *Ethics:* "He who has a Body capable of a great many things has a mind whose greatest part is eternal." One has "a body capable of a great many things" the more of the universe is one's "blind man's stick."
6. *Waiting for God,* p. 158.
7. Cf. Wittgenstein, *Culture and Value,* p. 3^e: "You cannot lead people to what is good; you can only lead them to some place or other. The good is outside the space of facts."
8. In *On Science, Necessity and the Love of God,* pp. 3–43.
9. Ibid., p. 21.
10. Ibid., p. 5.
11. The importance of the idea of "measuring against a standard" is reflected in her tendency to speak now in terms of "aspirations" rather then "desires." The connection between an aspiration and the actions which express it is different, and in a sense less immediate, than that characteristic of desire and action.
12. *On Science, Necessity and the Love of God,* p. 5.
13. Ibid., p. 12.
14. Ibid., pp. 11–12.
15. Ibid., pp. 15–16.
16. Ibid., p. 17.
17. Ibid., p. 20.
18. Ibid., p. 18.

19. Ibid., p. 21.
20. Simone Weil's understanding of the mechanism by which these conflicts are produced is closely parallel to that of Spinoza. Her essay on *The Iliad* might be thought of as a particular application of what Spinoza described in general terms in his account of "human bondage" in the *Ethics*. Where she diverges sharply from Spinoza is in her insistence that the true nature of this mechanism can only be understood from the point of view of a "supernatural" conception of justice, which is a point "outside the world." For Spinoza, of course, such a way of speaking would have been meaningless.
21. *Simone Weil: An Anthology*, p. 195.
22. Ibid., pp. 193–4.
23. Ibid., p. 184.
24. "A Medieval Epic Poem," in *Selected Essays, 1934–43*, pp. 35–43. For an impressive history of this episode, which fully bears out what Simone Weil says of it, see Zoé Oldenbourg, *Le Bûcher de Montségur* (Paris: Gallimard 1959), trans. P. Green, *Massacre at Montségur* (New York: Pantheon, 1962).
25. *Simone Weil: An Anthology*, p. 191.

12. Incommensurability

1. Think for instance of what Vico says about the significance of funerary rites in *The New Science*. In a different but connected context see Cora Diamond, "Eating Meat and Eating People," *Philosophy* 53 (1978): 465–79.
2. *Simone Weil: An Anthology*, p. 187.
3. George Eliot, *Middlemarch* (London: Chatto & Windus, 1978), p. 311.
4. "The Romanesque Renaissance," *Selected Essays 1934–43*, p. 49. My use of the phrase "the one through the other" in the sentence immediately preceding this quotation is a deliberate echo of Wittgenstein, *Philosophical Investigations*, pt. II, sect. v: "'I noticed that he was depressed.' Is that a report on behaviour or on a state of mind? ('The sky looks threatening': is that about the present or the future?) Both; but not alongside each other; rather about the one through the other."
5. *Selected Essays 1934–43*, p. 36.
6. *Massacre at Montségur*, pp. 363–4.
7. I am grateful to Marina Barabaš for a remark she once made to me in a conversation which showed me the importance of our reactions to this case.
8. *Culture and Value*, p. 35ᵉ.
9. *Without Proof or Evidence*, ed. J. L. Craft and R. E. Hustwit (Lincoln: University of Nebraska Press, 1984), p. 3.
10. *Culture and Value*, p. 58ᵉ.
11. *Notebooks*, vol. II, p. 490. Cf. *First and Last Notebooks*, p. 316. But similar examples are legion.
12. "Reflections on the Right Use of School Studies," in *Waiting for God*, p. 72.
13. *First and Last Notebooks*, pp. 349–50.

14. Ibid., p. 24.
15. *Simone Weil: An Anthology*, p. 199.
16. Ibid., p. 210.
17. Ibid., p. 208.

13. Beauty

1. *Waiting for God*, p. 158.
2. *On Science, Necessity and the Love of God*, pp. 15–16.
3. *The Need for Roots*, p. 95.
4. *L'enracinement*, pp. 123–4.
5. *The Need for Roots*, p. 89.
6. See *On Science, Necessity and the Love of God*, passim.
7. *Culture and Value*, p. 17ᵉ.
8. On this see Rush Rhees, *Without Answers* (London: Routledge & Kegan Paul, 1969), ch. 1, "A Scientific Age"; ch. 2, "Science and Questioning"; and ch. 3, "Philosophy and Science."
9. *The Need for Roots*, p. 93.
10. *Intuitions pré-chrétiennes*, pp. 22ff. Cf. David Hume, *Dialogues Concerning Natural Religion*.
11. *Waiting for God*, pp. 158–81. The quoted passage is on pp. 165–6. Some of her ideas at this point are strongly reminiscent of Kant, though the direction in which she takes them is different.
12. Cf. Wittgenstein, *Culture and Value*, p. 1ᵉ: "The human gaze has a power of conferring value on things; but it makes them cost more too." The cost has to be understood as a *condition* of the conferring of value.
13. Ibid., p. 4ᵉ.
14. "Essai sur la notion de lecture," p. 19.
15. *Waiting for God*, p. 165.
16. *On Science, Necessity and the Love of God*, p. 12.
17. Ibid., p. 17.
18. Wittgenstein, in a different – but not very different – connection, remarked of the relation between a measuring rod's corporality and its capacity to measure that one cannot say: "'Of course the ruler measures length in spite of its corporality; actually, a ruler that had only length would be the ideal, as it were a *pure* ruler.' No, if a body has length, there can be no length without a body – and even if I understand that in a certain sense it is only the length of the ruler that measures, still the fact remains that what I put in my pocket is the ruler, the body, not the length" (*Philosophical Remarks*, pt. v, §48).
19. *Waiting for God*, p. 167.
20. *Massacre at Montségur*, p. 95.
21. *Notebooks*, vol. I, p. 38.
22. Cf. *Waiting for God*, p. 166: "It may be that vice, depravity and crime are nearly always, or even perhaps always, in their essence, attempts to eat beauty, to eat what we should only look at. Eve began it. If she caused humanity to be lost eating the fruit, the opposite attitude,

looking at the fruit without eating it, should be what is required to save it. 'Two winged companions,' says an Upanishad, 'two birds are on the branch of a tree. One eats the fruit, the other looks at it.' These two birds are the two parts of our soul." The characteristic yielding to temptation ("nearly always, or even perhaps always") should not make us overlook the marvellous insight.

23. *Notebooks,* vol. I, p. 38.
24. Ibid., pp. 38–9. In another passage she remarks that Spinoza's injunction "neither to laugh, nor weep, nor be indignant about human affairs" is not, "as I used to think," opposed to social action: what one has to "understand" are the *necessities* to which one *then* has to respond in action (*First and Last Notebooks,* p. 42).

14. Justice

1. "Human personality," in *Simone Weil: An Anthology,* p. 81. And on p. 77 she says that such expressions are "valid in their own region, which is that of ordinary institutions. But for the sustaining inspiration of which all institutions are, as it were, the projection, a different language is needed."
2. Ibid., p. 83.
3. Ibid., p. 80.
4. Ibid., p. 93.
5. A work that raises such questions, in a horrifying but illuminating way, is Heinrich von Kleist's *Michael Kohlhaas.*
6. *Simone Weil: An Anthology,* p. 90.
7. Ibid., p. 72.
8. Ibid., p. 91.
9. "The Legitimacy of the Provisional Government," p. 94.
10. Ibid., p. 88.
11. "Are We Struggling for Justice?" p. 6.
12. Ibid.
13. "The Legitimacy of the Provisional Government," p. 89.
14. *Simone Weil: An Anthology,* p. 93.
15. *First and Last Notebooks,* p. 5.
16. Ibid., p. 173. Cf. *Waiting for God,* p. 163, which speaks of beauty as

> the trap which enticed Cora. All the heavens were smiling at the scent of the narcissus, so was the entire earth and all the swelling ocean. Hardly had the poor girl stretched out her hand before she was caught in the trap. She fell into the hands of the living God. When she escaped she had eaten the seed of the pomegranate which bound her for ever. She was no longer a virgin; she was the spouse of God.

On the grain of mustard see, e.g., Luke 14:31f.:

> Another parable put he forth unto them, saying, The kingdom of heaven is like to a grain of mustard seed, which a man took, and sowed in his field:

Which indeed is the least of all seeds: but when it is grown, it is the greatest among herbs, and becometh a tree, so that the birds of the air come and lodge in the branches thereof.

15. *"A supernatural virtue"?*

1. Kierkegaard has a quite interesting suggestion about this in *The Concept of Anxiety.*
2. For a discussion of this kind of issue see "Darwin, *Genesis* and Contradiction," in Winch, *Trying To Make Sense.* By chance while writing the present chapter I came on a remark about Genesis in an article about the current state of scientific theory concerning the origin of the universe: "Nice idea, shame about the facts" (*The Economist*, 1–7 November 1986, p. 88).
3. Thucydides, *The Peloponnesian War*, trans. R. Warner (Harmondsworth: Penguin, 1980), v. 7.
4. See "Three Letters on History," in *Selected Essays, 1934–43*, p. 77.
5. "The Great Beast," ibid., p. 115.
6. See "Are We Struggling for Justice?" p. 3. I have quoted Saint Paul (Philippians 2:6–11) somewhat more fully than does she, and in the translation of the Authorized Version.
7. "Are We Struggling for Justice?" p. 3.
8. I again intentionally echo a phrase of Wittgenstein's, this time *Tractatus*, 5.473: "Logic must look after itself *(Die Logik muß für sich selber sorgen).*" Cf. also 5.551–5.5521.

    There is continuity between this central tenet of the *Tractatus* and the way Wittgenstein in *Philosophical Investigations* repeatedly counters philosophical objections to certain ways of speaking with the rejoinder "This language game is played." Cf. too the important passage in *Philosophical Grammar* (p. 184) in which Wittgenstein discusses the idea that "the use of language is in a certain sense autonomous, as cooking and washing are not."
9. Alasdair MacIntyre expresses a similar view concerning our usual ways of expressing our moral views in *After Virtue.*
10. *Waiting for God*, p. 148.
11. *First and Last Notebooks*, pp. 146–8.
12. I think, for instance, that Simone Weil would have agreed with Socrates' astounding remark to Polus in the *Gorgias* that "I think that you and all men think the same as I do" (viz., that it is better to suffer than to do evil). In calling this "astounding," I do not mean to imply that I think it obviously false; neither, of course, do I think it obviously true.
13. *First and Last Notebooks*, p. 315.
14. Ibid., pp. 349–50. It was Rush Rhees who, a long time ago, with a characteristically sure diagnosis of the confusions I was in, drew my attention to this important passage.
15. *Waiting for God*, pp. 200–8.
16. Ibid., p. 200.
17. Ibid. The italics are mine.

18. Ibid., pp. 204, 205, 206.
19. Ibid., p. 203. Concerning all these examples it is good to bear in mind Wittgenstein's remark (*Culture and Value*, p. 1ᵉ): "The human gaze has a power of conferring value on things; but it makes them cost more too."
20. *Waiting for God*, p. 206.
21. Ibid., p. 142. The italics are mine.
22. Ibid., p. 144.
23. *Culture and Value*, p. 73ᶜ.
24. Ibid., p. 3ᶜ.
25. 1 John 4:12, 20.
26. *Waiting for God*, pp. 104–5.
27. Ibid., p. 148.
28. Wittgenstein, *Culture and Value*, p. 33ᶜ.
29. Ibid., p. 85ᶜ.
30. *Waiting for God.*, p. 127.
31. Ibid., p. 128.

BIBLIOGRAPHY

Austin, J. L., *How To Do Things with Words*, ed. J. O. Urmson (Oxford: Oxford University Press, 1962)

Bouwsma, O. K., *Without Proof or Evidence*, ed. J. L. Craft and R. E. Hustwit (Lincoln: University of Nebraska Press, 1984)

Diamond, Cora, "Eating Meat and Eating People," *Philosophy* 53 (1978): 465–79

Eliot, George, *Middlemarch* (London: Chatto & Windus, 1978)

Frege, Gottlob, *Logical Investigations*, ed. P. T. Geach (Oxford: Blackwell Publisher, 1977)

Goethe, Johann Wolfgang von, *Faust* (Berlin and Weimar: Aufbau Verlag, 1986)

Hume, David, *Dialogues Concerning Natural Religion*, ed. N. Kemp Smith (London: Nelson, 1947)

   Enquiry Concerning Human Understanding, ed. L. A. Selby-Bigge (Oxford: Clarendon Press, 1955)

Kant, Immanuel, *Critique of Pure Reason*, trans. N. Kemp Smith (London: Macmillan, 1963)

Kierkegaard, Søren, *Kierkegaard's Writings*, ed. E. H. Hong and H. V. Hong, vol. VIII: *The Concept of Anxiety*, ed. and trans. R. Thomte and A. B. Anderson (Princeton, N.J.: Princeton University Press, 1980)

Kripke, Saul A., *Wittgenstein on Rules and Private Language* (Oxford: Blackwell Publisher, 1982)

Perrin, J.-M. and Thibon, Gustave, *Simone Weil telle que nous l'avons connue* (Paris: Fayard, 1967)

Oldenbourg, Zoé, *Le bûcher de Montségur* (Paris: Gallimard, 1959). Trans. Peter Green as *Massacre at Montségur* (New York: Pantheon, 1962)

Rhees, Rush, *Without Answers* (London: Routledge & Kegan Paul, 1969)

Rousseau, Jean-Jacques, *The Social Contract and Discourses* (London: Dent, 1947)

Spinoza, Benedict de, *Ethics*, in *The Collected Works of Spinoza*, vol. I, ed. and trans. E. Curley (Princeton, N.J.: Princeton University Press, 1985)

Thucydides, *The Peloponnesian War,* trans. R. Warner (Harmondsworth: Penguin, 1980)

Weil, Simone, "Are We Struggling for Justice?" trans. Marina Barabas, *Philosophical Investigations* 53 (January 1987): 1–10 (translation of "Luttons-nous pour la justice?" in *Écrits de Londres,* pp. 45–57)

Attente de Dieu (Paris: Fayard, 1966)

Cahiers, vols. I–III (Paris: Plon, 1970–4)

Écrits de Londres (Paris: Gallimard, 1957)

L'enracinement (Paris: Gallimard, 1949)

"Essai sur la notion de lecture," *Études Philosophiques* (Marseilles), N.S. 1 (January–March 1946): 13–19

First and Last Notebooks, trans. Richard Rees (Oxford: Oxford University Press, 1970) (translation of parts of *Cahiers*)

Formative Writings 1929–41, ed. and trans. Dorothy Tuck McFarland and Wilhelmina van Ness (London: Routledge & Kegan Paul, 1987) (Includes translation of "Science et perception dans Descartes")

Intimations of Christianity Among the Ancient Greeks, ed. and trans. Elisabeth Chase Geissbuhler (London: Routledge & Kegan Paul, 1957) (translation of chapters from *La source grecque* and *Intuitions pré-chrétiennes*)

Intuitions pré-chrétiennes (Paris: La Colombe, 1951)

Leçons de philosophie (Paris: Plon, 1959)

Lectures on Philosophy, transcribed Anne Reynaud-Géricault, trans. Hugh Price with an introduction by Peter Winch (Cambridge: Cambridge University Press, 1978) (translation of *Leçons de philosophie*)

"The Legitimacy of the Provisional Government," trans. Peter Winch, *Philosophical Investigations* 53 (April 1987): 87–98 (translation of "Légitimité du gouvernement provisoire," in *Écrits de Londres,* pp. 58–73)

The Need for Roots, trans. Arthur Wills with a preface by T. S. Eliot (Boston: Beacon Press, 1955) (translation of *L'enracinement*)

The Notebooks, vols. I–II, trans. Arthur Wills (London: Routledge & Kegan Paul, 1956) (translation of parts of *Cahiers*)

On Science, Necessity and the Love of God, ed. and trans. Richard Rees (Oxford: Oxford University Press, 1968) (includes material translated from *Sur la science*)

Oppression and Liberty, trans. Arthur Wills and John Petrie (London: Routledge & Kegan Paul, 1958) (translation of *Oppression et liberté*)

Oppression et liberté (Paris: Gallimard, 1955)

Poèmes (Paris: Gallimard, 1968)

Selected Essays, 1934–43, ed. and trans. Richard Rees (Oxford: Oxford University Press, 1962)

Seventy Letters, ed. and trans. Richard Rees (Oxford: Oxford University Press, 1965)

Simone Weil: An Anthology, ed. Siân Miles (London: Virago, 1986)

La source grecque (Paris: Gallimard, 1953)

Sur la science (Paris: Gallimard, 1966)

Waiting for God, trans. Emma Craufurd with an introduction by Leslie
    A. Fiedler (New York: Harper & Row, 1973) (translation of *Attente
    de Dieu*)
Winch, Peter, *Ethics and Action* (London: Routledge & Kegan Paul, 1972)
    Trying To Make Sense (Oxford: Blackwell Publisher, 1987)
Wittfogel, Karl August, *Oriental Despotism* (New Haven, Conn.: Yale Uni-
    versity Press, 1959)
Wittgenstein, Ludwig, *The Blue and Brown Books* (Oxford: Blackwell Pub-
    lisher, 1969)
    "Cause and Effect: Intuitive Awareness," ed. Rush Rhees, trans. Peter
    Winch, *Philosophia* 6, nos. 3–4 (September–December 1976): 391–
    445
    Culture and Value, ed. G. H. von Wright, trans. Peter Winch (Oxford:
    Blackwell Publisher, 1980)
    Philosophical Grammar, ed. Rush Rhees, trans. Anthony Kenny (Oxford:
    Blackwell Publisher, 1958)
    Philosophical Investigations, ed. G. E. M. Anscombe and G. H. von
    Wright, trans. G. E. M. Anscombe (Oxford: Blackwell Publisher,
    1958)
    Philosophical Remarks, ed. Rush Rhees, trans. Raymond Hargreaves and
    Roger White (Oxford: Blackwell Publisher, 1973)
    Remarks on the Foundations of Mathematics, ed. G. H. von Wright, Rush
    Rhees, and G. E. M. Anscombe, trans. G. E. M. Anscombe
    (Oxford: Blackwell Publisher, 1974)
    Tractatus Logico-Philosophicus, trans. D. F. Pears and B. McGuiness
    (London: Routledge & Kegan Paul, 1961) (first published 1922)
    Wittgenstein's Lectures on the Foundations of Mathematics, Cambridge 1939,
    ed. Cora Diamond (Brighton: Harvester, 1976)

INDEX